D0619647

ANSI C Made Easy

Herbert Schildt

Osborne **McGraw-Hill**

Berkeley   New York   St. Louis   San Francisco
Auckland   Bogotá   Hamburg   London   Madrid
Mexico City   Milan   Montreal   New Delhi   Panama City
Paris   São Paulo   Singapore   Sydney
Tokyo   Toronto

Osborne **McGraw-Hill**
2600 Tenth Street
Berkeley, California 94710
U.S.A.

For information on translations and book distributors outside of the
U.S.A., please write to Osborne **McGraw-Hill** at the above address.

A complete list of trademarks appears on page 445.

ANSI C Made Easy

1234567890 DOC 8987

ISBN 0-07-881500-2

Acquisitions Editor	Jeffrey Pepper
Technical Reviewer	Jeff Hsu
Project Editor	Nancy Beckus
Cover art	Bay Graphics Design Associates
Screens	InSet Systems, Inc.

This book was printed and bound by R.R. Donnelley & Sons Company,
Crawfordsville, Indiana.

Contents

PREFACE

Welcome to the world of ANSI C. In this book you will learn about one of the most exciting and powerful computer languages in existence. You will see how C unlocks the power within the computer and puts you, the programmer, in full control.

The story of the C language is a success story unlike that of most other programming languages. Since its conception in the 1970s, its popularity has continued to increase. Futhermore, this popularity is due almost entirely to grass-roots support. Unlike languages such as FORTRAN, COBOL, OR ADA, C did not have any large institution supporting it. Instead, C grew in popularity for one basic reason: it is simply one of the best programming languages ever devised. With the advent of the ANSI standard for C, the last cornerstone to ensuring C's place in the programming world has been laid.

This book assumes that you have never programmed in C. Although not necessary, it will be helpful if you have programmed even a little in some computer language. However, even if you are a complete novice, you will be able to use this book.

The C language is not as easy to learn as some other languages, (BASIC, for instance). Do not become discouraged. Just work your way through this book, one example at a time. If you are persistent, by the time you reach the end you will be able to call yourself a C programmer.

The examples in this book can be compiled using any ANSI-standard C compiler. For the development and testing of the example programs I used both Borland's Turbo C and Microsoft's C.

There are many useful and interesting functions and programs contained in this book. If you're like me, you probably would appreciate using them, but hate typing them into the computer. When I key in routines from a book it always seems that I type something wrong and spend hours trying to get the program to work. For this reason, I am offering the source code on diskette for all the functions and programs contained in this book for $24.95. Just fill in the order blank on the next page and mail it, along with your payment, to the address shown. Or, if you're in a hurry, just call (217) 586-4021 (the number of my consulting office) and place your order by telephone. (Visa and Mastercard are accepted.)

HS
Mahomet, Illinois
Dec, 1988

Please send me _____ copies, at $24.95 each, of the source code to the programs in *ANSI C Made Easy*. Please add $5 for the shipping and handling of foreign orders.

Name _____

Address _____

City _____ State _____ Zip _____

Telephone _____

Diskette size (check one): 5 1/4" _____ 3 1/2" _____

Method of payment: check _____ Visa _____ MC _____

Credit card number: _____

Expiration date: _____

Signature: _____

Send to: Herbert Schildt
            RR 1, Box 130
            Mahomet, Il 61853

            or phone: (217) 586-4021

Osborne/McGraw-Hill assumes NO responsibility for this offer. This is solely an offer of Herbert Schildt and not of Osborne/McGraw-Hill.

1

GETTING ACQUAINTED WITH C

Before beginning to explore the exciting world of ANSI standard C you should understand how it relates to other programming languages. This chapter presents a brief history of the C programming language, its origins, uses, and philosophy. If you already know something about C and are an experienced programmer, you might want to skip to Chapter 2.

THE ORIGINS OF C

C was invented and first implemented by Dennis Ritchie on a DEC PDP-11 using the UNIX operating system. The development of C

started with an older language called BCPL, developed by Martin Richards. (BCPL is still in use, primarily in Europe.) BCPL influenced a language called B, invented by Ken Thompson, which led to the development of C in the 1970s.

For many years, the de facto standard for C was the one supplied with the UNIX version 5 operating system and described in *The C Programming Language* by Brian Kernighan and Dennis Ritchie (Englewood Cliffs, N.J.: Prentice-Hall, 1978). With the popularity of microcomputers, a large number of C implementations were created. Amazingly, most of these implementations were highly compatible on the source-code level. However, because no standard existed, there were always some discrepancies. To remedy this situation, a committee was established in the summer of 1983 to create an ANSI standard that would once and for all define the C language. As of this writing, the proposed standard is very nearly complete and its adoption by ANSI is expected soon.

It is important to understand that the ANSI C standard is a superset of the original UNIX standard. Because of this, programmers transferring from a UNIX-based compiler to an ANSI standard compiler will find all the features they have come to rely on. In addition, they will find some new things that will make programming a little easier.

Now that you know C's lineage, let's look at what kind of programming language it is.

C AS A MIDDLE-LEVEL LANGUAGE

C is often called a "middle-level" computer language. This does not mean that C is less powerful, harder to use, or less developed than a "high-level" language, or that it is as difficult to use as a low-level language, such as *assembly language*. (Assembly language, or *assembler* as it is often called, is simply a symbolic representation of the actual machine code that a computer can read.) C is considered a middle-level language because it combines elements of high-level languages, such as Pascal or Modula-2, with the functionality of assembler. Table 1-1 shows C in relation to some other computer languages.

Theoretically, a high-level language attempts to supply everything the programmer could possibly want, already built into the language.

Level	Language
High	Ada
	FORTRAN
	Pascal
	COBOL
	Modula-2
Middle	C
	FORTH
Low	Macro Assembler
	Assembler

TABLE 1-1   C's Place in the World of Languages

A low-level language provides nothing other than access to the actual machine instructions. A middle-level language offers a concise set of tools and allows the programmer to develop higher-level constructs. Thus, a middle-level language gives the programmer built-in power coupled with flexibility.

Another way of looking at it is that middle-level languages are sometimes thought of as "building block" languages because the programmer first creates routines to perform almost all functions necessary to the program and then puts them together.

C, as a middle-level language, allows you to manipulate the bits, bytes, addresses, and ports that comprise your computer. That is, C does not significantly buffer the machine's hardware from your program. For example, unlike many high-level languages that can operate directly on strings of characters to perform a multitude of string manipulations, C operates on characters. Most high-level languages have built-in statements to read and write disk files. In C, these procedures are performed by calls to functions that are not technically part of the C language. Although all ANSI standard compilers supply functions capable of performing disk I/O, your C programs can bypass them if you choose. C offers you greater flexibility than most other languages.

C allows—indeed requires—the programmer to define routines to perform high-level routines. These routines are called *functions,*

and are very important in the C language. You can easily tailor a library of C functions to perform the various tasks used by your program. In this sense, you can personalize C to fit your needs.

C has very few statements to remember—only 32 keywords as defined by ANSI. (By comparison, the IBM PC version of BASIC has approximately 159.) This means that C compilers can be relatively easy to write, and that there is generally one available for whatever machine you are using. For this reason the first compilers available for a new computer tend to be C compilers. Since C operates on the same data types as the computer, the code output from a C compiler tends to be very efficient and fast. In fact, C can be used in place of assembler for most tasks.

C code is very portable. *Portability* means you may adapt software written for one type of computer to another. This is important if you ever need to move an application to a new computer that uses a different processor, operating system, or both. Most application programs will only need to be recompiled with a C compiler written for the new processor. This can save countless hours and dollars.

Uses of C

C was first used primarily for system programming. *System programming* refers to a class of programs that are either part of or work closely with the operating system of the computer. System programs are the programs that make the computer capable of performing useful work. Some examples are

- Operating Systems
- Language Compilers
- Assemblers
- Text Editors
- Print Spoolers
- Network Drivers
- Modem Programs

- Data Bases
- Language Interpreters
- Utilities

C is used for system programming for several reasons. First, system programs often must run very quickly. Programs compiled by most C compilers can run almost as fast as those written in assembler. In the past, most system software had to be written in assembly language because the available computer languages could not create programs that ran fast enough. Writing in assembly language is long, hard, tedious work. Since C code can be written much more quickly than the assembly code, using the C code reduces development costs tremendously.

Second, C is a "programmer's language." Professional programmers are attracted to C because of the lack of restrictions and its easy manipulation of bits, bytes, and addresses. In addition, the system programmer needs C's direct control of the I/O and memory management functions.

In recent years C has also been used as a general-purpose language because of its popularity with programmers. Once you are familiar with C, you can follow the precise flow and logic of a program and verify the general operation of subroutines fairly easily. C program listings tend to look clear yet intriguing. In contrast, a language such as BASIC can look cluttered and confusing. Perhaps the main reason why C has become a general-purpose language is that it is simply fun to use!

C as a Structured Language

C is a structured language. A *structured language* is distinguished by its use of blocks. A *block* is a set of statements that are logically connected. For example, imagine an IF statement that, if successful, will execute five discrete statements. If these statements can be grouped together and referenced as an indivisible unit, then they form a block.

A structured language allows a variety of programming possibilities. It supports the concept of subroutines with local variables. A *local variable* is simply a variable that is known only to the subroutine in which it is defined. A structured language also supports several loop constructs, such as **while, do/while,** and **for**. (The use of **goto** is either prohibited or discouraged and is not the common form of program control in the same way as it is in BASIC or FORTRAN.) A structured language allows you to indent statements and does not require a strict field concept (as in early versions of FORTRAN).

The following are some examples of structured and non-structured languages:

Non-Structured	Structured
FORTRAN	Pascal
BASIC	Ada
COBOL	C

Structured languages are generally more recent than non-structured ones. In fact, a mark of an older computer language is that it is not structured. It is widely considered that programs in structured languages are not only easier to program *in* but also much easier to maintain.

COMPILERS VERSUS INTERPRETERS

The terms *compiler* and *interpreter* refer to the way that a program is executed. Any programming language can, in theory, be either compiled or interpreted. Although some languages are usually executed one way or the other, the way a program is executed is not defined by the language it is written in.

Interpreters and compilers are simply sophisticated programs that operate on your program's source code. *Source code* is the program text that you write. An interpreter reads the source code of your program one line at a time and performs the specific instructions contained in that line. A compiler first reads the entire program and then converts it into object code, a form that can be

directly executed by the computer. Object code is also referred to as *binary* or *machine code*. Once the program is compiled, a line of source code may no longer be meaningful to the execution of your program.

For example, BASIC is usually interpreted and C is almost always compiled. An interpreter must be present each time you run your program. In BASIC, you first have to execute the BASIC interpreter, load your program, and then type **RUN** each time you want to use the program. A compiler, on the other hand, converts your program into object code that can be directly executed by your computer. Since the compiler translates your program only once, all you need to do is execute your program directly, usually by just typing its name.

Compiled programs run much faster than interpreted ones. The compiling process itself takes some extra time, but this is offset by the time you save while using the program.

In addition to advantages in speed, compilers protect your source code from tampering and theft. Compiled code bears no resemblance to your source code. For this reason, commercial software houses use compilers almost exclusively.

Two terms that you will see often in this book and in your C compiler manual are *compile time* and *run time*. Compile time refers to the compilation process. Run time refers to program execution. Unfortunately, you will often see them used in connection with the word "errors," as in *compile time errors* and *run time errors*.

CREATING AND COMPILING A C PROGRAM

How you create and compile a program is determined to a large extent by which compiler you are using and what operating system it is running under. If you are using a PC, then you have a choice of several excellent compilers that contain integrated program development environments, such as Turbo C and Quick C. If you are using such an environment, you can edit, compile, and run your programs directly inside it. (For beginners this is an excellent option.) Just follow the instructions supplied with your compiler.

If you are using a traditional command-line compiler, such as the UNIX C compiler, then you need to follow these steps to create and compile a program.

1. Create your program using an editor.

2. Compile the program.

3. Link your program with any necessary libraries.

4. Execute your program.

The exact method to accomplish these steps will be explained in your compiler's user manual.

Most compilers supply at least one sample program, so before continuing, it is a good idea for you to compile, link, and run a sample program to make sure you know how to do it.

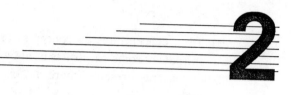

AN OVERVIEW
OF C

By far the hardest thing about learning a programming language is that no element of a language exists independently. Rather, all the components of a language work in relation to one another.

You will need to have a general idea of what constitutes a C program—including some basic control structures, forms, and functions—to understand the example programs that are used to illustrate the various aspects of the language in later chapters. To demonstrate these language elements, this chapter provides an overview of a C program, showing several simple examples. (Working through the examples on your computer is recommended, since most people learn best by doing.) This chapter does not go into much

detail but concentrates on concepts common to any C program. It also introduces some constructs used by almost all C programs. Most of the concepts presented here are examined more closely later in the book.

YOUR FIRST C PROGRAM

Before discussing any theory, let's look at a simple C program. Enter and execute the following:

```
/* Program #1 - My first C program. */

#include "stdio.h"

main()
{
   printf("This is my first C program.");
}
```

When run, this program displays "This is my first C program." on the screen.

A Line-by-Line Explanation

Let's examine the function of each line in the program. First, the program begins with the line

```
/* Program #1 - My first C program. */
```

This is a *comment*. In C, as in most other programming languages, you can enter a remark into a program's source code that is ignored by the compiler. The purpose of a comment is to provide an explanation of what the program—or a part of the program—is doing. A comment that starts this program simply identifies the program. In

more complex programs, comments are used to help explain what each feature of the program is for and how it functions. In other words, you can use comments to provide a "play-by-play" description of what your program does.

In C, a comment begins with a slash followed by an asterisk; that is, the symbol pair /*. A comment is concluded by the same pair in reverse, */. Anything within the comment symbols is ignored by the compiler. A comment may be several lines long.

The next line of code looks like this:

```
#include "stdio.h"
```

The C language defines several files, called *header files,* that contain information either necessary or useful to your program. For this program the file STDIO.H is needed. This file comes with your compiler and it must be on the same disk that you use to compile your program. Later in this book you will learn more about header files and why they are important.

The next line in the program is

```
main()
```

All C programs are composed of building blocks called *functions.* A program may consist of one or several functions. (See "Functions," later in this chapter for a complete discussion.) Each C function must have a name and the only function that any C program *must* have is the one called **main( )**. The **main( )** function is where program execution begins and, usually, ends. In technical terms, a C program begins with a call to **main( )** and ends (in most cases) when **main( )** returns.

The opening brace that follows **main( )** marks the start of the **main( )** function code.

The next line in the program is

```
printf("This is my first C program.");
```

This line causes the message "This is my first C program." to be displayed on the screen. It does this by calling the standard **printf( )**

function, which is supplied by your compiler. In its simplest form, **printf( )** displays the string specified between double quotes. Notice that this statement ends with a semicolon. In general, most C statements end with a semicolon.

The brace at the very end concludes the program. Although the brace is not actually part of the object code of the program, you can think of the program ending when the closing brace is executed. (It is possible to terminate the execution of a C program in several different ways. However, for simple programs like the ones used in the first chapters of this book, the other ways are not used.)

HANDLING ERRORS

If you incorrectly enter something in your program, the compiler will give you a syntax error message when it tries to compile it. But, since most C compilers will attempt to make sense out of your source code, no matter what you have written, the reported error may not reflect the actual mistake. For example, with some compilers, a missing opening brace in the **main( )** function in the preceding sample program will cause the **printf( )** statement to be reported as an incorrect identifier. So keep in mind that when you receive syntax error messages, you should look at the last few lines of code in your program to find the cause of the error.

Many C compilers report not only actual errors but also warning errors. The C language was designed to be very forgiving and to allow virtually anything that is syntactically correct to be compiled. However, some things, even though correct in syntax, are highly suspect. When the compiler encounters such a situation, it prints a warning. You, as the programmer, then decide whether its suspicions are justified. Unfortunately, some compilers can be a bit too helpful and will flag warnings on perfectly correct C statements.

Some compilers allow you to turn on options that report information you might want to know about your program. Sometimes, this type of information is reported as a warning message, even though there is nothing to be warned about. The programs in this book comply with the ANSI standard for C and will not generate any

warning messages about which you need be concerned. If you use your compiler's default error checking, you shouldn't see any warning messages.

ASSIGNING VALUES TO VARIABLES

Aside from the general form of a program, no other construct is as important in a programming language as the way values are assigned to variables. This is the subject of the next program.

The following program creates a variable called **value**, gives it the value 1023, and then displays this value on the screen.

```
/* Program #2 - A variable example. */

#include "stdio.h"

main()
{
  int value;

  value = 1023;

  printf("This program prints the value %d", value);
}
```

The message "This program prints the value 1023" will be displayed on the screen.

This program introduces three new things. First, the statement

```
int value;
```

declares a variable called **value** of type integer. In C, all variables must be named (or *declared*) before they are used. Further, the *type* of the variable must be specified, restricting the values the variable may hold. In this case, **value** may hold only integer values. (For most

compilers, this means the whole number values between $-32,768$ and 32,767.) To declare a variable to be of type integer, precede its name with the keyword **int**. C supports a wide range of variable types.

The next line of code

```
value = 1023;
```

assigns the value 1023 to **value**. In C, the assignment operator is the single equal sign.

Finally, the **printf( )** statement introduces another **printf( )** feature. This call to **printf( )** contains not one, but two, arguments. The first is the quoted string and the other is the variable **value**. Notice that the arguments are separated by a comma. In general, when there is more than one argument to a function the arguments are separated by commas.

The operation of the **printf( )** function is as follows. The first argument is a quoted string that may contain either normal characters or format codes that begin with the percent sign. Normal characters are simply displayed as is on the screen, in the order in which they are encountered. A format code informs **printf( )** that a non-character item is to be displayed. In this case, the **%d** means that an integer is to be output in decimal format. The value to be displayed is found in the second argument, in this case **value**. This value is then output to the screen at the point at which the format code is found in the string. To understand the relationship between the normal characters and the format codes, change the line to read

```
printf("This %d program displays the value", value);
```

Now the program displays "This 1023 program displays the value" on the screen. Thus, the value associated with a format code is displayed at the point where the code is encountered in the string that is the first argument to **printf( )**. But, as you will see shortly, **printf( )** is substantially more powerful than this example shows.

A MORE PRACTICAL EXAMPLE

Your first two programs, although illustrating several important features of the C language, are not very useful. The next sample

program performs a useful task: it converts gallons to liters.

```
/* This program converts gallons to liters. */

#include "stdio.h"

main()
{
  int gallons, liters;

  printf("Enter number of gallons: ");
  scanf("%d", &gallons);

  liters = gallons * 4;

  printf("%d liters", liters);
}
```

The program first prints the prompting message on the screen and waits for you to enter the number of gallons in whole numbers. (Integer types cannot have fractional components.) The program then displays the approximate liter equivalent. There are actually 3.7854 liters in a gallon, but since integers are used in this example, the conversion is rounded to four liters per gallon. For example, if you enter 1 gallon, the program will respond with a metric equivalent of 4 liters.

The first new thing you see in this program is that two variables are declared following the **int** keyword using a comma-separated list. In general, you can declare any number of variables of the same type by separating them by commas. (The program could have also used multiple **int** statements to accomplish the same thing.)

The next new statement is the call to the standard function **scanf( )**. This function is included with your compiler. It is used to read values from the keyboard. As it appears in this program, **scanf( )** takes two arguments. The first is a quoted string that contains only the format code **%d**. (Notice that **printf( )** and **scanf( )** use the same format code.) This tells **scanf( )** to read an integer and to place the results in the variable that follows. The ampersand (&) in front of gallons is necessary for **scanf( )** to work properly. You will learn why later in this book.

A New Data Type

Although the gallons-to-liters program is fine for rough approximations, it leaves something to be desired when a more accurate answer is needed, since integer data types cannot be used to represent fractions. If you need to use fractions, then you must use a floating-point data type. One of these is called **float**. Data of this type will typically be in the range 3.4E−38 to 3.4E+38. Operations on floating-point numbers preserve any fractional part of the outcome and thus provide a more accurate conversion.

The following version of the conversion program uses floating-point values to compute the number of liters.

```
/* This program converts gallons to liters using
   floating-point numbers. */

#include "stdio.h"

main()
{
  float gallons, liters;

  printf("Enter number of gallons: ");
  scanf("%f", &gallons);

  liters = gallons * 3.7854;

  printf("%f liters", liters);
}
```

There are three changes to this program from the previous version. First, *gallons* and *liters* are declared as **floats**. Second, in the **printf( )** and **scanf( )** statements, %fs have been substituted for the %ds. When using **printf( )** to display or **scanf( )** to input floating-point data, you must specify the %f format code because this code tells the functions to expect floating-point data. Finally, notice that the conversion coefficient is now specified as 3.7854, allowing a more accurate conversion. Whenever C encounters a number containing a decimal point, it automatically knows it is a floating-point constant. Hence, it uses both the integer and fractional part of the number.

Now try the program. Enter **1 gallon** when prompted. The equivalent number of liters is 3.7854.

A QUICK REVIEW

Before proceeding, let's review the most important things you have learned.

- All C programs must have a **main( )** function. This begins program execution.

- All variables must be declared before they are used.

- C supports a variety of data types, including integer and floating point.

- The **printf( )** function is used to output information to the screen.

- The **scanf( )** function reads information from the keyboard.

- The program stops executing when it encounters the end of **main( )**.

FUNCTIONS

As mentioned earlier, the C language is based on the concept of building blocks called functions. A C program is a collection of one or more functions. To write a program, you first create functions and then put them together.

In C, a function is a subroutine that contains one or more C statements and performs one or more tasks. (In well-written C code, each function performs only one task.) Each function has a name that is used to call it. In general, you can give a function any name you please. However, remember that **main( )** is reserved for the function that begins execution of your program. Also, the keywords that comprise the C language cannot be used.

If you have programmed in Pascal or Modula-2, one of the most important things to remember about C functions is that you cannot create a function within another function. Unlike Pascal, Modula-2, and some other languages that allow the nesting of functions, all C functions are separate entities (although one function may call another).

When denoting functions, this book uses a notational convention that is standard when writing about C: functions have parentheses after their name. For example, if a function's name is **max**, then it

will be written **max( )** when its name is used in text. This notation will help you distinguish function names from variable names in this book.

In your first programs, **main( )**, **printf( )**, and **scanf( )** are functions. As stated earlier, **main( )** is the first function executed when your program begins to run. It is a function that must be written by you. However, **printf( )** and **scanf( )** are functions that are supplied with your compiler and are part of the standard C function library. In general, programs you write will be a mix of functions you create and those supplied by the compiler.

Since functions form the foundation of C, let's take a closer look at them now.

The General Form of C Functions

All C functions share a common form, of which **main( )** in the preceding programs is an example. Below is the general form of a C function.

```
return-type function_name(parameter list)
{
    .
    . body of the function
    .
}
```

Let's look closely at the different parts of this general form.

In C, a function may return information back to the calling routine. Just as there are different types of variables, there are different types of return values. (So far return values haven't been used, but you will see some examples later in the chapter.) If the return type is not specified, as in the **main( )** functions in the preceding examples, the C compiler assumes an integer value is returned. That is, by default a function may return an integer. Keep in mind, however, that no function has to return a value. In fact, none of the programs you have seen so far do so. But if the function does return a value, then it must be of a type that is compatible with the function's return type. (This will be discussed further in "Functions Returning Values," later in the chapter.)

All functions need to be named. To call a function you simply use its name. Inside the parentheses following the function name is the parameter list. The *parameter list* specifies the names and types of variables to which information will be passed. If a function has no parameters, the parentheses are empty.

Next, braces surround the body of the function. The *body of the function* is composed of C statements that define what the function does. The function terminates and returns to the calling procedure when the closing brace is reached.

A PROGRAM WITH TWO FUNCTIONS

The following program contains two functions: **main( )** and **myfunc( )**. Before trying this program or reading the description that follows, try to figure out exactly what it prints on the screen.

```
/* This program contains two functions: main()
   and myfunc().
*/
#include "stdio.h"

main()
{
  printf("in main()");
  myfunc();
  printf("back in main()");
}

myfunc()
{
  printf(" inside myfunc() ");
}
```

The program works as follows. First, **main( )** begins execution and calls the first **printf( )** statement. Next, **main( )** calls **myfunc( )**. Notice how this is achieved: the function's name, **myfunc**, is followed by a pair of parentheses followed by a semicolon. (A function call is a C statement and so must end with a semicolon.) Then **myfunc( )** calls **printf( )** and returns to **main( )** at the line of code immediately

following the call. Finally, **main( )** calls **printf( )** the second time and then terminates. Thus, the output on the screen is

in main( ) inside myfunc( ) back in main( )

Function Arguments

In your first program, the function **printf( )** has one argument: the string that will be printed on the computer screen. Functions in C can have several arguments or none at all. (The upper limit is determined by the compiler you are using, but ANSI specifies that a function must be able to take at least 31 arguments.) An *argument* is a value that is passed into a function. When a function is defined, variables that will receive argument values must also be declared. These are called the *formal parameters* of the function. For example, the function listed below prints the product of the two integer arguments used to call it.

```
mul(int x, int y)
{
   printf("%d", x * y);
}
```

Each time **mul( )** is called, it will multiply the value passed to **x** times the value passed to **y**. Remember, however, that **x** and **y** are simply the function's operational variables that receive the values you use when calling the function. Consider this short program which illustrates how to call **mul( )**.

```
/* A simple program that demonstrates mul(). */

#include "stdio.h"

main()
{
   mul(10, 20);
   mul(5, 6);
   mul(8, 9);
}
```

```
mul(int x, int y)
{
  printf("%d ", x * y);
}
```

This program will print "200," "30," and "72" on the screen. When **mul( )** is called, the C compiler copies the value of each argument into the matching parameter. That is, in the first call to **mul( )**, 10 is copied into **x** and 20 is copied into **y**. In the second call, 5 is copied into **x** and 6 into **y**. In the third call, 8 is copied into **x** and 9 into **y**.

If you have never worked with a language that allows parameterized functions, then the preceding process may seem a bit strange. Don't worry, as you see more examples of C programs, the concept of arguments, parameters, and functions will become clear.

It is important to keep two terms straight. First, *argument* refers to the value that is passed to a function. Remember, the variable that receives the value of the arguments used in the function call is the formal parameter of the function. Functions that take arguments are called *parameterized functions*. The variable used as an argument in a function call has nothing to do with the formal parameter that receives its value.

In C functions, arguments are always separated by commas. In this book, the term *argument list* will refer to comma-separated arguments. The argument list for **mul( )** is *x, y*.

Functions Returning Values

Many of the C library functions you will use return a value. Also, functions you write may return values to the calling routine. In C, a function may return a value using **return**. The general form of the **return** statement is

return *value*;

where *value* is the value being returned.

To illustrate, the foregoing program that prints the product of two numbers can be rewritten as follows. Notice the value is assigned to a variable by placing the function on the right side of an assignment statement.

```
/* A program that uses return. */

#include "stdio.h"

main()
{
  int answer;

  answer = mul(10, 11); /* assign return value */

  printf("The answer is %d\n", answer);
}

/* This function returns a value. */
mul(int x, int y)
{
  return x * y;
}
```

In this example, **mul( )** returns the value of **x*y** using the **return** statement. This value is then assigned to **answer**. Thus, the value returned by the **return** statement becomes **mul( )**'s value in the calling routine.

Note: As stated earlier, there are different types of variables just as there are different types of return values. The type returned by the **mul( )** routine is **int** by default. Return values of different types will be explained later.

It is possible to cause a function to return by using the **return** statement without any value attached to it, making the returned value undefined. There can also be more than one **return** in a function.

The main( ) Function

As you know, the **main( )** function is special because it is the first function called when your program executes. It signifies the beginning of your program. Unlike some programming languages that always begin at the top of the program, a C program begins with a

call to the **main( )** function, no matter where that function is in your program. It is, however, good form for **main( )** to be the first function in your program.

There can only be one **main( )** in a program, since, if there were more than one, your program would not know where to begin. Actually, most compilers will catch an error like that before you ever reach the execution stage.

A CLOSER LOOK AT printf( )

Nearly every program example in this book that writes data to the screen uses the **printf( )** function. You have already seen how to print an integer, a decimal number, and a floating-point number on your computer screen. Now, let's take a closer look at this important library function.

The general form of **printf( )** is

printf("*control string*", *argument list*)

In the **printf( )** function the control string contains characters to be displayed on the screen, or format commands that tell how to display the rest of the arguments, or both. The format codes you have learned so far are **%d** and **%f**. One more will be introduced here and the rest will be discussed in later chapters.

Format control commands may be embedded anywhere in the control string. When you call **printf( )**, the control string is scanned by **printf( )**. All regular characters are printed on the screen as is. When a format command is encountered, **printf( )** remembers and uses it when printing the appropriate argument. Format commands and arguments are matched up left to right. The number of format commands in the control string tells **printf( )** how many subsequent arguments to expect.

Since the percent sign (%) is used to signal the beginning of a format command, if you wish to print a % as a character embedded in the control string, you must use two percent signs next to each other, that is, %%.

If you wish to print a single character using **printf( )**, use the **%c** format code. In C, all character constants must be enclosed in single

quotes. For example, this call to **printf( )** prints the letters "A," "B," and "C."

```
printf("%c %c %c". 'A', 'B', 'C');
```

The following examples show the **printf( )** function in action.

printf("this is a string %d", 100);
displays: this is a string 100

printf("%d is decimal, %f is float.",10, 110.789);
displays: 10 is decimal, 110.789 is float

printf("this is %c in uppercase %c", 'a', 'A');
displays: this is a in uppercase A

You *must* have the same number of arguments as format commands in the control string. If you don't, errors will occur.

Up to now you haven't needed to output a carriage return-linefeed sequence. However, the need for this will arise very soon. In C, the carriage return-linefeed sequence is generated using the *newline* character. To put a newline character into a string that can be used by **printf( )**, you must use the code **\n**. This is a backslash followed by a lowercase "n." To see an example of this, try the following program:

```
/* This program demonstrates the \n code which
    generates a new line.
*/
#include "stdio.h"

main()
{
  printf("one\n");
  printf("two\n");
  printf("three");
  printf("four");
}
```

The program produces this output.

```
one
two
threefour
```

One thing to keep in mind is that the newline character can go anywhere in the string—not just at the end. You might want to try experimenting with it a little now to make sure you understand exactly what it does.

A CLOSER LOOK AT scanf( )

The **scanf( )** function is one of C's input functions. Although it can be used to read virtually any type of data entered at the keyboard, you will often use it to input integers or floating-point numbers. The general form of **scanf( )** is

```
scanf("control string", argument list);
```

For now, assume that the control string may only contain format codes. (Until you study **scanf( )** in detail later in this book, it's best not to put anything in the control string other than the format codes. Otherwise you might get some confusing results.)

The two codes you have learned about are **%d** and **%f**, which tell **scanf( )** to read an integer and a floating-point number, respectively. The argument list must contain exactly the same number of arguments as there are format codes in the control string. If this is not the case, various things could occur— including a program crash! The variables following the control string will contain the values you entered at the keyboard after the call to **scanf( )** returns.

The variables that will be receiving the values read from the keyboard must be preceded by an **&** in the argument list. It is too complicated to explain at this time why the **&** is necessary, except to say that it lets **scanf( )** place a value into the argument.

IDENTIFIERS IN C

In C, an identifier is a name for a function, a variable, or any other user-defined item. Identifiers can be one or several characters long.

The ANSI standard specifies that at least the first 31 characters be significant. Variable names may start with any letter of the alphabet or an underscore (_). Next may come a letter, a digit, or an underscore. The underscore can be used to make a variable name more readable, as in **first_name**. To C, uppercase and lowercase are different—**count** and **COUNT** are separate names. Here are some examples of acceptable identifiers:

first	last	Addr1	top_of_file
name23	_temp	t	s23e3

You cannot use any of the C keywords as identifier names. *Keywords* are the words that make up the C programming language. Also, you should not use the name of a standard function, such as **printf( )**, for an identifier. Beyond these two restrictions, good programming practice dictates that you should use identifier names that reflect the function's or variable's meaning or usage.

TWO SIMPLE COMMANDS

To understand the examples in the next few chapters, you need to understand two C commands: **if** and **for**, at least in their simplest form. In later chapters these commands will be explored completely.

The if Statement

The C **if** statement operates much the same way an IF statement operates in any other language. Its simplest form is

if(*condition*) statement;

where *condition* is an expression that evaluates to either true or false. In C, true is non-zero and false is zero. If the condition is true, the statement will execute. If the condition is false, the statement will not be executed. The following fragment prints the phrase "10 is less than 11" on the screen.

```
if(10 < 11) printf("10 is less than 11");
```

The comparison operators are similar to those in other languages, such as < for "less than," or >= for "greater than or equal to." However, in C, the equality operator is ==. Therefore, this statement does not print the message "hello".

```
if(10==11) printf("hello"):
```

The following program shows an example of the **if** statement:

```
/* This program illustrates the if statement. */

#include "stdio.h"

main()
{
  int a, b;

  printf("enter first number: ");
  scanf("%d", &a);
  printf("enter second number: ");
  scanf("%d", &b);

  if(a < b) printf("First number is less than second");
}
```

The for Loop

The **for** loop in C can operate much like the FOR loop in other languages, including Pascal and BASIC. Its simplest form is

for(*initialization, condition, increment*) statement;

where *initialization* is used to set the loop control variable to an initial value. *Condition* is an expression that is tested each time the loop repeats. As long as it is true (non-zero) the loop keeps running. The *increment* portion is added to the loop control variable. For example, this program prints the numbers 1 through 100 on the screen.

```
/* A program that illustrates the for loop. */

#include "stdio.h"

main()
{
  int count;

  for(count=1; count<=100; count=count+1)
    printf("%d ", count);
}
```

As you can see, **count** is initialized to 1. Each time the loop repeats the condition **count<=100** is tested. If it is true, the **printf( )** statement is executed and **count** is increased by one. When **count** is greater than 100, the condition is false and the loop stops.

In professionally written C code, you will never see a statement like **count=count+1** because C supports a shorthand, **count++**, for this sort of statement. The ++ is a special operator in C that tells the compiler to increment the variable by one. The complement of ++ is − −, which decrements by one. These operators will be discussed later in the book. They are mentioned here because you may see them in **for** statements of programs in other books and magazines. For example, the preceding **for** statement will generally be written this way:

```
for(count=1; count<=100; count++) printf("%d ", count);
```

This is also the form that will be used in this book from this point onward.

BLOCKS OF CODE

Because C is a structured language it supports the creation of blocks of code. A *code block* is a logically connected group of program statements that is treated as a unit. In C, a code block is created by placing a sequence of statements between opening and closing braces. In this example,

```
if(x<10) {
  printf("too low, try again");
  scanf("%d", &x);
}
```

the two statements after the **if** and between the braces are both executed if **x** is less than ten. These two statements with the braces represent a block of code. They are a logical unit: one of the statements cannot execute without the other also executing. In C, the target of most commands may be either a single statement or a code block. Not only do code blocks allow many algorithms to be implemented with greater clarity, elegance, and efficiency but they also help the programmer conceptualize the true nature of the routine.

The program that follows uses a block of code. Enter and run the program so you can see the effect of the block.

```
/* This program demonstrates a block of code. */

#include "stdio.h"

main()
{
  int a, b;

  printf("enter first number: ");
  scanf("%d", &a);
  printf("enter second number: ");
  scanf("%d", &b);

  if(a < b) {
    printf("First number is less than second.\n");
    printf("Their difference is: %d", b-a);
  }
}
```

If the first number is less than the second number, then both **printf( )** statements are executed. Otherwise, both are skipped. At no time can just one of them execute.

SEMICOLONS, POSITIONING, AND COMMENTS

You may be wondering why so many statements end with a semicolon. In C, the semicolon is a statement *terminator*. That is, each individual statement must end with a semicolon. It indicates the end of one logical entity. (For those of you who know Pascal, *be careful*. The semicolon in Pascal is a statement *separator;* in C it is a statement *terminator*.)

As you know, a block is a set of logically connected statements that are inside opening and closing braces. If you consider a block a group of statements with a semicolon after each statement, it makes sense that the blocks are not followed by a semicolon. (This is why there are no semicolons following the closing brace of a function.)

C does not recognize the end of the line as a terminator. This means there are no constraints on the positioning of statements. For example,

```
x = y;

y = y+1;

mul(x, y);
```

is the same as

```
x = y;   y = y+1;   mul(x, y);
```

to a C compiler.

Comments in C may be placed anywhere in a program and are enclosed between two markers. As stated earlier, the start comment marker is /* and the end comment marker is */.

INDENTATION PRACTICES

As you may have noticed in the previous examples, some statements were indented. The C language is free-form because it does not

matter where you place statements relative to each other on a line.

However, over the years, a common and accepted indentation style has evolved that makes programs very readable. This book will follow that style and it is recommended that you do so as well. Using this style, you indent one level after each opening brace and move back out one level at each closing brace. There are also certain statements that encourage some additional indenting. These will be covered later.

C KEYWORDS

Now that you have seen an overview of the C language, it is time for you to see the keywords that comprise it. ANSI standard C has 32 keywords that may not be used as variable or function names. These words, combined with the formal C syntax, form the C programming language. They are listed in Table 2-1.

In addition, many C compilers have several additional keywords that are used to take better advantage of the 8086/8088 family of

Keyword List

auto	double	int	struct
break	else	long	switch
case	enum	register	typedef
char	extern	return	union
const	float	short	unsigned
continue	for	signed	void
default	goto	sizeof	volatile
do	if	static	while

TABLE 2-1 The 32 Keywords as Defined by the Proposed ANSI Standard

asm	_cs	_ds	_es
interrupt	cdecl	far	huge
	near	pascal	

asm	_cs	_ds	_es
_ss	cdecl	far	huge
interrupt	near	pascal	

TABLE 2-2   Some Common C Extended Keywords

processors' memory organization. These keywords also give support for inter-language programming and interrupts. The most commonly used extended keywords are shown in Table 2-2.

Note: C requires that all keywords be in lowercase. For example, **RETURN** will not be recognized as the keyword **return**.

THE STANDARD C LIBRARY

In the discussion of the sample programs, it was mentioned that **printf( )** and **scanf( )** were provided with your C compiler. Neither **printf( )** nor **scanf( )** is part of the C language, per se, yet they are included with every ANSI C compiler. These functions, and others, are found in the *standard C library*.

The ANSI standard defines a rather large set of functions that will be provided by the C compiler. These functions are designed to perform many common tasks, including I/O operations. The designers of your C compiler have already written most of the general purpose functions that you will use. When you use a function that is not part of the program you wrote, the C compiler remembers its name. A piece of the compiler finds the missing function and adds it to your object code. The linker performs this process and the action is called *linking*. Some C compilers have their own linker; others use the standard linker supplied by your operating system.

The linking process adds already compiled code into your program. The functions that are kept in the library are in *relocatable*

format. This means the memory addresses for the various machine-code instructions have not been absolutely defined; rather, only offset information has been kept. When your program links with the functions in the standard library, these memory offsets are used to create the actual addresses used. There are several technical manuals and books that explain this process in more detail. However, you do not need any further understanding of the actual relocation process to program in C.

Many of the functions you will need are already written. They act as building blocks that you simply assemble. If you write a function that you will use again and again, it too can be placed into a library. Some compilers will allow you to place it in the standard library; others will make you create an additional one. Either way, the code will be there for you to use over and over.

One key point to remember is that the ANSI standard only specifies a *minimum* standard library. Most compilers supply libraries that contain far more functions than those defined by ANSI.

EXERCISES

1. If you haven't done so already, run the first program. Confirm that you can successfully compile a program with your C compiler.

2. Write a short program that prints the following output on the screen:

   This is line one.
   This is line two.

3. Write **printf( )** statements that will display the following on your screen:

   This is a test. 1 2 3
   123.23

4. Show the declaration statements that will declare these variables as shown here:

up, down as integers
first, last as floating point

5. Rework the gallons-to-liters program so that it converts from liters to gallons.

Answers

2.
```
main()
{
   printf("This is line one.\n");
   printf("This is line two.");
}
```

3.
```
printf("This is a test. %d %d %d", 1, 2, 3);

printf("%f", 123.23);
```

4.
```
a int up, down;
float first, last;
```

5.
```
/* This program converts liters to gallons using
      floating-point numbers. */

#include "stdio.h"

main()
{
   float gallons, liters;
```

```
    printf("Enter number of liters: ");
    scanf("%f", &liters);

    gallons = liters / 3.7854;

    printf("%f gallons", gallons);
}
```

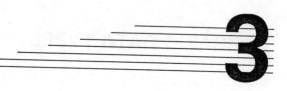

INTRODUCING VARIABLES, CONSTANTS, AND OPERATORS

Variables and constants are manipulated by operators to form expressions. This process forms the basis of most programming. Unlike some other computer languages that take a simple — and limited — approach to these elements, C places a much greater value on them. This chapter introduces these concepts as they relate to the C programming language. You should read this chapter thoroughly because it discusses some of the most fundamental aspects of C.

THE BASIC DATA TYPES

As you saw in Chapter 2, all variables in C must be declared prior to their use. This is necessary because the compiler needs to know what type of data a variable is before it can properly compile any statement the variable is used in. In ANSI standard C there are five basic data types: character, integer, floating point, double floating point, and valueless. The keywords used to declare variables of these types are **char**, **int**, **float**, **double**, and **void**, respectively. The size and range of each data type is shown in Table 3-1. These numbers will apply to most C compilers for the PC, but remember, your compiler may vary slightly.

Variables of type **char** are used to hold 8-bit ASCII characters such as "A," "B," "C," or any other 8-bit quantity. To specify a character you must enclose it in single quotation marks ("). Variables of type **int** can hold quantities that do not require a fractional component. Variables of this type are often used for controlling loops and conditional statements. Variables of the types **float** and **double** are employed when a fractional component is required or when your application requires very large numbers. The difference between a **float** and a **double** variable is the size of the largest and smallest numbers they can hold. As Table 3-1 shows, a **double** in C can store a number approximately ten times larger than a **float**. The purpose of the **void** type is discussed later in this book.

Type	Bit Width	Range
char	8	-128 to 127
int	16	$-32,768$ to $32,767$
float	32	$3.4E-38$ to $3.4E+38$
double	64	$1.7E-308$ to $1.7E+308$
void	0	Valueless

TABLE 3-1   The Common Size and Range of C's Basic Types

DECLARATION OF VARIABLES

The general form of a variable declaration statement is shown here:

type variable_list;

Here, *type* must be a valid C data type and *variable_list* may consist of one or more identifier names, separated by commas. Some declarations are shown here:

```
int i, j, k;

char ch, chr;

float f, balance;

double d;
```

In C, the name of a variable has nothing to do with its type.

The ANSI standard guarantees that at least the first 31 characters of any identifier name (including variable names) will be significant. To understand why the number of significant characters is important, consider these two identifiers:

this_is_a_very_long_identifier_name
this_is_a_very_long_identifier_name_too

These names have the first 35 characters in common. Consequently, for most C compilers they will appear to be the same because any character after the 31st will be ignored.

There are three basic places where variables will be declared: inside functions, in the definition of function parameters, or outside of all functions. These variables are called local variables, formal parameters, and global variables, respectively. The importance of these places in declaring variables will be discussed in greater detail later in this book. However, let's take a brief look at these three categories of variables now.

Local Variables

Variables declared inside a function are called local variables. These may be referenced only by the statements that are inside the function in which the variables are declared. Local variables are not known to other functions outside their own. For example:

```
#include "stdio.h"

main()
{
  int x;

  x = 10;
  func();
  printf("%d", x);
}

func()
{
  int x;

  x = -199;
  printf("%d\n", x);
}
```

The integer variable **x** was declared twice, once in **main( )** and once in **func( )**. The **x** in **main( )** has no bearing on, nor relationship to, the **x** in **func( )**. That is, inside **main( )**, **x** is given the value 10 and the call to **func( )** does not change its value. Thus, this program will print −199 and 10 on the screen.

In C, local variables are "created" when the function is called and "destroyed" when the function is exited. Correspondingly, the storage for these local variables is created and destroyed dynamically. Local variables are sometimes called *dynamic* or *automatic variables*. However, this book will continue to use the term "local variable" since it is the more common term.

Formal Parameters

As you saw in Chapter 2, if a function has arguments, those arguments must be declared. These are called the formal parameters of

the function. As shown in the following program fragment, the declaration occurs after the function name, inside the parentheses.

```
func1(int first, int last, char ch)
{
    .
    .
    .
}
```

The **func1( )** function has three arguments called **first, last,** and **ch.** You must tell C what type of variables these are by declaring them as shown above. Once this has been done, they receive the information passed to the function. They may also be used inside the function as normal local variables. For example, you may make assignments to a function's formal parameters or use them in any valid C expression. Even though these variables perform the special task of receiving the value of the arguments passed to the function, they can be used like any other local variable. Like other local variables, their value is lost once the function terminates.

Global Variables

You may have been wondering how to make a variable and its data stay in existence throughout the execution of your program. You can do this in C by using *global variables.* Unlike local variables, global variables will hold their value the entire time your program is running. You create global variables by declaring them outside of any function. A global variable can be accessed by any function.

In the following program, you can see that the variable **count** has been declared outside of all functions. Its declaration was before the **main( )** function. However, it could have been placed anywhere, as long as it was not within a function. Remember, though, that since you must declare a variable before you use it, it is best to declare global variables at the top of the program.

```
#include "stdio.h"

int count;    /* this is a global variable */
```

```
main()
{
  int i;    /* this is a local variable */

  for(i=0; i<10; i++) {
    count = i * 2;
    func1();
  }
}

func1()
{
  printf("count: %d", count); /* access global count */
  func2();
}

func2()
{
  int count;   /* this is a local variable */

  for(count=0; count<3; count++) printf(".");
}
```

Looking closely at this program, it should be clear that although neither **main( )** nor **func1( )** has declared the variable **count**, both may use it. In **func2( )**, however, a local variable called **count** is declared. When **func2( )** references **count**, it will be referencing only its local variable, not the global one. It is very important to remember that if a global variable and a local variable have the same name, all references to that variable name inside the function where the local variable is declared will refer to that local variable and have no effect on the global variable. (Try this program and observe its output to convince yourself that it operates as expected.)

SOME TYPE MODIFIERS

Except for type **void**, C allows the basic data types to have various *modifiers* preceding them. A modifier is used to alter the meaning of

the base type to more precisely fit the needs of a specific situation. A list of the modifiers is shown here:

signed
unsigned
long
short

The modifiers **signed, unsigned, long,** and **short** may be applied to character and integer base types. However, **long** may also be applied to **double.** Table 3-2 shows all the allowed combinations of the basic types and modifiers. The table also shows the most common size for each type and its most common range.

Although allowed, the use of **signed** on integers is redundant because the default integer declaration assumes a signed number.

The difference between signed and unsigned integers is the way the high-order bit of the integer is interpreted. If a signed integer is specified, then the C compiler will generate code that assumes the high-order bit of an integer is to be used as a *sign flag.* If the sign flag is 0, then the number is positive; if it is 1, the number is negative. Negative numbers are represented using the *two's complement* approach. In this method, all bits in the number (except the sign flag) are reversed and then 1 is added to the number. Finally, the sign flag is set to 1.

Signed integers are important for a great many algorithms, but they have only half the absolute magnitude of their unsigned brothers. For example, here is 32,767:

0 1 1 1 1 1 1 1 1 1 1 1 1 1 1 1

If the high-order bit were set to 1, the number would then be interpreted as −1 (assuming two's complement format). However, if you had declared this to be an **unsigned int,** then when the high-order bit is set to 1, the number becomes 65,535.

To understand the difference in the ways signed and unsigned integers are interpreted by C, you should run this short program:

```
#include "stdio.h"

/* This program shows the difference between
```

```
  signed and unsigned integers.
*/
main()
{
  int i;    /* a signed integer */
  unsigned int j; /* an unsigned integer */

  j = 60000;
  i = j;
  printf("%d %u", i, j);
}
```

Type	Bit Width	Range
char	8	−128 to 127
unsigned char	8	0 to 255
signed char	8	−128 to 127
int	16	−32768 to 32767
unsigned int	16	0 to 65535
signed int	16	−32768 to 32767
short int	8	−128 to 127
unsigned short int	8	0 to 255
signed short int	8	−128 to 127
long int	32	−2147483648 to 2147483649
signed long int	32	−2147483648 to 2147483649
unsigned long int	32	0 to 4294967296
float	32	3.4E−38 to 3.4E+38
double	64	1.7E−308 to 1.7E+308
long double	80	3.4E−4932 to 1.1E+4932

TABLE 3-2   Combinations, Size, and Range of C's Basic Types and Modifiers

When this program is run the output is "−5536 60000." This is because the bit pattern that represents 60000 as an unsigned integer is interpreted as −5536 by a signed integer. As you know, the **%d** tells **printf( )** to display an integer in decimal form. The **%u** is another format code that tells **printf( )** an **unsigned int** is to be displayed.

C allows a shorthand notation for declaring **unsigned, short,** or **long** integers. You may simply use the word "unsigned," "short," or "long" without the **int**. The **int** is implied. For example,

```
unsigned x;
unsigned int y;
```

both declare unsigned integer variables.

Variables of type **char** may be used to hold values other than just the ASCII character set. A **char** variable can also be used as a "small" integer with the range −128 through 127 and can be used in place of an integer when larger numbers are not required. For example, the following program uses a **char** variable to control the loop that prints the alphabet on the screen.

```
/* Program prints the alphabet in reverse order. */

#include "stdio.h"

main()
{
  char letter;

  for(letter = 'Z'; letter >= 'A'; letter--)
    printf("%c ", letter);
}
```

If the **for** loop seems odd to you, keep in mind that the character "A" is represented inside the computer as a number and that the values from A to Z are sequential in ascending order.

CONSTANTS

In C, constants refer to fixed values that may not be altered by the program. However, for the most part, constants, and their usage, are so intuitive that they have been used in some form in all the preceding sample programs. Now, the time has come to cover them formally.

C constants can be of any of the basic data types. The way each constant is represented depends on its type. Character constants are enclosed between single quotes. For example "a," and "%" are both character constants. As some of the examples have shown, if you wish to assign a character to a variable of type **char**, you will use a statement similar to this:

```
ch = 'Z';
```

Remember, when you use **printf( )** to display a character, use the %c format code.

Integer constants are specified as numbers without fractional components. For example, 10 and −100 are integer constants. Floating-point constants require the use of the decimal point followed by the number's fractional component. For example, 11.123 is a floating- point constant. C also allows you to use scientific notation for floating-point numbers.

There are two floating-point types: **float** and **double**. Also, there are several flavors of the basic types that are generated using the type modifiers. The question is, how does the compiler determine the type of a constant? For example, is 123.23 a **float** or a **double**? The answer to this is both simple and complex.

By default, the C compiler fits a numeric constant into the smallest compatible data type that will hold it. Therefore, 10 is an **int** by default, but 60000 is **unsigned** and 100000 is a **long**. Even though the value 10 could be fit into a character, the compiler will not do this because it would mean crossing type boundaries. The only exception to the smallest type rule is floating-point constants, which are assumed to be **double**. For virtually all programs you will write as a beginner, the compiler defaults are perfectly adequate. However, it is possible to specify precisely the type of constant you want.

In cases where the assumption that C makes about a numeric constant is not what you want, C allows you to specify the exact type of numeric constant by using a suffix. For floating-point types, if you follow the number with an "F," the number is treated as a **float**. If you follow it with an "L," the number becomes a **long double**. For integer types, the "U" suffix stands for **unsigned** and the "L" for **long**. Some examples are shown here:

Data Type	Constant Examples
int	1 123 21000 −234
long int	35000L −34L
short int	10 −12 90
unsigned int	10000U 987U 40000
float	123.23F 4.34e−3F
double	123.23 12312333 −0.9876324
long double	1001.2L

Hexadecimal and Octal Constants

As you probably know, in programming it is sometimes easier to use a number system based on 8 or 16 instead of 10. The number system based on 8 is called *octal* and it uses the digits 0 through 7. In octal the number 10 is the same as 8 in decimal. The base 16 number system is called *hexadecimal* and uses the digits 0 through 9 plus the letters "A" through "F," which are equivalent to 10, 11, 12, 13, 14, and 15 in decimal. The hexadecimal number 10 is 16 in decimal. Because of the frequency with which these two number systems are used, C allows you to specify integer constants in hexadecimal or octal instead of decimal. A hexadecimal constant must begin with 0x (a zero followed by an "x") and then the constant in hexadecimal form. An octal constant begins with 0. Here are some examples:

```
int hex = 0xFF;   /* 255 in decimal */

int oct = 011;    /* 9 in decimal */
```

String Constants

C supports one other type of constant in addition to the predefined data types: the *string*. A string is a set of characters enclosed in double quotes. For example, "this is a test" is a string. You have seen examples of strings in some of the **printf( )** statements in the sample programs. Keep in mind one important fact: although C allows you to define string constants, it does not formally have a string data type as many other languages do. Instead, as you will see a little later in this book, strings are supported in C as character arrays.

Don't confuse the strings with characters. A single character constant is enclosed by single quotes, as with "a." However, "a" is a string containing only one letter.

You can use **printf( )** to display a string constant using the %s format code. For example, this program prints the sentence "this is a test." on the screen.

```
/* Demonstrate the %s printf() format code. */

#include "stdio.h"

main()
{
   printf("%s %s %s %s", "this", "is", "a", "test.");
}
```

The preceding example is contrived simply to illustrate the %s format code; it could obviously be written in a more straightforward fashion. The %s, as you will see later, is most often used in printing string variables.

Backslash Character Constants

Enclosing character constants in single quotes works for most printing characters, but a few, such as the carriage return, are impossible to enter from the keyboard. For this reason, C has created the special backslash character constants.

You have already learned that "\n" stands for newline. C supports several special backslash codes (listed in Table 3-3) so you can easily enter these characters as constants. Use the backslash codes instead of their ASCII equivalents to help ensure portability. For example, the following program outputs newline, a backslash, and a backspace.

```
#include "stdio.h"

main()
{
  printf("\n\\b");
}
```

Code	Meaning
\b	Backspace
\f	Form feed
\n	Newline
\r	Carriage return
\t	Horizontal tab
\"	Double quote
\'	Single quote character
\0	Null
\\	Backslash
\v	Vertical tab
\a	Alert
\N	Octal constant (where N is an octal constant)
\xN	Hexadecimal constant (where N is a hexidecimal constant)

TABLE 3-3   Backslash Codes

VARIABLE INITIALIZATION

You can give a value to most variables in C when they are declared by placing an equal sign and a constant after the variable name. This is called *initialization*. The general form of initialization is

type variable _ name = constant;

Some examples are

```
char ch = 'a';

int first = 0;

float balance = 123.23F;
```

Global variables are initialized only at the start of the program. Local variables are initialized each time the function in which they are declared is entered. All global variables are initialized to zero if no other initializer is specified. Local variables that are not initialized will have unknown values until the first assignment is made to them.

The main advantage of initializing variables is that it slightly reduces the amount of code in the program. As a simple example of variable initialization, this program requests a number and then sums all the numbers between 1 and that number.

```
/* An example using variable initialization. */

#include "stdio.h"

main()
{
  int t;

  printf("enter a number: ");
  scanf("%d", &t);
  total(t);
}

total(int x)
```

```
{
  int sum=0;  /* initialize sum */
  int i, count;

  for(i=0; i<x; i++) {
    sum = sum + i;
    for(count=0; count<10; count++) printf(".");
    printf("the current sum is %d\n", sum);
  }
}
```

OPERATORS

C is very rich in built-in operators. An *operator* is a symbol that tells the compiler to perform specific mathematical or logical manipulations. C has three general classes of operators: *arithmetic, relational and logical,* and *bitwise.* In addition, C has some special operators for particular tasks.

This chapter will concentrate on the arithmetic and relational and logical operators. The more advanced operators are discussed later in this book.

Arithmetic Operators

Table 3-4 lists the arithmetic operators allowed in C. The operators +, −, *, and / all work the same way in C as they do in any other computer language (or algebra, for that matter). They can be applied to any built-in data type allowed by C. When / is applied to an integer or character, any remainder will be truncated. For example, 10/3 will equal 3 in integer division.

The modulus operator % also works in C the way that it does in other languages. Remember that the modulus operation yields the remainder of an integer division. This means that the % cannot be used on type **float** or **double.** The following program will illustrate its use.

```
#include "stdio.h"

main()
{
  int x, y;

  x = 10;
  y = 3;
  printf("%d", x/y);   /* will display 3 */
  printf("%d", x%y);   /* will display 1, the remainder
                          of  the integer division */


  x = 1;
  y = 2;
  printf("%d %d", x/y, x%y); /*  will display 0 1 */

}
```

The last line prints a 0 and a 1 because 1/2 in integer division is 0 with a remainder of 1. Thus, 1%2 yields the remainder 1.

The unary minus (−), in effect, multiplies its single operand by −1. That is, any number preceded by a minus sign switches its sign.

Operator	Action
−	Subtraction, also unary minus
+	Addition
*	Multiplication
/	Division
%	Modulus
− −	Decrement
+ +	Increment

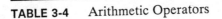

TABLE 3-4   Arithmetic Operators

Increment and Decrement

C allows two very useful operators not generally found in other computer languages. These are the increment and decrement operators, + + and — —. These operators were mentioned in passing in Chapter 2, when the **for** loop was introduced. The + + adds 1 to its operand, and — — subtracts 1. Therefore,

```
x = x+1;
```

is the same as

```
++x;
```

and

```
x = x-1;
```

is the same as

```
--x;
```

The increment and decrement operators may either precede or follow the operand. For example,

```
x = x+1;
```

can be written as

```
++x;
```

or as

```
x++;
```

There is, however, a difference when they are used in an expression. When an increment or decrement operator precedes its operand, C will perform that operation before using the operand's value. If the operator follows its operand, C will use the operand's value before incrementing or decrementing it. Consider the following:

```
x = 10;

y = ++x;
```

In this case, **y** will be set to 11. However, if the code had been written as

```
x = 10;

y = x++;
```

y would have been set to 10. In both cases, **x** is still set to 11; the difference is when it happens. There are significant advantages in being able to control when the increment or decrement operation takes place.

Most C compilers produce very fast, efficient object code for increment and decrement operations that is better than the code generated by using an assignment statement. Thus, it is a good idea to use increment and decrement operators when you can.

Here is the precedence of the arithmetic operators.

Highest	++ --
	- (unary minus)
	* / %
Lowest	+ -

Operators on the same precedence level are evaluated by the compiler from left to right. Of course, parentheses may be used to alter the order of evaluation. Parentheses are treated by C in the same way they are by virtually all other computer languages: they force an operation, or set of operations, to a higher precedence level.

Relational	
Operator	**Action**
>	Greater than
>=	Greater than or equal to
<	Less than
<=	Less than or equal to
==	Equal
!=	Not equal to

Logical	
Operator	**Action**
&&	AND
||	OR
!	NOT

TABLE 3-5   Relational and Logical Operators

Relational and Logical Operators

In the terms "relational operator" and "logical operator," "relational" refers to the relationships that values can have and "logical" refers to how these relationships can be connected. Because relational and logical operators often work together, they will be discussed together here.

The key to the concepts of relational and logical operators is the idea of true and false. In C, true is any value other than 0 and false is 0. However, expressions that use relational or logical operators will evaluate to 0 when false and 1 when true. The relational and logical operators are shown in Table 3-5. Notice that in C, not equal is != and equality is the double equal sign, ==.

The logical operators are used to support the basic logical operations of AND, OR, and NOT, according to this truth table. The table uses 1 for true and 0 for false.

p	q	p AND q	p OR q	NOT p
0	0	0	0	1
0	1	0	1	1
1	1	1	1	0
1	0	0	1	0

Although C does not contain a built-in exclusive-OR (XOR) operator, it is easy to construct one. The XOR operation uses this truth table.

p	q	XOR
0	0	0
0	1	1
1	0	1
1	1	0

The XOR operation produces a true result when one and only one operand is true. The following function uses the AND and OR operators to construct an XOR operation. The result is returned by the function.

```c
xor(int a, int b)
{
   return (a || b) && !(a && b);
}
```

The following program uses this function. It displays the results of AND, OR, and XOR for the values you enter.

```c
/* This program demonstrates the xor() function. */
#include "stdio.h"

main()
{
  int p, q;

  printf("enter P (0 or 1): ");
```

```
    scanf("%d", &p);
    printf("enter Q (0 or 1): ");
    scanf("%d", &q);

    printf("P AND Q: %d\n", p && q);
    printf("P OR Q: %d\n", p || q);
    printf("P XOR Q: %d\n", xor(p, q));
}

xor(int a, int b)
{
    return (a || b) && !(a && b);
}
```

The relational and logical operators are lower in precedence than the arithmetic operators. This means that an expression like 10 > 1 + 12 is evaluated as if it were written 10 > (1 + 12). The result is, of course, false.

You may link any number of relational operations using logical operators. For example, the expression joins three relational operations.

```
    var>15 || !(10<count) && 3<=item
```

The following list shows the precedence of the relational and logical operators.

Highest	!
	> >= < <=
	== !=
	&&
Lowest	||

Remember, all relational and logical expressions produce a result of either 0 or 1. Therefore, the following program is not only correct, but will also print the number 1 on the display.

```
#include "stdio.h"

main()
```

```
{
  int x;

  x = 100;
  printf("%d", x>10);
}
```

EXPRESSIONS

Operators, constants, and variables constitute *expressions*. An expression in C is any valid combination of those pieces. You probably already know the general form of expressions from your other programming experience or from algebra. But there are a few aspects of expressions that relate specifically to C and these will be discussed now.

Type Conversion in Expressions

When constants and variables of different types are mixed in an expression, they are converted to the same type. The C compiler will convert all operands "up" to the type of the largest operand. This is done on an operation by operation basis. For example, if one operand is a **char** and the other an **int**, then the **char** is promoted to an integer. Or, if either operand is a **double**, the other operand is promoted to **double**. This means that such unlikely conversions as **char**s to **double**s are perfectly valid. Once a conversion has been applied, each pair of operands will be of the same type and the result of each operation will be of the same type as both operands. Also, when expressions are evaluated, all **char**s are automatically converted to **int**, and **float** s is converted to **double**.

For example, consider the type conversions that occur in Figure 3-1. First, the character **ch** is converted to an integer and **float f** is converted to **double**. Then the outcome of **ch/i** is converted to a **double** because **f*d** is **double**. The final result is **double** because, by this time, both operands are **double**.

Casts

It is possible to force an expression to be of a specific type by using a construct called a *cast*. The general form of a cast is

(type) expression

where *type* is a valid C data type. For example, if you wished to make sure the expression **x/2** was evaluated to type **float** you could write it in the following way:

```
(float) x / 2
```

Casts are often considered operators. As an operator, a cast is unary and has the same precedence as any other unary operator.

There are times when a cast can be very useful, for example, when you wish to use an integer for loop control, but to perform computation on it requires a fractional part, as in this example program.

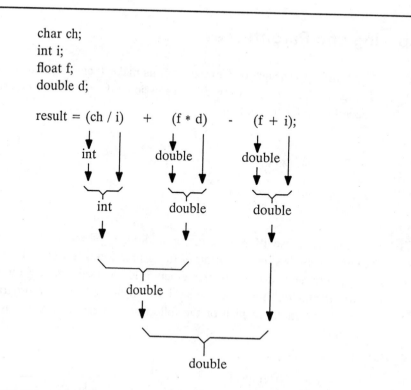

FIGURE 3-1   Type conversion example

```
#include "stdio.h"

main() /* print i and i/2 with fractions */
{
  int i;

  for(i=1; i<=100; ++i )
    printf("%d / 2 is: %f\n",i,(float) i /2);
}
```

Without the cast (**float**), only an integer division would have been performed. The cast ensures that the fractional part of the answer will be displayed on the screen.

Spacing and Parentheses

Tabs and spaces included in expressions make them easier to read. For example, the following two expressions are the same, but the second is easier to read.

```
x=10/y*(127/x);

x = 10 / y * (127/x);
```

Likewise, use of redundant or additional parentheses will not cause errors or slow execution of the expression. It's a good idea to use parentheses to clarify the exact order of evaluation, both for yourself and for others who may have to figure out your program later. For example, which of the following two expressions is easier to read?

```
x = y/3 - 34*temp&127;

x = (y/3) - ((34*temp) & 127);
```

EXERCISES

1. List the seven built-in data types in C.

2. What types can have the **unsigned** modifier applied to them?

3. Write a function called **add( )** that has two integer arguments. The function will return the sum of these two arguments.

4. Write a program that requests two numbers from the user and then divides the first number by the second. However, it will not allow a division by zero.

5. Show how to specify a **float** constant given the number 123.309.

6. Write a program that prints the odd numbers from 1 to 100.

7. Evaluate the following expressions, indicating which ones are true or false.

   a. 10= =9+1

   b. 10 && 8

   c. 8 || 0

   d. 0 && 0

   e. let x=10; y=9;

   x >= 8 && y<=x

Answers

1. char
   int
   float
   double
   void

2. char, int, long, and short

3.
```
    add(int x, int y)
    {
       return(x+y);
    }
```

4.
```
    #include "stdio.h"

    main()
    {
       int a, b;

       printf("Enter two numbers: ");
       scanf("%d%d", &a, &b);

       if(b!=0) printf("%d", a / b);
    }
```

5. 123.309F

6.
```
    #include "stdio.h"

    main()
    {
       int i;

       for(i=1; i<=100; i++)
         if((i%2)==1) printf("%d ", i);
    }
```

7. a. true
   b. true
   c. true
   d. false
   e. true

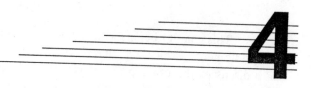

SELECTION, ITERATION, AND JUMP STATEMENTS

In this chapter you will learn about the statements that control a C program's flow of execution. In a very real sense, program control statements define the character of a language. The ANSI standard breaks the program control statements into three specific categories: *selection statements*, which include **if** and **switch**; *iteration statements*, which include the **for, while,** and **do-while** loops; and *jump statements*, which include **break, continue, return,** and **goto.**

This chapter discusses all but two of the program control statements. Since C programmers seldom use **goto,** it is not discussed here. However, you will find a description of it in Appendix A. An in-depth discussion of the **return** statement is deferred until Chapter 7, when functions are examined.

This chapter begins with a thorough examination of the **if** and **for** statements, which you have already been introduced to. It then discusses the other program control statements, with the exception of **goto** and **return**. This chapter is one of the most important in this book, and you should read it carefully and experiment with the examples.

THE if STATEMENT

Chapter 2 introduced the **if** statement. Now it is time to examine it in detail. The general form of the **if** statement is

```
if(condition) statement;
else statement;
```

where the objects of **if** and **else** are single statements. The **else** clause is optional.

The objects of both **if** and **else** can also be blocks of statements. The general form of **if** with blocks of statements as objects is

```
if(condition)
{
    statement block1
}
else
{
    statement block2
}
```

If the *condition* is true (i.e., anything other than 0), the target of the **if** will be executed. Otherwise, if it exists, the target of the **else** will be executed. At no time will both be executed.

According to the ANSI standard, the conditional statement controlling the **if** must produce a scalar result. A *scalar* is an integer, character, or floating-point type. However, floating-point numbers are rarely used to control conditional statements because execution

time is slowed considerably. (It takes the CPU several instructions to perform a floating-point operation; relatively few are required to perform an integer or character operation.)

As an example, consider the program below, which plays a simple number guessing game. The program prints the message "** Right **" when you guess the magic number. This program also introduces another standard C library function called **rand( )**, which returns a random number in the range of 0 through 32767. It uses the header file called STDLIB.H.

```c
/* Magic number program. */
#include "stdio.h"
#include "stdlib.h"

main()
{
    int magic;   /* magic number */
    int guess;   /* user's guess */

    magic = rand(); /* get a random number */

    printf("Enter your guess: ");
    scanf("%d", &guess);

    if (guess == magic) printf("** Right **");
}
```

The program uses the relational operator == to determine whether the guess entered matches the magic number. If it does, the message prints on the screen.

Taking the magic number program further, the next version also prints a message when the wrong number is picked.

```c
/* Magic number program: 1st improvement. */

#include "stdio.h"
#include "stdlib.h"

main()
{
```

```
int magic;   /* magic number */
int guess;   /* user's guess */

magic = rand(); /* get a random number */

printf("Enter your guess: ");
scanf("%d", &guess);

if (guess == magic) printf("** Right **");
else printf("..Sorry, you're wrong..");
}
```

The Conditional Expression

Sometimes newcomers to C are confused by the fact that any valid C expression can be used to control **if**. That is, the type of expression is not restricted to those involving the relational and logical operators (as it is in languages like BASIC or Pascal). The expression must simply evaluate to either a zero or non-zero value. For example, the following program reads two integers from the keyboard and displays the quotient. To avoid a "divide by zero" error, an **if** statement, controlled by the second number, is used.

```
/* Divide the first number by the second. */

#include "stdio.h"

main()
{
  int a, b;

  printf("enter two numbers: ");
  scanf("%d%d", &a, &b);

  if(b) printf("%d\n", a/b);
  else printf("cannot divide by zero\n");
}
```

This approach works because if **b** is zero, the condition controlling the **if** is false and the **else** executes. Otherwise, the condition is true (non-zero) and the division takes place. It is not necessary (and is considered extremely bad style) to write this **if** as in

```
if(b != 0) printf("%d\n", a/b);
```

because it is redundant and potentially inefficient.

Nested ifs

A *nested* **if** is an **if** that is the target of another **if** or **else**. Nested **if**s are very common in programming. The main thing to remember about nested **if**s in C is that an **else** statement always refers to the nearest **if** statement that is within the same block as the **else** and is not already associated with an **if**. For example:

```
if(i) {
  if(j) statement 1;
  if(k) statement 2; /* this if */
  else  statement 3; /* is associated with this else */
}
else statement 4; /* associated with if(i) */
```

As the comments describe, the final **else** is not associated with **if(j)** because it is not in the same block. Rather, the final **else** is associated with **if(i)**. Also, the inner **else** is associated with **if(k)** because that is the nearest **if**.

The ANSI standard specifies that at least 15 levels of nesting must be supported. In practice, most compilers will allow substantially more.

You can use a nested **if** to add a further improvement to the magic number program. This addition provides the player with feedback about a wrong guess.

```
/* Magic number program: 2nd improvement. */

#include "stdio.h"
#include "stdlib.h"

main()
{
  int magic;   /* magic number */
  int guess;   /* user's guess */

  magic = rand(); /* get a random number */
  printf("Enter your guess: ");
  scanf("%d", &guess);

  if (guess == magic) {
    printf("** Right **");
    printf(" %d is the magic number\n", magic);
  }
  else {
    printf("..Sorry, you're wrong..");
    if(guess > magic) printf(" Your guess is too high\n");
    else printf(" Your guess is too low\n");
  }
}
```

THE for LOOP

A simple form of the **for** loop was introduced in Chapter 2. But you might be surprised at just how powerful and flexible the **for** loop is in C. Let's begin by reviewing the basics, starting with the most traditional forms of the **for**.

The general form for repeating a single statement with the **for** is

for(*initialization*; *condition*; *increment*) *statement*;

To repeat a block, the general form is

```
for(initialization; condition; increment)
{
    code to be repeated
}
```

The *initialization* is usually an assignment statement used to set the loop control variable. The *loop control variable* is the variable that acts as the counter that controls the loop. The *condition* is a relational expression that determines when the loop will exit. The *increment* defines how the loop control variable changes each time the loop repeats. These three major sections must be separated by semicolons. The **for** loop will continue to execute as long as the condition tests true. Once the condition becomes false, program execution resumes on the statement following the **for** block.

The following program uses a **for** loop to print the square roots of the numbers between 1 and 100.

```
#include "stdio.h"
#include "math.h"

main()
{
    int num;
    double sq_root;

    for(num=1; num<100; num++) {
        sq_root = sqrt((double) num);
        printf("%d %lf\n", num, sq_root);
    }
}
```

This program introduces another of C's standard functions: **sqrt( )**, which returns the square root of its argument. The argument must be of type **double** and the function returns a value of the same type. Notice that the file MATH.H has been included. This file is needed to support the **sqrt( )** function.

The **for** loop can proceed in a positive or negative fashion and can increment the loop control value by any amount. For example, the following program prints the numbers 100 to −95 by increments of five.

```
#include "stdio.h"

main()
{
  int i;

  for(i=100; i>-100; i = i-5) printf("%d ", i);
}
```

An important point about **for** loops in C is that the conditional test is always performed at the top of the loop. This means the code inside the loop may not execute at all if the condition is false to begin with. Here's an example:

```
x = 10;

for(y=10; y!=x; ++x)
{
  printf("%d", y);   /* this statement will not execute */
}
printf("%d", y);
```

This loop will never execute because **x** and **y** are equal when the loop is first entered. After the loop, **y** will still have the value 10 assigned to it, and the output will be the number 10 printed once.

Some for Loop Variations

The **for** is one of the most versatile statements in the C language because it allows a wide range of variation from the traditional use

described in the preceding section. For example, multiple loop variables can be used. Consider the following fragment of code:

```
for(x=0, y=10; x<=10; ++x, --y) printf("%d %d\n",x,y);
```

Here, commas separate the two initialization statements and the two increment expressions. This is necessary for the compiler to understand that there are two of each statement. In C, the comma is an operator that essentially means "do this and this." (Other uses for the comma operator will be examined later in this book.) A common use is in the **for** loop. You can have any number of initialization and increment statements, but in practice more than two or three make the **for** unwieldy and difficult to read.

THE kbhit( ) FUNCTION The loop condition may be any relational or logical C statement. It is not limited to only testing the loop control variable. In the following example, the loop continues to execute until the user presses a key. An important function, **kbhit( )**, is also introduced. This function returns false if no key has been pressed, true if a key has been struck. It does not wait for a key press, thus allowing the loop to continue execution. The **kbhit( )** function uses the header file CONIO.H.

```
#include "stdio.h"
#include "conio.h"

main()
{
  int i;

  /* print numbers until a key is pressed */
  for(i=0; !kbhit(); i++) printf("%d ", i);
}
```

Each time through the loop, **kbhit( )** is called. If a key has been pressed, then a true value is returned, which causes **!kbhit( )** to be false and the loop to stop. If no key has been pressed, the **kbhit( )** returns false and **!kbhit( )** is true, allowing the loop to continue.

The **kbhit( )** function is not defined by ANSI because not all environments support this high a level of interactivity. However, this function is supported by virtually all mainstream C compilers, although it may have a slightly different name. Remember one important point: a compiler manufacturer is free — in fact, encouraged — to provide more library functions than are defined by ANSI, because ANSI only defines a minimally acceptable set of functions. You should feel free to use all the functions supplied by your compiler. In the case of **kbhit( )**, this or a similar function is so important in creating the interactive programs common in today's business environment that its use should not be overlooked. Later in this book you will see several more examples of functions not defined by ANSI, but found in virtually all commercial C compilers.

The difference may seem one of semantics, but ANSI makes a distinction between things that are *non-standard* and ones that are simply *not defined* by the standard. Using a library function that is not defined by ANSI does not violate the requirements of the standard, but may affect the portability of your program to a different environment where such a function is not supported. However, since most of what you do will be directed towards a specific environment, such as UNIX, DOS, or OS/2, portability may be less important than other factors. For example, making a program interactive for a DOS environment is more important than making it portable to some non-interactive environment.

Missing Pieces

Another aspect of the **for** loop that is different in C than in many computer languages is that pieces of the loop definition can be left out. For example, if you wanted to write a loop that would run until the number 123 is entered, it could look like this:

```
#include "stdio.h"

main()
{
  int x;

  for(x=0; x!=123; )
```

```
{
    printf("enter a number: ");
    scanf("%d", &x);
  }
}
```

The increment portion of the **for** definition is blank. This means that each time the loop repeats, **x** is tested to see if it equals 123, but no further action takes place. If, however, you type 123, the loop condition is false and the loop exits. The C **for** loop will not modify the loop control variable if no increment portion of the loop is present.

Another variation on the **for** is to move the initialization section outside the loop, as this fragment shows:

```
x = 0;

for( ; x<10; )
{
  printf("%d", x);
  ++x;
}
```

Here, the initialization section has been left blank and **x** is initialized before the loop is entered. The initialization is usually placed outside the loop only when the initial value is derived through a process too complex to be easily contained inside the **for** statement.

The Infinite Loop

You can create an infinite loop (a loop that never terminates) using this **for** construct.

```
for(;;)
{
  .
  .
  .
}
```

Although there are some programming tasks that require an infinite loop, such as operating system command processors, most so-called "infinite loops" are really just loops with special termination requirements. In "Exiting Loops Using **break**," later in this chapter, you will see how to halt a loop of this type.

Time Delay Loops

Time delay loops are often used in programs. These are loops that perform no other function than to kill time. For example:

```
for(x=0; x<1000; x++) ;
```

This example increments **x** 1000 times, but does nothing else. The semicolon that terminates the line is necessary because the **for** expects a statement, which can be empty.

THE switch

Before looking at C's other loop constructs, let's examine its other selection statement, the **switch**. Although a series of nested **if**s can perform multi-way tests, in many situations a more efficient approach can be used. C has a built-in multiple branch decision statement called **switch**. It tests a variable against a list of integer or character constants. When a match is found, the statement sequence associated with that match is executed. The general form of the **switch** statement is

```
switch(variable) {
    case constant1:
        statement sequence
        break;
    case constant2:
        statement sequence
        break;
```

```
case constant3:
    statement sequence
    break;
    .

    .

    .

default:
    statement sequence
}
```

where the **default** statement sequence is performed if no matches are found. The **default** is optional and, if it's not present, no action takes place if all matches fail. When a match is found, the statements associated with that **case** are executed until the **break** is encountered or, in the case of the **default** or the last **case**, the end of the **switch** is reached.

There are four important things to keep in mind about the **switch** statement:

1. The **switch** differs from the **if** in that **switch** can only test for equality, whereas the **if** conditional expression can be of any type.

2. No two **case** constants in the same **switch** can have identical values. Of course, a **switch** statement enclosed by an outer **switch** may have **case** constants that are the same.

3. A **switch** statement is more efficient than nested **if**s.

4. The statement sequences associated with each **case** are *not* blocks. This will be explained shortly.

The ANSI standard specifies that a **switch** be able to contain at least 257 **case** statements. For efficiency, you will want to limit the amount of **case** statements to a smaller number.

The **switch** statement is often used to process keyboard commands, such as menu selection. As shown here, the function **menu( )** will display a menu for a spelling checker program and call the proper procedures.

```
menu()
{
  int i;

  printf("1. Check Spelling\n");
  printf("2. Correct Spelling errors\n");
  printf("3. Display Spelling Errors\n");
  printf("Strike Any Other Key to Skip\n");
  printf("       Enter your choice: ");

  scanf("%d", &i);

  switch(i) {
    case 1:
      check_spelling();
      break;
    case 2:
      correct_errors();
      break;
    case 3:
      display_errors();
      break;
    default :
      printf("No option selected");
  }
}
```

Technically, the **break** statement is optional, although most applications of the **switch** will use it as described earlier. The **break** statement, when used inside each **case** of the **switch**, causes the program flow to exit the entire **switch** statement and continue onto the next statement outside the **switch**. However, if a **break** statement does not end the statement sequence associated with a **case**, then all the statements at and below the match will be executed until a **break** or the end of the **switch** is encountered. As an example, study the following program carefully. Can you figure out what is shown on the screen?

```
#include "stdio.h"

main()
{
```

```
int i;

for(i=0; i<5; i++) {
  switch(i) {
    case 0: printf("less than 1\n");
    case 1: printf("less than 2\n");
    case 2: printf("less than 3\n");
    case 3: printf("less than 4\n");
    case 4: printf("less than 5\n");
  }
  printf("\n");
}
}
```

The program displays the following output:

```
less than 1
less than 2
less than 3
less than 4
less than 5

less than 2
less than 3
less than 4
less than 5

less than 3
less than 4
less than 5

less than 4
less than 5

less than 5
```

As this program illustrates, execution will continue into the next **case** if no **break** statement is present.

You can also have empty cases. For example:

```
switch(i) {
  case 1:
  case 2:
  case 3: do_somthing();
    break;
  case 4: do_something_else();
    break;
```

In the preceding fragment, if **i** has a value of 1, 2, or 3, then **do_something( )** is called. If **i** is 4, then **do_something_else( )** is called. The stacking of cases, as shown in this example, is very common when several cases share common code.

Nested switch Statements

It is possible to have a **switch** as part of the statement sequence of an outer **switch**. Even if the **case** constants of the inner and outer **switch**es contain common values, no conflicts will arise. For example, the following code fragment is perfectly acceptable.

```
switch(x) {
  case 1:
    switch(y) {
      case 0: printf("divide by zero error");
              break;
      case 1: process(x, y);
    }
    break;
  case 2:
    .
    .
    .
```

The ANSI standard specifies that at least 15 levels of nesting be allowed for **switch** statements.

THE while LOOP

Another of C's loops is the **while** loop. The general form of the **while** loop is

while(*condition*) *statement*;

where *statement* may be a single statement or a block of statements. The *condition* may be any expression, with true being any non-zero value. The statement is performed while the condition is true. When the condition becomes false, program control passes to the line after the loop code.

The following program illustrates the **while** in a short but interesting program. Virtually all PCs and a large number of mini-and mainframe computers support a set of characters beyond that defined by ASCII. These extended sets often contain special symbols such as foreign language characters and scientific notations. The ASCII characters use codes from 0 through 127. The extended character set begins at 128 and continues to 255. This program prints all characters between 1 and 255. You will probably see some very interesting ones!

```
/* This program displays all printable characters,
   including the extended character set, if one
   exists.
*/

#include "stdio.h"

main()
{
  char ch;

  ch = 1;
  while(ch!=0) {
    printf("%c", ch);
    ch++;
  }
}
```

Like the **for** loop, **while** loops check the test condition at the top of the loop, which means the loop code may not execute at all. This eliminates the need to perform a separate test before the loop. The following program illustrates this. It displays a line of periods equal to the length of the number entered by the user. The program does not allow lines longer than 80 characters. This test is performed in the loop conditional test, not outside of it.

```c
#include "stdio.h"

main()
{
  int len;

  printf("enter length (1 to 79)");
  scanf("%d", &len);

  while(len>0 && len<80)  {
    printf(".");
    len--;
  }
}
```

There need not be any statements at all in the body of the **while** loop. For example:

```c
while(rand()!=1001) ;
```

This loop iterates until the random number generated by **rand( )** equals 1001.

THE do/while LOOP

Unlike the **for** and **while** loops that test the loop condition at the top of the loop, the **do/while** loop checks its condition at the bottom of the loop. This means that a **do/while** loop will always execute at least once. The general form of the **do/while** loop is

```
do {
    statements;
} while(condition);
```

Although the braces are not necessary when only one statement is present, they are often used to improve readability of the **do/while** construct, avoiding confusion with the **while**. For example, the following program loops until the number 100 is entered.

```
#include "stdio.h"

main()
{
  int num;

  do {
    scanf("%d", &num);
  } while(num!=100);
}
```

Perhaps the most common use of the **do/while** is in a menu selection routine, where the user chooses from a menu displayed on the screen. In the case of a menu function you will always want it to execute at least once. When a valid response is typed it is returned as the value of the function. Invalid responses will cause a re-prompt. The following shows an improved version of the spelling checker menu function developed earlier in this chapter.

```
menu()
{
  int i;

  printf("1. Check Spelling\n");
  printf("2. Correct Spelling Errors\n");
  printf("3. Display Spelling Errors\n");
  printf("Strike Any Other Key to Skip\n");
  printf("      Enter your choice: ");
  do {
    scanf("%d", &i);
    switch(i) {
```

```
      case 1:
        check_spelling();
        break;
      case 2:
        correct_errors();
        break;
      case 3:
        display_errors();
        break;
    }
  } while(i!=1 && i!=2 && i!=3);
}
```

Using a **do-while** loop, we can also further improve the magic number program. This time, the program loops until you guess the number.

```
/* Magic number program: 3rd improvement. */

#include "stdio.h"
#include "stdlib.h"

main()
{
  int magic;  /* magic number */
  int guess;  /* user's guess */

  magic = rand(); /* get a random number */

  do {
    printf("Enter your guess: ");
    scanf("%d", &guess);

    if (guess == magic) {
      printf("** Right **");
      printf(" %d is the magic number\n", magic);
    }
    else {
      printf("..Sorry, you're wrong..");
      if(guess > magic) printf(" Your guess is too high\n");
      else printf(" your guess is too low\n");
```

```
    }
  } while(guess != magic);
}
```

USING continue

The **continue** statement forces the next iteration of the loop, skipping any code between itself and the test condition of the loop. For
example, this program prints the even numbers between 0 and 100.

```
#include "stdio.h"

main()
{
  int x;

  for(x=0; x<=100; x++) {
    if(x%2) continue;
    printf("%d ", x);
  }
}
```

An odd number will cause the loop to perform the termination test,
x< =100, and start over again.

In **while** and **do-while** loops, a **continue** statement will cause
control to go directly to the test condition and then continue the
looping process. In the case of the **for**, the increment part of the
loop is performed, then the condition test is executed, and the loop
continues. If you expanded the preceding example so that it will
repeat no more than 100 times, it could be written this way:

```
#include "stdio.h"

main()
{
  int i, x;
```

```
printf("enter 100 to quit\n");
for(i=0, x=0; i<100 && x!=100; i++) {
  printf(": ");
  scanf("%d", &x);
  if(x<0) continue;
  printf("%d ", x);
}
}
```

Notice that x is initialized to 0 in the **for**. Since it is used in the conditional portion of the **for** statement, it must have a known starting value.

EXITING LOOPS USING break

As you saw, it is possible to create an infinite loop in C using the **for** statement. (You can also create infinite loops using the **while** and the **do-while**, but the **for** is the traditional method.) In order to break out of an infinite loop, you must use the **break** statement. You can also use **break** to terminate from a non-infinite loop as well.

When the **break** statement is encountered inside a loop, the loop is immediately terminated and program control resumes at the next statement following the loop. A simple example is shown here:

```
#include "stdio.h"

main()
{
  int t;

  /* loop until user enters 10 */
  for(; ; ) {
    scanf("%d", &t);
    if(t==10) break;
  }
}
```

This program will print the numbers 0 through 10 on the screen before ending.

The **break** statement is commonly used in loops in which a special condition can cause immediate termination. This is an example of such a situation, where a key press can stop the execution of the program:

```
for(i=0; i<1000; i++) {
  /* do something */
  if(kbhit()) break;
}
```

A **break** will cause an exit from only the innermost loop. This, for example,

```
#include "stdio.h"

main()
{
  int t, count;

  for(t=0; t<100; t++) {
    count = 1;
    for(;;) {
      printf("%d ", count);
      count++;
      if(count==10) break;
    }
  }
}
```

will print the numbers 1 through 10 on the screen 100 times. Each time the **break** is encountered, control is passed back to the outer **for** loop.

A **break** used in a **switch** statement will affect only that **switch** and not any loop the **switch** is in.

NESTED LOOPS

As you have seen in some of the preceding examples, loops may be nested inside each other. The ANSI standard stipulates that at least 15 levels of nesting be supported; most compilers will allow more. Nested loops are used to solve a wide variety of programming problems. For example, a nested **for** loop is used to find the prime numbers from 2 to 1000 in this program.

```
/* This program finds the prime numbers from
    2 to 1000.
*/

#include "stdio.h"

main()
{
  int i, j;

  for(i=2; i<1000; i++) {
    for(j=2; j <= i/2; j++)
      if(!(i%j)) break;
    if(j>i/2) printf("%d is prime\n", i);
  }
}
```

One way to determine if a number is prime or not is to successively divide it by the numbers between 2 and half its value. (You can stop there because a number larger than one-half another number could not be a factor of the number.) If any division is even, the number is not prime. If the loop completes, the number is prime.

PUTTING TOGETHER THE PIECES

This next example shows the final version of the magic number game. It uses much of what has been described in this chapter; you should be able to understand all of the concepts in it before going

on. The program allows you to generate a new number, to play the game (giving you up to 100 guesses), and then quit.

```c
/* Magic number program: final improvement. */

#include "stdio.h"
#include "stdlib.h"
main()
{
  int option;
  int magic;

  magic = rand();

  do {
    printf("1. Get a new magic number\n");
    printf("2. Play\n");
    printf("3. Quit\n");
    do {
      printf("Enter your choice: ");
      scanf("%d", &option);
    } while(option<1 || option>3);

    switch(option) {
      case 1:
        magic = rand();
        break;
      case 2:
        play(magic);
        break;
      case 3:
        printf("Goodbye\n");
        break;
    }
  } while(option!=3);
}

play(int m)
{
  int t, x;

  for(t=0; t<100; t++) {
    printf("Guess the number: ");
```

```
    scanf("%d", &x);
    if(x==m) {
      printf("*** Right ***\n");
      return;
    }
    else
      if(x<m) printf("Too low\n");
      else printf("Too high\n");
  }
  printf("You used up all your guesses...try again\n");
}
```

EXERCISES

1. Write a function called **max** that returns the value of the larger of its two integer arguments. (Hint: Use the **if** statement.)

2. Write a function called **look_up( )** that takes one integer argument. If the argument is any of the following, return the characters indicated. Otherwise, return the character '0'.

   Hint: You should use the **switch** statement.

Argument	Return
1	a
2	b
3	c
4	d

3. Write the **look_up( )** function from Exercise 2, using nested **if**s.

4. Show three ways to write a function called **count( )** that simply prints the numbers 0 to 99 on the screen.

5. Write a program that gets an integer from the keyboard and then prints the message "hello" as many times as the number.

6. Compile and run the final magic number game. Improve the magic number game so that it tells the player how many guesses they've used.

Answers

1.
```
max(int a, int b)
{
    if(a>b) return(a);
    else return(b);
}
```

2.
```
look_up(int i)
{
  switch(i) {
    case 1: return('a');
    case 2: return('b');
    case 3: return('c');
    case 4: return('d');
    default:  return('0');
  }
}
```

3.
```
look_up(int i)
{
    if (c==1) return('a');
    else if (c==2) return('b');
    else if (c==3) return('c');
    else if (c==4) return('d');
    else return('0');
}
```

4.
```
count1()
{
    int t;

    for(t=0; t<100; ++t) printf("%d", t);
}

count2()
```

```
{
  int t;

  t = 0;
  while(t<100) {
    printf("%d", t);
    t++;
  }
}


count3()
{
  int t;

  t = 0;

  do {
    printf("%d", t);
    t++;
  } while(t<100);
}
```

5.
```
#include "stdio.h"

main()
{
  int t;

  printf("Enter a number: ");
  scanf("%d", &t);

  for( ; t>0; t--) printf("hello\n");
}
```

6.
```
/* Magic number program: final improvement,
     exercise version. */

#include "stdio.h"
#include "stdlib.h"
```

```
main()
{
  int option;
  int magic;

  magic = rand();

  do {
    printf("1. Get a new magic number\n");
    printf("2. Play\n");
    printf("3. Quit\n");
    do {
      printf("Enter your choice: ");
      scanf("%d", &option);
    } while(option<1 || option>3);

    switch(option) {
      case 1:
        magic = rand();
        break;
      case 2:
        play(magic);
        break;
      case 3:
        printf("Goodbye\n");
        break;
    }
  } while(option!=3);
}

play(int m)
{
  int t, x;

  for(t=0; t<100; t++) {
    printf("Guess the number: ");
    scanf("%d", &x);
    if(x==m) {
      printf("*** Right ***\n");
      printf("You used %d guesses.\n", t+1);
      return;
    }
    else
```

```
        if(x<m) printf("Too low\n");
        else printf("Too high\n");
    }
    printf("You used up all your guesses...try again\n");
}
```

5

ARRAYS AND STRINGS

An array is a collection of variables of the same type that are referenced by a common name. In C, all arrays consist of contiguous memory locations, with the lowest address corresponding to the first element, and the highest address to the last element. Arrays may have one or several dimensions. Each specific element in an array is accessed by an index.

The array that you will most often use is the character array. Because there is no built-in string data type in C, arrays of characters are used. As you will soon see, this approach to strings allows greater power and flexibility than are available in languages that use a special string type.

SINGLE-DIMENSION ARRAYS

The general form of a single-dimension array declaration is

type var__name[size];

Here, *type* declares the base type of the array. The *base type* determines the data type of each element in the array. *Size* defines how many elements the array will hold. For example, the following declares an integer array named **sample** that is ten elements long.

```
int sample[10];
```

In C, all arrays have zero as the index of their first element. Therefore, this declares an integer array that has ten elements, **sample[0]** through **sample[9]**. For example, the following program loads an integer array with the numbers 0 through 9.

```
main()
{
  int x[10];   /* this reserves 10 integer elements */
  int t;

  for(t=0; t<10; ++t) x[t]=t;
}
```

Single-dimension arrays are essentially lists of information of the same type. For example, after running this program

```
int i[7];

main()
{
  int j;

  for(j=0; j<7; j++) i[j] = j;
}
```

i looks like this:

i[0]	i[1]	i[2]	i[3]	i[4]	i[5]	i[6]
0	1	2	3	4	5	6

For a single-dimension array, the total size of an array in bytes is computed as shown here.

total bytes = number of bytes in type * number of elements

Arrays are very common in programming because they let you deal easily with a large number of related variables. For example, the following program creates an array of ten elements, assigns each element a random value, and then displays the minimum and maximum values.

```c
#include "stdio.h"
#include "stdlib.h"

main()
{
  int i, min_value, max_value;
  int list[10];

  for(i=0; i<10; i++) list[i] = rand();

  /* find minimum value */
  min_value = 32767;
  for(i=0; i<10; i++)
    if(min_value>list[i]) min_value = list[i];
  printf("minimum value generated is %d\n", min_value);

  /* find maximum value */
  max_value = 0;
  for(i=0; i<10; i++)
    if(max_value<list[i]) max_value = list[i];
  printf("maximum value generated is %d\n", max_value);
}
```

In C, you cannot assign one array to another. For example, the following is illegal:

```
int a[10], b[10];
    .
    .
    .
a = b;
```

To transfer the contents of one array into another, you must assign each value individually.

No Bounds-Checking

C performs no bounds-checking on arrays: nothing will stop you from overrunning the end of an array. If this happens during an assignment operation, you could assign values to another variable's data, or even into a piece of the program code. In other words, an array of size N can be indexed beyond N without causing any compile or run-time error messages, even though your program will probably crash. As the programmer, you need to ensure that all arrays are large enough to hold what the program will put in them, and provide bounds-checking when it is needed. For example, C will compile and run this program even though the array **crash** is being overrun. (Do *not* try this example. It will probably crash your system!)

```
/* An incorrect program.  Do Not Execute! */

main()
{
  int crash[10], i;

  for(i=0; i<100; i++) crash[i]=i;
}
```

In this case, the loop will still iterate 100 times, even though **crash** is only ten elements long! This could cause important information to be overwritten, resulting in a program failure.

You may wonder why C, or the C language in general, does not provide boundary checks on arrays. Since C was designed to replace assembly language coding, little error checking was included because it slows program execution. Instead, the programmer is expected to prevent array overruns in the first place.

TWO-DIMENSIONAL ARRAYS

C allows multidimensional arrays. The simplest form of multidimensional array is the two-dimensional array, which is, in essence, a list of one-dimensional arrays. To declare a two-dimensional integer array **twod** of size 10,20 you would write

```
int twod[10][20];
```

Notice that in the declaration, unlike most computer languages that use commas to separate the array dimensions, C places each dimension in its own set of brackets.

Similarly, to access point 3,5 of array **twod**, you would use **twod[3][5]**. In the following example, a two-dimensional array is loaded with the numbers 1 through 12.

```
main()
{
  int t,i, num[3][4];

  for(t=0; t<3; ++t)
    for(i=0; i<4; ++i)
      num[t][i] = (t*4)+i+1;
}
```

In this example, **num[0][0]** will have the value 1, **num[0][1]** the value 2, **num[0][2]** the value 3, and so on. The value of **num[2][3]** will be 12.

Two-dimensional arrays are stored in a row-column matrix, where the first index indicates the row and the second the column. This means the right index changes faster than the left when accessing elements in the order they are stored in memory.

Remember that storage for global array elements is allocated at compile time. The memory used to hold an array is needed the entire time your program is executing. This formula will compute the amount of memory for a two-dimensional array:

bytes = row * column * number of bytes in type

Therefore, an integer array with dimensions 10,5 would have

10 x 5 x 2
or 100

bytes allocated.

MULTIDIMENSIONAL ARRAYS

C allows arrays with more than two dimensions. The general form of a multidimensional array declaration is

type name[size1][size2]. . .[sizeN];

For example, this creates a 4 x 10 x 3 integer array:

```
int multidim[4][10][3];
```

Arrays of three or more dimensions are not often used because of the amount of memory they require. As stated before, storage for global array elements is allocated throughout the execution of your program. For example, a four-dimensional character array with dimensions 10,6,9,4 would require

10 x 6 x 9 x 4
or 2,160 bytes

If the array is of 2-byte integers, 4,320 bytes would be needed. If the array is **double** (8 bytes long), then 34,560 bytes would be required. The storage required increases exponentially with the number of dimensions. A program with arrays of more than three or four dimensions may quickly run out of memory!

ARRAY INITIALIZATION

C allows the initialization of arrays. The general form of array initialization is similar to that of other variables, as shown here:

type-specifier array_name[size1]. . .[sizeN] = { *value-list* };

The *value-list* is a comma-separated list of constants that are of a type compatible with the array's base type. The first constant is placed in the first position of the array, the second constant in the second position, and so on. Note that a semicolon follows the closing brace (}). In the following example, a ten-element integer array is initialized with the numbers 1 through 10.

```
int i[10] = {1, 2, 3, 4, 5, 6, 7, 8, 9, 10};
```

This means that **i[0]** will have the value 1 and **i[9]** will have the value 10.

Character arrays that will hold strings allow a shorthand initialization that takes the form

char *array_name[size]* = *"string"*;

For example, this code fragment initializes **str** to the phrase "hello."

```
char str[6] = "hello";
```

This is the same as writing

```
char str[6] = {'h', 'e', 'l', 'l', 'o', '\0'};
```

Because strings in C must end with a null, you must make sure the array you declare is long enough to include it. This is why **str** is six characters long, even though "hello" is only five. When a string constant is used, the compiler automatically supplies the null terminator.

Multidimensional arrays are initialized in the same way as single-dimension arrays. For example, the following initializes **sqrs** with the numbers 1 through 10 and their squares:

```
int sqrs[10][2] = {
  1, 1,
  2, 4,
  3, 9,
  4, 16,
  5, 25,
  6, 36,
  7, 49,
  8, 64,
  9, 81,
  10, 100
};
```

The **sqrs** array appears in memory as shown in Figure 5-1.

The following program uses the **sqrs[ ]** array to find the square of a number entered by the user. It first looks up the number in the array, and then prints the corresponding square.

```
#include "stdio.h"

int sqrs[10][2] = {
  1, 1,
  2, 4,
  3, 9,
  4, 16,
  5, 25,
  6, 36,
  7, 49,
  8, 64,
  9, 81,
  10, 100
};
```

	0	1
0	1	1
1	2	4
2	3	9
3	4	16
4	5	25
5	6	36
6	7	49
7	8	64
8	9	81
9	10	100

FIGURE 5-1   The initialized **sqrs** array

```
main()
{
  int i, j;

  printf("enter a number between 1 and 10: ");
  scanf("%d", &i);

  /* look up i */
  for(j=0; j<10; j++)
    if(sqrs[j][0]==i) break;
  printf("the square of %d is %d\n", i, sqrs[j][1]);
}
```

As you recall, global variables are initialized when the program begins, but local variables are initialized each time the function containing them is called. For example:

```
#include "stdio.h"

main()
{
  f1(); f1();
```

```
}

f1()
{
  char s[80]="this is a test\n";

  printf(s);
  strcpy(s, "hello");
  printf(s);
}
```

The array **s** is initialized each time **f1( )** is called. The fact that **s** is changed in the function does not affect its reinitialization upon subsequent calls. This means that **f1( )** prints "this is a test" each time it is entered.

Unsized Array Initializations

Imagine you are using array initialization to build a table of error messages, as shown here:

```
char el[14] = "Divide by 0\n";
char e2[23] = "End-of-File\n";
char e3[21] = "Access Denied\n";
```

As you might guess, it can be very tedious to determine the correct array dimension by counting the characters in each message. Fortunately, it is possible to let C automatically dimension the arrays in this example through the use of *unsized arrays*. If, in an array initialization statement, the array size is not specified, then C will automatically create an array big enough to hold all the initializers present. Using this approach, the message table becomes

```
char el[] = "Divide by 0\n";
char e2[] = "End-of-File\n";
char e3[] = "Access Denied\n";
```

Besides being less tedious, the unsized array initialization method allows you to change a message without fear of miscounting the characters.

Unsized array initializations are not restricted to single-dimension arrays. For multidimensional arrays, you must specify all but the leftmost dimension for C to properly index the array. In this way you can build tables of varying length, with the compiler automatically allocating enough storage. For example, the declaration of **sqrs** as an unsized array is shown here:

```
int sqrs[][2] = {
  1, 1,
  2, 4,
  3, 9,
  4, 16,
  5, 25,
  6, 36,
  7, 49,
  8, 64,
  9, 81,
  10, 100
};
```

The advantage of this declaration over the sized version is that you can change the table length without changing the array dimensions.

A LONGER EXAMPLE

Two-dimensional arrays are commonly used to simulate board game matrices, as in chess and checkers. While it is beyond the scope of this book to present a chess or checkers program, a tic-tac-toe game will be developed. The tic-tac-toe matrix will be represented by a three-by-three character array. You are X and the computer is O.

The computer plays a very simple game. When it is the computer's turn to move, it uses **get_computer_move( )** to scan the matrix for an unoccupied cell. When it finds one, it puts an O there. If it cannot find an empty location, it reports a draw game and exits. The

get_player_move( ) function prompts you to give the location where you want an X placed. The upper-left corner is location 1,1; the lower-right corner is 3,3.

The **get_player_move( )** function introduces a new standard library function: **exit( )**. This function immediately terminates your program and returns the integer value of its argument to the operating system. By convention, a return value of zero means the program terminated normally. Other values are used to indicate errors. The **exit( )** function can be placed anywhere in a program.

The matrix array is initialized to contain spaces. This makes it easy to display the matrix on the screen.

Each time a move has been made, the program calls the **check( )** function. It returns a space if there is no winner yet, an X if you have won, or an O if the computer has won. It scans the rows, the columns, and then the diagonals looking for a line containing all Xs or all Os.

The **disp_matrix( )** function displays the current state of the game. You should be able to see how initializing the matrix with spaces simplified this function. Remember, the **%c** format code tells **printf( )** to output a character.

The entire tic-tac-toe program is shown here. The routines in this example all access the array **matrix** in different ways. Study them to make sure you understand each array operation.

```
/* A simple Tic Tac Toe game. */
#include "stdio.h"
#include "stdlib.h"

char matrix[3][3];   /* the tic tac toe matrix */

main()
{

  char done;

  printf("This is the game of tic tac toe.\n");
  printf("You will be playing against the computer.\n");

  done = ' ';

  init_matrix();
```

```
    do {
      disp_matrix();
      get_player_move();
      done = check(); /* see if winner */
      if(done!=' ') break; /* winner!*/
      get_computer_move();
      done = check(); /* see if winner */
    } while(done==' ');

    if(done=='X') printf("You won!\n");
    else printf("I won!!!!\n");

    disp_matrix(); /* show final positions */
}


/* Initialize the matrix. */
init_matrix()
{
  int i, j;

  for(i=0; i<3; i++)
    for(j=0; j<3; j++) matrix[i][j] = ' ';
}

/* Get a player's move. */
get_player_move()
{
  int x, y;

  printf("Enter coordinates for your X: ");
  scanf("%d%d",&x,&y);

  x--; y--;

  if(matrix[x][y]!=' ') {
    printf("Invalid move, try again.\n");
    get_player_move();
  }
  else matrix[x][y] = 'X';
}

/* Get a move from the computer. */
```

```
get_computer_move()
{
  int i, j;

  for(i=0; i<3; i++) {
    for(j=0; j<3; j++)
      if(matrix[i][j]==' ') break;
    if(matrix[i][j]==' ') break;
  }

  if(i*j==9)  {
    printf("draw\n");
    exit(0);
  }
  else
    matrix[i][j] = 'O';
}

/* Display the matrix on the screen. */
disp_matrix()
{
  int t;

  for(t=0; t<3; t++) {
    printf(" %c | %c | %c ",matrix[t][0],
            matrix[t][1], matrix [t][2]);
    if(t!=2) printf("\n---|---|---\n");
  }
  printf("\n");
}

/* See if there is a winner. */
check()
{
  int i;

  for(i=0; i<3; i++)  /* check rows */
    if(matrix[i][0]==matrix[i][1] &&
       matrix[i][0]==matrix[i][2]) return matrix[i][0];

  for(i=0; i<3; i++)  /* check columns */
    if(matrix[0][i]==matrix[1][i] &&
       matrix[0][i]==matrix[2][i]) return matrix[0][i];
```

```
/* test diagonals */
if(matrix[0][0]==matrix[1][1] &&
  matrix[1][1]==matrix[2][2])
  return matrix[0][0];

if(matrix[0][2]==matrix[1][1] &&
  matrix[1][1]==matrix[2][0])
  return matrix[0][2];

return ' ';
}
```

STRINGS

By far the most common use for single-dimension arrays is to create character strings. In C, a *string* is defined as a character array that is terminated by a null. A null is specified using '\0' and, in virtually all C compilers, is zero. As mentioned before, because of the null terminator, you need to declare character arrays one character longer than the largest string they will hold. For example, if you wished to declare an array **str** that could hold a ten-character string, you would write

```
char str[11];
```

This makes room for the null at the end of the string.

As you learned earlier, although C does not have a string data type, it allows string constants. A *string constant* is a list of characters enclosed between double quotes, such as

"hello there" "this is a test"

You don't need to add the null onto the end of string constants — the C compiler does this for you automatically. Thus the string "Hello" will appear in memory like this.

H	e	l	l	o	'\0'

Reading a String from the Keyboard

The easiest way to input a string from the keyboard is with the **gets( )** library function. The general form of a **gets( )** call is

gets(*array-name*);

To read a string, call **gets( )**, with the name of the array, without any index, as its argument. Upon return from **gets( )**, the array will hold the string input at the keyboard. The **gets( )** function will continue to read characters until you enter a carriage return. The header file used by **gets( )** is STDIO.H.

For example, the following program simply displays the string you enter at the keyboard. This program introduces a new **printf( )** format code: %s. This code tells **printf( )** to display a string argument.

```
/* A simple string example. */

#include "stdio.h"

main()
{
  char str[80];

  printf("enter a string: ");
  gets(str); /* read a string from the keyboard */

  printf("%s", str);
}
```

Notice that **str** can be used as an argument to **printf( )**, and that the array name is used without an index. The name of a character array,

without an index, that holds a string can be used anywhere a string constant can be used. The reasons for this will be clear after you have read a few more chapters.

Keep in mind that **gets( )** does not perform any bounds-checking on the array that it is called with. Therefore, if the user enters a string longer than the size of the array, the array will be overwritten.

Some String Library Functions

ANSI C supports a wide range of string manipulation functions. The most common are

strcpy( )
strcat( )
strcmp( )
strlen( )

The string functions all use the same header file: STRING.H. Let's look at these functions now.

strcpy( )

A call to **strcpy( )** takes this general form:

strcpy(*to, from*);

The **strcpy( )** function is used to copy the contents of the string **from** into **to**. Remember, the array that forms **to** must be large enough to hold the string contained in **from**. If it isn't, the array will be overrun and this will probably crash your system.

(The **strcpy( )** function does return a value; its meaning will be explained in Chapter 6.)

The following program will copy "hello" into string **str**.

```
#include "stdio.h"
#include "string.h"

main()
{

  char str[80];

  strcpy(str, "hello");
  printf("%s", str);
}
```

strcat( )

A call to **strcat( )** takes this form:

    strcat(s1, s2);

The **strcat( )** function appends **s2** to the end of **s1**; **s2** is unchanged. Both strings must be null terminated and the result is null terminated. For example, this program will print "hello there" on the screen.

```
#include "stdio.h"
#include "string.h"

main()
{

  char s1[20], s2[10];

  strcpy(s1, "hello");
  strcpy(s2, " there");
  strcat(s1, s2);
  printf("%s", s1);

}
```

Like **strcpy( )**, **strcat( )** returns a value that will be explained in Chapter 6.

strcmp( )

A call to **strcmp( )** takes this general form:

strcmp(s1, s2);

The **strcmp( )** function compares two strings and returns a zero if they are equal. If **s1** is lexicographically greater than **s2**, then a positive number is returned. If it is less than **s2**, a negative number is returned.

The **password( )** function, shown in this program, is a password verification routine. It uses **strcmp( )** to check user input against a password.

```
#include "string.h"
#include "stdio.h"

main()
{
  if(password()) printf("logged on\n");
  else printf("access denied\n");
}

/* Return true if password accepted; false otherwise.*/
password()
{
  char s[80];

  printf("enter password: ");
  gets(s);

  if(strcmp(s, "password")) {  /* strings different */
    printf("invalid password\n");
    return 0;
  }

  /* strings compared the same */
  return 1;
}
```

The key to using **strcmp( )** is that it returns false when the strings match. Therefore, you will need to use the NOT operator if you wish something to occur when the strings are equal. For example, this program continues to request input until you type the word "quit."

```c
#include "stdio.h"
#include "string.h"

main()
{
  char s[80];

  for(;;) {
    printf("Enter a string: ");
    gets(s);
    if(!strcmp("quit", s)) break;
  }
}
```

strlen( )

The general form of a call to **strlen( )** is

```c
strlen(s);
```

where **s** is a string. The **strlen( )** function returns the length of the string pointed to by **s**.

The following will print the length of the string you enter at the keyboard:

```c
#include "stdio.h"
#include "string.h"

main()
{
  char str[80];

  printf("enter a string: ");
```

```
     gets(str);

     printf("%d", strlen(str));

}
```

For example, if you entered the string "Hi there", this program would display 8. The null terminator is not counted by **strlen( )**.

The following program prints the string entered at the keyboard in reverse. For example, "hello" will print as "olleh." Remember that strings are simply character arrays; each character may be referenced individually.

```
/* Print a string backwards. */
#include "stdio.h"
#include "string.h"

main()
{
  char str[80];
  int i;

  printf("enter a string: ");
  gets(str);

  for(i=strlen(str)-1; i>=0; i--) printf("%c", str[i]);
}
```

As a final example, the following program illustrates the use of all four string functions.

```
#include "stdio.h"
#include "string.h"

main()
{
  char s1[80], s2[80];

  printf("enter two strings: ");

  gets(s1); gets(s2);
```

```
printf("lengths: %d %d\n", strlen(s1), strlen(s2));

if(!strcmp(s1, s2)) printf("The strings are equal\n");
else printf("not equal\n");

strcat(s1, s2);
printf("%s\n", s1);

strcpy(s1, s2);
printf("%s %s are now the same\n", s1, s2);
}
```

If this program is run and the strings "hello" and "there" are entered, then the output will be

```
lengths: 5 5
not equal
hello there
there there are now the same
```

It is important to remember that **strcmp( )** returns false if the strings are equal, so be sure to use a ! to reverse the condition, as shown in this example, if you are testing for equality.

Using the Null Terminator

The fact that all strings are null terminated can often be used to simplify various operations on strings. For example, look at how little code is required to transform every character in a string to uppercase.

```
/* Convert a string to uppercase. */
#include "stdio.h"
#include "string.h"
#include "ctype.h"

main()
{
  char str[80];
  int i;
```

```
    strcpy(str, "this is a test");

    for(i=0; str[i]; i++) str[i] = toupper(str[i]);

    printf("%s", str);
}
```

This program will print "THIS IS A TEST." It uses the library function **toupper( )**, which returns the uppercase equivalent of its character argument, to convert each character in the string. The **toupper( )** function uses the CTYPE.H header file. Note that the test condition of the **for** loop is simply the array indexed by the control variable. This works because a true value is any non-zero value. Therefore, the loop runs until it encounters the null terminator, which is zero. Since the null terminator marks the end of the string, the loop stops precisely where it is supposed to. As you progress you will see many examples that use the null terminator similarly.

A printf( ) Variation

Until now, to display the string held in a character array using **printf( )**, this basic format was used:

    printf("%s", *array-name*);

where the **%s** is the format code that tells **printf( )** a string argument follows. However, remember that the first argument to **printf( )** is a string, and all characters that are not format commands are printed. Therefore, if you only want to print one string, you can use this form:

    printf(*array-name*);

For example, the following program prints "I like C" on the screen.

```
#include "stdio.h"
#include "string.h"

main()
{
   char str[80];

   strcpy(str, "I like C");
   printf(str);
}
```

Arrays of Strings

It is not uncommon in programming to use an array of strings. For instance, the input processor to a database may verify user commands against a string array of valid commands. To create an array of strings, a two-dimensional character array is used. The size of the left index determines the number of strings and the size of the right index specifies the maximum length of each string. The following declares an array of 30 strings, each having a maximum length of 80 characters.

```
char str_array[30][80];
```

Accessing an individual string is quite easy: you simply specify only the left index. For example, this statement calls **gets( )** with the third string in **str _ array**.

```
gets(str_array[2]);
```

To better understand how string arrays work, study the following short program. It accepts lines of text entered at the keyboard and redisplays them when a blank line is entered.

```
/* Enter and display strings. */
#include "stdio.h"

main()
{
```

```
int t, i;
char text[100][80];

for(t=0; t<100; t++) {
  printf("%d: ", t);
  gets(text[t]);
  if(!text[t][0]) break; /* quit on blank line */
}

/* redisplay the strings */
for(i=0; i<t; i++)
  printf("%s\n", text[i]);
}
```

Notice how the program checks for the entry of a blank line. The **gets( )** function returns a zero-length string if the only character you type is a carriage return. This means the first byte in that string will be the null character. A null value is always false, thus allowing the **if** condition to be true.

An Example Using String Arrays

Arrays of strings are commonly used to handle tables of information, such as an employee database that stores each employee's name, telephone number, hours worked per pay period, and wage. Assuming there are ten employees, to create such a program you must define these four arrays (the first two of which are string arrays):

```
char name[10][80];   /* array holds employee names */
char phone[10][20];  /* their phone numbers */
float hours[10];     /* hours worked per week */
float wage[10];      /* wage */
```

To enter information about each employee, you could use a function like **enter( )**, shown here:

```
enter()
{
  int i;
```

```
char temp[80];

for(i=0; i<10; i++) {
  printf("enter name: ");
  gets(name[i]);
  printf("enter phone number: ");
  gets(phone[i]);
  printf("enter number of hours worked: ");
  gets(temp);
  hours[i] = atof(temp);
  printf("enter wage: ");
  gets(temp);
  wage[i] = atof(temp);
}
}
```

This function introduces a new library function called **atof( )**, which returns the floating-point equivalent of the numeric string used as its argument. The **atof( )** function uses the header file STDLIB.H. You will recall that **scanf( )** can be used to read a floating- point number. However, due to some unusual attributes of **scanf( )**, for many C compilers **gets( )** and **scanf( )** do not work properly together. (You will understand why after you have read a few more chapters.) Since this program has to use **gets( )** to input the employee's name and telephone number, **scanf( )** had to be avoided. Therefore, to input the wage and hours information, the function uses a temporary string variable called **temp**, into which the user enters the numeric information. This string is then converted into a floating-point value using **atof( )**.

Once information has been entered, the database can report the data and calculate the amount of pay each employee is to receive using the **report( )** function, shown here:

```
report()
{
  int i;

  for(i=0; i<10; i++) {
    if(!*name[i]) break;
    printf("%s %s\n", name[i], phone[i]);
```

```
      printf("pay for the week: %f\n", wage[i] * hours[i]);
  }
}
```

The entire employee database program follows. Pay special attention to how each array is accessed. (This version of the program
is not particularly useful as is, since the information is lost when the
program terminates. Later in this book you will learn how to store
information in a disk file.)

Notice that **menu( )** introduces another conversion function
called **atoi( )**. This function works like **atof( )**, except that it converts
a numeric string into an integer. It is used here to avoid the interac-
tion problems of using **scanf( )** and **gets( )** in the same program.

```
/* A simple employee database program. */

#include "stdio.h"
#include "stdlib.h"

char name[10][80];   /* array holds employee names */
char phone[10][20];  /* their phone numbers */
float hours[10];     /* hours worked per week */
float wage[10];      /* wage */

main()
{
  int choice;

  do {
    choice = menu(); /* get selection */
    switch(choice) {
      case 0: break;
      case 1: enter();
        break;
      case 2: report();
        break;
      default: printf("try again");
    }
  } while(choice!=0);
}

/* Return a user's choice. */
```

```
menu()
{
  char str[80];
  int i;

  printf("0. Quit\n");
  printf("1. Enter information\n");
  printf("2. Report information\n");
  printf("\nchoose one: ");
  gets(str);
  i = atoi(str);
  printf("\n");
  return i;
}

enter()
{
  int i;
  char temp[80];

  for(i=0; i<10; i++) {
    printf("enter name: ");
    gets(name[i]);
    printf("enter phone number: ");
    gets(phone[i]);
    printf("enter number of hours worked: ");
    gets(temp);
    hours[i] = atof(temp);
    printf("enter wage: ");
    gets(temp);
    wage[i] = atof(temp);
  }
}

report()
{
  int i;

  for(i=0; i<10; i++) {
    if(!*name[i]) break;
    printf("%s %s\n", name[i], phone[i]);
```

```
    printf("pay for the week: %f\n",wage[i] * hours[i]);
  }
}
```

EXERCISES

1. Write a function called **load( )** that loads a 10-byte character array, **a,** with the letters *A* through *J.*

2. Write the declaration portion of a function called **func( )** that will receive array **num,** declared here:

```
int num[100][1234];
```

3. What is wrong with this statement?

```
int i[] = 1, 2, 3;
```

4. How many bytes of memory will the following arrays need? Assume that integers are 2 bytes and floats are 8 bytes.

```
a. char s[80];

b. char s[80][10];

c. int n[10];

d. float f[10][5];

e. char x[10][9][8][7];
```

5. What is wrong with the following function fragment?

```
f(int s[10][4][])
{
  int t;
```

```
        t = s[3][2][4];
    .
    .
    .
    }
```

6. Improve the tic-tac-toe program to play a better game. Or, just for fun, rewrite the tic-tac-toe game so the computer plays against itself. Try to make each game different.

Answers

1.
```
    load()
    {
        int t;

        for(t=0; t<10; ++t) a[t] = 'A'+t;
    }
```

2.
```
    func(int n[][1234])
    {
```

3. The initialization list needs to be enclosed in braces, as shown here:

```
    int i[] = {1, 2, 3};
```

4. a. 80
   b. 800
   c. 20
   d. 400
   e. 5040

5. The array dimension to the farthest right is missing. This dimension is necessary for the function to properly handle array indexing.

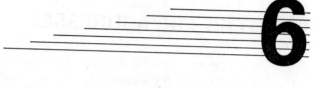

POINTERS

Pointers are without a doubt one of the most important—and troublesome—aspects of C. A large measure of C's power is derived from pointers. They allow C to support such things as linked lists and dynamic memory allocation, and they allow a function to alter the contents of the argument it is called with. These and other uses of pointers will be introduced in subsequent chapters. In this chapter you will learn the basics about pointers, how to manipulate them, and some potential problems to avoid.

In a few places in this chapter it is necessary to refer to the size of several of C's basic data types. For the sake of discussion, assume that characters are 1 byte long, integers are 2 bytes long, **float**s 4 bytes long, and **double**s 8 bytes long.

POINTERS ARE ADDRESSES

A *pointer* is a variable that contains a memory address. Very often this address is the location of another variable. For example, if **x** contains the location of **y**, then **x** is said to "point to" **y**.

Pointer variables must be declared as such. The general form of this declaration is

```
type *var-name;
```

where *type* is a valid C type and *var-name* is the name of the pointer variable. For example, to declare **p** to be a pointer to an integer, use this declaration:

```
int *p;
```

For a **float** pointer, use

```
float *p;
```

THE POINTER OPERATORS

There are two special operators that are used with pointers: * and &. The & is a unary operator that returns the memory address of its operand. (A unary operator requires only one operand.) For example,

```
address = &balance;
```

places into **address** the memory address of the variable **balance**. This address is the computer's internal location of the variable. It has nothing to do with the *value* of **balance**. The operation of the & can be thought of as returning the address of the variable it precedes.

Therefore, the above assignment statement could be written as "**address** receives the address of **balance**." To better understand this assignment, assume the variable **balance** is located at address 100. Then, after the above assignment, **address** will have the value 100.

The second operator is *; it is the complement of the **&**. It is a unary operator that returns the *value of the variable located at the address that follows*. Continuing with the same example, if **address** contains the memory address of the variable **balance**, then

```
value = *address;
```

will place the value of **balance** into **value**. For example, if **balance** originally had the value 3200, then **value** will have the value 3200 because that is the value stored at location 100, the memory address assigned to **address**. The operation of the * can be thought of as "at address." In this case, then, the statement could be read as "**value** receives the value at address **address**."

This program executes the sequence of operations just described.

```
#include "stdio.h"

main()
{
   int balance;
   int *address;
   int value;

   balance = 3200;
   address = &balance;
   value = *address;
   printf("balance is: %d\n", value);
}
```

It is unfortunate that the multiplication symbol and the "at address" sign are the same, since it sometimes confuses newcomers to C. These operators are not related. Both * and **&** have a higher precedence than the arithmetic operators, except for the unary minus, which has the same level of precedence.

The act of using a pointer is often called *indirection* because you access a location in memory indirectly through another variable.

The Base Type Is Important

In the preceding discussion, you saw it was possible to assign **value** the value of **balance** indirectly through a pointer. This raises an important question: how does C know how many bytes to copy into **value** from the address pointed to by **address**? Or, more generally, how does the compiler transfer the proper number of bytes for any assignment using a pointer? The answer is that the base type of the pointer determines the type of data the compiler assumes the pointer is pointing to. In this case, because **address** is an integer pointer, C copies 2 bytes of information into **value** from the address pointed to by **address**. If it had been a **double** pointer, then 8 bytes would have been copied.

Make sure your pointer variables always point to the correct type of data. For example, when you declare a pointer to be of type **int**, the compiler assumes that any address it holds will point to an integer variable. Because C allows you to assign any address to a pointer variable, the following code fragment will compile with no error messages issued by most compilers, but it will not work correctly.

```
#include "stdio.h"

/* This program will not work correctly. */
main()
{
  float x, y;
  int  *p;

  x = 123.23
  p = &x;
  y = *p;
  printf("%f", y);
}
```

This will *not* assign the value of **x** to **y**. Because **p** is declared to be an integer pointer, only 2 bytes of information will be transferred to **y**, not the 4 that make up a floating-point number.

Assigning Values Using a Pointer

You can use a pointer on the right-hand side of an assignment statement to assign a value to the location pointed to by the pointer. Assuming that **p** is an integer pointer, the following assigns the value 101 to the location pointed to by **p**.

```
*p = 101;
```

This assignment could be stated as "at the location pointed to by **p**, assign the value 101."

You can increment or decrement the value at the location pointed to by a pointer using a statement such as this:

```
(*p)++;
```

The parentheses are necessary because the * operator has lower precedence than the ++ operator. The following program illustrates an assignment using a pointer that prints "100 101 100" on the screen.

```
#include "stdio.h"

main()
{
    int *p, num;

    p = &num;

    *p = 100;
    printf("%d ", num);
    (*p)++;
    printf("%d ", num);
    (*p)--;
    printf("%d ", num);
}
```

POINTER EXPRESSIONS

Pointers may be used in most valid C expressions. However, some special rules apply. You may also need to surround some parts of a

pointer expression with parentheses in order to ensure that the outcome is what you want.

Pointer Arithmetic

There are only four arithmetic operators that can be used on pointers: $++, +, --$, and $-$. To understand what occurs in pointer arithmetic, let **p1** be an integer pointer with a current value of 2000. After the expression

```
p1++;
```

p1's contents will be 2002, not 2001. Each time **p1** is incremented, it will point to the next integer. The same is true of decrements. For example,

```
p1--;
```

will cause **p1** to have the value 1998, assuming that it was previously 2000.

Remember, each time a pointer is incremented it will point to the memory location of the next element of its type. Each time it is decremented it will point to the location of the previous element of its type.

In the case of pointers to characters, an increment or decrement will appear as "normal" arithmetic because, generally, characters are 1 byte long. However, all other pointers will increase or decrease by the length of the data type they point to.

You are not limited to increment and decrement operations. You may add or subtract integers to or from pointers. The expression

```
p1 = p1 + 9
```

will make **p1** point to the ninth element of **p1**'s type beyond the one it currently points to.

Besides addition and subtraction of pointers and integers, no other arithmetic operations can be performed on pointers. Specifically, you can not multiply, divide, add, or subtract pointers; apply the bitwise operators to them, or add or subtract type **float** or **double** to them.

To see the actual effects of pointer arithmetic, execute the following program. It prints the actual physical address that a character, integer, or floating-point pointer is pointing to. It does this by using another of **printf( )**'s format codes, **%p**. This code causes the value of a pointer to be printed in the form most common to the computer you are using.

```c
#include "stdio.h"

main()
{
  char *c, ch[10];
  int *i, j[10];
  float *f, g[10];
  int x;

  c = ch;
  i = j;
  f = g;

  for(x=0; x<10; x++)
    printf("%p %p %p\n", c+x, i+x, f+x);

}
```

Pointer Comparisons

Pointers can be involved in relational and logical expressions. Conceptually, two pointers that refer to separate types of variables have no relationship because ANSI C does not specify where in memory a variable will be. For example, if **p1** and **p2** are pointers that point to two separate and unrelated variables, then any comparison between **p1** and **p2** is meaningless. However, if both **p1** and **p2** point to variables that are related to each other, such as elements of the same array, then **p1** and **p2** can be meaningfully compared. In a short while, you will see an example of pointer comparisons.

POINTERS AND ARRAYS

As you may have guessed, there is a close relationship between pointers and arrays. Consider the following fragment.

```
char str[80];
char *pl;

pl = str;
```

Here, **pl** has been set to the address of the first array element in **str**. In C, using the name of an array without an index generates a pointer to the first element in the array. Thus the assignment **pl = str** assigns the address of the array to **pl**. This is a very important point. When an unindexed array name is used in an expression, it is a pointer to the first element of the array.

If you wished to access the fifth element in **str** you could write

```
str[4]
```

or

```
*(pl+4)
```

Both statements will return the fifth element. Remember, arrays start at 0, so a 4 is used to index **str** to reach the fifth element. You also add 4 to the pointer **pl** to get the fifth element because **pl** currently points to the first element of **str**.

The parentheses surrounding **pl+4** are necessary because the * operation has a higher priority than the + operation. Without them, the expression would first find the value pointed to by **pl** (the first location in the array) and then add 4 to it. It is very easy to forget this point, and if you do, it is hard to find the problem because your program looks correct. So it never hurts to add parentheses when in doubt.

In effect, C allows two methods of accessing array elements. This is important because pointer arithmetic can be faster than array indexing. Since speed is often a consideration in programming, the use of pointers to access array elements is very common in C programs.

To give you an idea of the difference between using array indexing and pointers, two versions of the same program will be shown.
The programs extract words, separated by spaces, from a string. For
example, given "Hello Tom," the program would extract "Hello"
and "Tom." Programmers often refer to these extracted words as
tokens. The program scans the input string, copying characters from
the string into another array, called **token**, until a space is encountered. It then prints that token and repeats the process until the null
at the end of the string is reached. For example, if you enter "This is
a test." the program displays

> This
> is
> a
> test.

Here is the pointer version of this program:

```
/* Tokenizing program: pointer version. */
#include "stdio.h"

main()
{
  char str[80];
  char token[80];
  char *p, *q;

  printf("Enter a sentence: ");
  gets(str);

  p = str;

  /* Read a token at a time from the string. */
  while(*p) {
    q = token;  /* set q pointing to start of token */

    /* Read characters until either a space or the
       null terminator is encountered.
    */
    while(*p!=' ' && *p) {
      *q = *p;
```

```
        q++; p++;
    }
    if(*p) p++; /* advance past the space */
    *q = '\0'; /* null terminate the token */
    printf("%s\n", token);
  }
}
```

And here is the array indexing version:

```
/* Tokenizing program: array indexing version. */
#include "stdio.h"

main()
{
  char str[80];
  char token[80];
  int i, j;

  printf("Enter a sentence: ");
  gets(str);

  /* Read a token at a time from the string. */
  for(i=0; ; i++) {
    /* Read characters until either a space or the
       null terminator is encountered.
    */
    for(j=0; str[i]!=' ' && str[i]; j++, i++)
      token[j] = str[i];

    token[j] = '\0';  /* null terminate the token */
    printf("%s\n", token);
    if(!str[i]) break;
  }
}
```

Because of the way most C compilers generate code, these two programs are not equivalent in performance. It generally takes more instructions to index an array than to perform arithmetic on a pointer. Hence, in professionally written C code the pointer version is used more frequently. As a beginning C programmer, however, don't hesitate to use array indexing until you feel comfortable using pointers.

Indexing a Pointer

In C, it is possible to index a pointer as if it were an array. This further illustrates the close relationship between pointers and arrays. For example, this program is perfectly valid and prints "HELLO TOM" on the screen.

```
/* Indexing a pointer like an array. */

#include "stdio.h"
#include "ctype.h"

main()
{
  char str[20] = "hello tom";
  char *p;
  int i;

  p = str;

  for(i=0; p[i]; i++) printf("%c", toupper(p[i]));
}
```

String Constants

You may be wondering how a function such as **strlen( )** can be called with a string constant as an argument, since it requires a pointer to the string. For example, how does the following fragment work?

```
printf("C Compiler is %d bytes long",
       strlen("C Compiler"));
```

When a string constant is used, only a pointer to it is passed to **strlen( )**. The actual string is stored in the compiler's string table. More generally, when a string constant is used in any type of expression, it is treated as a pointer to the first character in the string. For example, this program is perfectly valid and prints the phrase "pointers are fun to use" on the screen.

```
#include "stdio.h"

main()
{
  char *s;

  s = "pointers are fun to use";

  printf(s);
}
```

The characters that make up a string constant are stored in a special string table maintained by the compiler. Your program uses a pointer to that table.

A COMPARISON EXAMPLE

Earlier you learned it is legal to compare the value of one pointer to another. Now that you know more about how pointers and arrays are related, here is an example.

The following program uses two pointer variables, one initially pointing to the beginning of an array and the other to the end. As the user enters keystrokes, the array is filled from beginning to end. Each keystroke entered into the array also causes the starting pointer to be incremented. To see if the array is full, the program simply compares the starting pointer with the ending pointer. If they are equal, the array has been filled. Once the array is full, the contents of the array are printed.

```
#include "stdio.h"
#include "conio.h"

main()
{
  char str[10];
  char *start, *end;

  start = str;
  end = &str[9];
```

```
while(start!=end) {
  *start = getche();
  start++;
}
start = str;  /* reset the starting pointer */
while(start!=end) {
  printf("%c", *start);
  start++;
}
}
```

ARRAYS OF POINTERS

Pointers may be arrayed like any other data type. The declaration for an **int** pointer array of size 10 is

```
int *x[10];
```

To assign the address of an integer variable called **var** to the third element of the pointer array, you would write

```
int var;

x[2] = &var;
```

Remember, you are working with an array of pointers. The only values the array elements can hold are the addresses of integer variables. To find the value of **var**, you would write

```
*x[2]
```

If you want to pass an array of pointers into a function, you can use the same method as for other arrays—simply call the function with the array name, without any index. For example, a function that will receive array **x**, declared above, would look like the following.

```
func1(int *q[])
{
  int t;

  t = *q[2];    /* gets value of integer pointed
                   to by the third pointer in q */
  .
  .
  .
}
```

You must use the [] to signify an array. In this case, **q** is not a pointer to integers, but rather a pointer to an array of pointers to integers. Never forget what kind of data you are dealing with.

A common use of pointer arrays is to hold pointers to messages. For example, you can create a function that will output a fortune by defining the messages in a pointer array, as shown here:

```
char *fortunes[] = {
  "Soon, you will come into some money.\n",
  "A new love will enter your life.\n",
  "You will live long and prosper.\n",
  "Now is a good time to invest for the future.\n",
  "A close friend will ask for a favor.\n"
};
```

Remember, C stores all string constants in its string table, so the array need only store pointers to them. To print the second message, use a statement such as this:

```
printf(fortunes[1]);
```

The entire "fortune cookie" program is shown here. It uses **rand( )** to generate a random number, and then uses the modulus operator to obtain a number between 0 and 4 to index the array.

```
#include "stdio.h"
#include "stdlib.h"
#include "conio.h"

char *fortunes[] = {
  "Soon, you will come into some money.\n",
```

```
    "A new love will enter your life.\n",
    "You will live long and prosper.\n",
    "Now is a good time to invest for the future.\n",
    "A close friend will ask for a favor.\n"
};

main()
{
    int chance;

    printf("To see your fortune, press a key: ");
    /* randomize the random number generator */
    while(!kbhit()) rand();
    printf("\n");

    chance = rand();
    chance = chance % 5;
    printf("%s", fortunes[chance]);
}
```

Notice that the program calls **rand( )** repeatedly until a key is pressed. Because the **rand( )** function always begins with the same sequence, it is necessary to have some way for the program to start using this sequence at a random point. Otherwise, the same fortune will be given each time the program is run. This is achieved by having **rand( )** called until a key is pressed. Remember, **kbhit( )** is a common extension provided by many compilers, but it is not defined by ANSI. If your compiler does not support the **kbhit( )** function, you need to ask the user for an arbitrary number and call **rand( )** that number of times.

This example uses a two-dimensional array of pointers to create the skeleton for a C help program. The program initializes a list of string pointers. The first dimension points to a C keyword, the second to a short description of the keyword. The list is terminated by two null strings, which mark the end of the list. Users input the keyword for which they need help and the program displays the description. As you can see, only a few keywords have been entered. You can expand the list as an exercise.

```
/* A simple C keyword help program. */
#include stdio.h
#include "string.h"
```

```
char *keyword[][2] = {
  "for", "for(initialization; condition; increment)",
  "if", "if(condition)...else...",
  "switch", "switch(value) { case-list }",
  "while", "while(condition)...",
  "", ""    /* terminate the list with nulls */
};

main()
{
  char str[80];
  int i;

  printf("Enter keyword: ");
  gets(str);
  for(i=0; keyword[i][0]; i++)
    if(!strcmp(keyword[i][0], str))
      printf(keyword[i][1]);
}
```

INITIALIZING POINTERS

After a pointer is declared, but before it has been assigned, it will contain an arbitrary value. If you try to use the pointer before giving it a value, you will probably crash not only your program, but even your computer's operating system — a very nasty error indeed.

By convention, a pointer may be initialized to null to signify that it points to nothing.

Pointer arrays, like any variable, may be initialized when they are declared, as you may recall from the **fortunes** array shown earlier in this chapter.

POINTERS AND THE 8086 FAMILY OF PROCESSORS

If you are using C on a computer that uses one of the 8086 family of processors, then you have six different ways to compile your program, each of which organizes memory differently. For somewhat

complex reasons, the way the program is compiled has some effect
on how pointers behave and what you can do with them. It is beyond
the scope of this book to discuss 8086 memory models and their
effects on pointers, except to say that for most applications, the
effect on pointer operations is not an issue. For example, all the
programs in this book compile and operate correctly no matter what
approach to memory is taken. As a beginner you do not have to
worry about the differences in memory organization. (However, this
advanced topic is discussed in depth in the book *Advanced C,*
Herbert Schildt (Berkeley, Ca.: Osborne/McGraw-Hill, 1988).)

MULTIPLE INDIRECTION

A pointer to a pointer is a form of multiple indirection, or a chain of
pointers. Consider Figure 6-1. As you can see, in the case of a
normal pointer the value of the pointer is the address of the variable
that contains the desired value. In the case of a pointer to a pointer,
the first pointer contains the address of the second pointer, which
points to the location that contains the desired value.

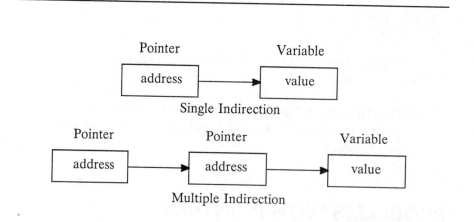

FIGURE 6-1   Single and multiple indirection

Multiple indirection can be carried on to the extent you desire, but more than a pointer to a pointer is seldom advised, or needed. Excessive indirection is difficult to follow and prone to conceptual errors. (Do not confuse multiple indirection with *linked lists,* which are used in databases and the like.)

A variable that is a pointer to a pointer must be declared as such by placing an additional asterisk in front of its name. For example, this declaration tells the compiler that **balance** is a pointer to a pointer of type **int**.

```
int **balance;
```

It is important to understand that **balance** is not a pointer to an integer, but rather a pointer to an **int** pointer.

Accessing the target value indirectly pointed to by a pointer to a pointer requires that the asterisk operator be applied twice, as is shown in this short example:

```
#include "stdio.h"

main()
{
  int x, *p, **q;

  x = 10;
  p = &x;
  q = &p;

  printf("%d", **q); /* print the value of x */
}
```

Here, **p** is declared as a pointer to an integer and **q** as a pointer to a pointer to an integer. The call to **printf( )** will print the number 10 on the screen.

PROBLEMS WITH POINTERS

Nothing will get you into more trouble than a "wild" pointer. Pointers are a mixed blessing. They give you tremendous power and are

necessary for several systems programs; but when a pointer contains a wrong value it can be the most difficult bug to track down.

The erroneous pointer itself is not the problem. The problem is that each time you perform an operation using it, you are reading or writing to some unknown piece of memory. If you read from it, the worst that can happen is that you get garbage. If you write to it, however, you will write over other pieces of your code or data. This may not show up until later in the execution of your program, and this may lead you to look for the bug in the wrong place. There may be little or no evidence to suggest that the pointer is the problem. In an effort to avoid pointer errors, let's see how they are created.

Uninitialized Pointers

The classic example of a pointer error is the *uninitialized pointer*. Consider

```
main() /* this program is wrong */
{
  int x, *p;

  x = 10;
  *p = x;
}
```

Here, **p** contains an unknown address because it has never been defined. You have no way of knowing where the value of **x** has been written. When your program is very small, as it is here, odds are that **p** will contain an address that is not in your code or data area, so most of the time your program will appear to work fine. However, as your program grows, the probability of **p** having a pointer into either your program code or data area increases. Eventually your program stops working. The solution is to make sure that a pointer is always pointing at something valid before it is used.

Misunderstanding Pointers

A second common error is caused by a simple misunderstanding of how to use a pointer. Let's look at the following.

```
#include "stdio.h"

main() /* this program is wrong */
{
  int x, *p;

  x = 10;
  p = x;
  printf("%d", *p);
}
```

The call to **printf( )** will not print the value of **x**, which is 10, onto the screen. It will print some unknown value. The reason is that the assignment

```
p = x;
```

is wrong. That statement assigned the value 10 to the pointer **p**, which was supposed to contain an address, not a value. To make the program correct, you would write

```
p = &x;
```

Pointers can cause tricky bugs when handled incorrectly; however, this is not a reason to avoid using them.

Invalid Pointer Comparisons

Comparisons between pointers that do not access the same array are generally invalid and often cause errors. You can never know where your data will be placed in memory, if it will be placed there the same way again, or whether different compilers will treat it the same way. Therefore, making comparisons between pointers to two different arrays can yield unexpected results. For example,

```
char s[80];
char y[80];
char *p1, *p2;
```

```
p1 = s;
p2 = y;
if(p1 < p2)...
```

is probably an invalid concept. You should write your applications so that they work no matter where data is located in memory.

A related error occurs when the programmer assumes that two back-to-back arrays may be indexed as one by simply incrementing a pointer across the array boundaries. For example:

```
int first[10];
int second[10];

int *p, t;

p = first;
for(t=0; t<20; ++t)  *p++=t;
```

This code *cannot* be used to initialize arrays **first** and **second** with the numbers 0 through 19. Even though it may work on some compilers under certain circumstances, it assumes that both arrays will be placed back-to-back in memory with **first** first. However, the ANSI standard does not specify this and it is up to each compiler implementor.

Forgetting to Reset a Pointer

The following incorrect program inputs a string from the keyboard and then displays the ASCII code for each character in the string. However, it has a serious bug. Can you find the error?

```
/* This program is wrong. */

#include "stdio.h"
#include "string.h"

main()
{
  char s[80];
```

```
  char *pl;
  pl = s;

  do {
    gets(s); /* read a string */
    /* print the ASCII values of each character */
    while(*pl) printf(" %d", *pl++);
  } while(strcmp(s, "done"));
}
```

pl is assigned the address of **s** once. This assignment is outside the loop. The first time through the loop, **pl** points to the first character in **s**. The second time through, however, it continues on from where it left off because it was not reset to the start of the array **s**. This next character may be part of the second string, or another variable, or a piece of the program. Eventually, it will crash the program.

The proper way to write the program is

```
/* This program is correct. */

#include "stdio.h"
#include "string.h"

main()
{
  char s[80];
  char *pl;

  do {
    pl = s;
    gets(s); /* read a string */
    /* print the ASCII values of each character */
    while(*pl) printf(" %d", *pl++);
  } while(strcmp(s, "done"));
}
```

Here, each time the loop iterates, **pl** is set to the beginning of the string. Remember, you must always know where your pointers are pointing.

EXERCISES

1. Let **x** be an integer and **p** be an integer pointer. Write a code fragment that will assign the value 10 to **x** using pointer **p1**.

2. What is wrong with this function?

```
func1()
{
  char *p;

  char s[80];

  p = s[0];
  gets(s);
  printf("%s ",p);
}
```

3. Write a short function that will print out the value of each element pointed to by an array of **float** pointers. Assume that the array is ten elements long.

4. Write your own version of the **strcmp( )** library function.

5. Is the following fragment valid C code?

```
int *p, i[100];

p = i;

*(p+10) = 10;
```

6. Expand and enhance the C keyword help program.

Answers

1.
```
    p = &x;
    *p = 10;
```

2. **p** is assigned the value of the first element of array **s**, not its address. The intention was to assign the address of the first element in the array.

3.
```
func1(float *f[])
{
  int t;

  for(t=0; t<10; ++t) printf("%f ", *f[t]);
}
```

4.
```
strcmp(char *s1, char *s2)
{
  while(*s1) {
    if(*s1!=*s2) break;
    s1++; s2++;
  }
  return *s1-*s2;
}
```

5. Yes, it assigns the eleventh element of **i** the value 10.

FUNCTIONS

Functions are the building blocks of C. Aside from the brief introduction given in Chapter 2, you have been using functions on faith. In this chapter you will study functions in detail, learning how to make a function modify its arguments, the scope rules and lifetime of variables, how to make recursive functions, and some special properties of the **main( )** function. You will also learn about function prototypes, one of the most important features added to C by the ANSI standard.

THE GENERAL FORM OF A FUNCTION

The general form of a function is

type-specifier function _name(parameter declarations)
{
   body of the function
}

The *type-specifier* designates the type of value the function will return using the **return** statement. It may be any valid type. If no type is specified, then, by default, the function is assumed to return an integer result. The programs in previous chapters have made use of this default. The *parameter declarations* list is a comma-separated list of variable types and names that will receive the values of the arguments when the function is called. A function may be without parameters, in which case the parameter list will be empty. However, even if there are no parameters, the parentheses are still required.

It is important to understand one thing about a function's parameter declarations list. Unlike variable declarations, in which many variables can be declared to be of a common type by using a comma-separated list of variable names, all function parameters must include both the type and variable name. That is, the parameter declaration list for a function takes this general form:

f(*type varname1, type varname2, . . . , type varnameN*)

SCOPE RULES OF FUNCTIONS

The *scope rules* of a language are the rules that govern whether a piece of code knows about, or has access to, another piece of code or data. In C, each function is a discrete block of code. A function's code is restricted to that function and cannot be accessed by statements in other functions except through a call to that particular function. (It is not possible, for instance, to use the **goto** to jump into the middle of another function.) The code comprising the body of a function is hidden from the rest of the program and, unless it uses global variables or data, it can neither affect nor be affected by other parts of the program except as specified by your program. Stated another way, the code and data that are defined within one function cannot interact with the code or data defined in another function unless explicitly specified because the two functions have a different scope.

As you recall, there are three types of variables: local variables, formal parameters, and global variables. The scope rules govern how each of these may be accessed by other parts of your program and establish their lifetimes. Let's look at how this works.

Local Variables

As you know, variables declared inside a function are called local variables. In reality, variables local to a function are simply a special case of the more general concept. A variable may be declared inside any block of code and is local to that block. (Remember, a block begins and ends with braces.) Local variables may be referenced only by statements that are inside the block in which they are declared. Stated another way, local variables are not known outside their own code block; their scope is limited to the block within which they are declared.

One of the most important things to understand about local variables is that they exist only while the block of code in which they are declared is executing. That is, a local variable is created when its block is entered and destroyed upon exit.

Local variables are most commonly declared in the function code block. For example, consider the following program:

```
#include "stdio.h"

main()
{
  char str[]="this is str in main()";

  printf("%s\n", str);
  f1();
  printf("%s\n", str);
}

f1()
{
```

```
    char str[80];

    printf("enter something: ");
    gets(str);
    printf("%s\n", str);
}
```

The character array **str** was declared twice, once in **main( )** and once in **f1( )**. The **str** in **main( )** has no bearing on, or relationship to, the one in **f1( )**. This is because each **str** is only known to the code within the same block as the variable's declaration. To confirm this, try the program. As you will see, the value of **str** in **main( )** remains unchanged.

The C language contains the keyword **auto**, which can be used to declare local variables. However, since all non-global variables are, by default, assumed to be **auto**, it is virtually never used. You will not see it in any examples in this book. If you choose to use it, place it immediately before the variable type. For example:

```
auto char ch;
```

It is common practice to declare all variables needed within a function at the start of that function's code block—mostly to make it easy for anyone reading the code to know what variables are used. However, a local variable may be declared within any block of code. Again, a variable declared within a block is local to that block. This means that the variable does not exist until the block is entered and is destroyed when the block is exited. Furthermore, no code outside that block—including other code in the function—may access that variable. Let's try the following program as another example:

```
/* This program illustrates how variables can be
   local to a block.
*/

#include "stdio.h"
#include "string.h"
#include "stdlib.h"

main()
{
```

```
char str[80];
int choice;

printf("(1) add numbers or ");
printf("(2) concatenate Strings?: ");
gets(str);
choice = atoi(str);
printf("\n");

if(choice == 1) {
  int a, b;  /* activate two integer vars */
  printf("Enter two numbers: ");
  scanf("%d%d", &a, &b);
  printf("Sum is %d", a+b);
}
else {
  char s1[80], s2[80];  /* activate two strings */
  printf("Enter two strings: ");
  gets(s1);
  gets(s2);
  strcat(s1, s2);
  printf("Sum is %s", s1);
}
}
```

This program adds two numbers or links two strings, depending upon what the user chooses. Notice the variable declarations for **a** and **b** in the **if** block, and those for **s1** and **s2** in the **else** block. As always, these variables only come into existence when their block is entered and will go out of existence when their block is exited. If the user chooses to add numbers, then **a** and **b** are created. If the user wants to link strings, **s1** and **s2** are created. Finally, none of these variables can be referenced elsewhere — even in other parts of the same function. For example, if you try to compile the following incorrect version of the program, you will receive an error message:

```
/* This program is incorrect. */

#include "stdio.h"
#include "string.h"
#include "stdlib.h"
```

```
main()
{
  char str[80];
  int choice;

  printf("(1) add numbers or ");
  printf("(2) concatenate Strings? (N or S): ");
  gets(str);
  choice = atoi(str);
  printf("\n");

  if(choice == 1) {
    int a, b;  /* activate two integer vars */
    printf("Enter two numbers: ");
    scanf("%d%d", &a, &b);
    printf("Sum is %d", a+b);
  }
  else {
    char s1[80], s2[80];  /* activate two strings */
    printf("Enter two strings: ");
    gets(s1);
    gets(s2);
    strcat(s1, s2);
    printf("Sum is %s", s1);
  }
  a = 10;  /* This line will be flagged as an error
              by the compiler.
           */
}
```

The main advantage to declaring a local variable within a conditional block is that memory will only be allocated if needed, since local variables do not come into existence until the block in which they are declared is entered. Although this is not important in most computer environments where plenty of RAM is available, it can really matter when code is being produced for dedicated controllers (such as a digitally controlled microwave oven) where RAM is in very short supply.

Because local variables are created and destroyed with each entry and exit from the block in which they are declared, their content is lost once the block is left. This is especially important to remember in terms of a function call. When a function is called, its

local variables are created, and upon its return, they are destroyed. Thus local variables cannot retain their values between calls. (There is an exception to this, which will be explained later in this book.)

Unless otherwise specified, storage for local variables is on the stack. The fact that the stack is a dynamic and changing region of memory explains why local variables cannot hold their values between function calls.

Formal Parameters

As you know, if a function is to use arguments, then it must declare variables, called formal parameters, that will accept the values of the arguments. Aside from receiving the function's input parameters, they behave like any other local variables inside the function. Remember, you must make sure that the formal parameters you declare are the same type as the arguments you will use to call the function. Also, even though these variables perform the special task of receiving the value of the arguments passed to the function, they can be used like any other local variable.

Global Variables

Unlike local variables, global variables are known throughout the program and may be used by any piece of code. They will also hold their value during the entire execution of the program. Global variables are created by declaring them outside of any function. They may be accessed by any expression regardless of what function that expression is in.

In the following program, you can see that the variables **count** and **num_right** have been declared outside of all functions. Common practice dictates it is best to declare global variables near the top of the program. However, technically, they simply have to be declared before they are first used. This program is a simple addition drill. It first asks you how many problems you want. For each drill, it calls **drill( )**, which generates two random numbers in the range 0 through 99. It prompts for and then checks your answer.

You get three tries per problem. At the end, the program displays the number of problems you answered correctly. Pay special attention to the variables.

```c
/* A simple addition drill program. */

#include "stdio.h"
#include "stdlib.h"

int count;  /* count and num_right are global. */
int num_right;

main()
{
  printf("How many practice problems: ");
  scanf("%d", &count);

  num_right = 0;
  do {
    drill();
    count--;
  } while(count);
  printf("You got %d right.\n", num_right);
}

drill()
{
  int count;  /* This count is local and unrelated to
                  the global one.
              */
  int a, b, ans;

  /* generate two numbers between 0 and 99 */
  a = rand() % 100;
  b = rand() % 100;

  /* The user gets three tries to get it right */
  for(count=0; count<3; count++) {
    printf("What is %d + %d? ", a, b);
    scanf("%d", &ans);
    if(ans==a+b) {
      printf("Right\n");
      num_right++;
```

```
        return;
      }
    }
    printf("You used up all your tries\n");
    printf("The answer is %d: \n", a+b);
}
```

Looking closely at this program, it should be clear that the reference to **count** in **main( )** is to the global **count**. However, **drill( )** has declared a local variable called **count**. When **drill( )** references **count**, it references only its local variable, not the global one. It is important to remember that if a global variable and a local variable have the same name, all references to that name inside the function where the local variable is declared will refer only to the local variable. This is often convenient; but forgetting it can cause your program to act very strangely, even though it looks correct. Finally, both **main( )** and **drill( )** have access to the global **num_right** because it is the only variable by that name declared in the program.

Storage for global variables is in a region of memory set aside for this purpose by C. Global variables are helpful when the same data is used in many functions in your program, but you should avoid using unnecessary global variables for three reasons:

- They take up memory the entire time your program is executing, not just when they are needed.

- Using a global where a local variable will do makes a function less general because it relies on something defined outside of itself.

- Using a large number of global variables can lead to program errors because of unanticipated side effects. (This is evidenced in BASIC, where all variables are global.)

A major problem in developing large programs is the accidental changing of a variable's value because it was used elsewhere in the program. This can happen in C if you use too many global variables in your programs.

One of the principal points of a structured language is the compartmentalization of code and data. In C, this separation is

achieved by using local variables and functions. For example, here are two ways to write **mul( )**—a simple function that computes the product of two integers.

```
General                     Specific

                            int x, y;
mul(int x, int y)           mul()
{                           {
  return(x*y);                return(x*y);
}                           }
```

Both functions will return the product of the variables **x** and **y**. However, the generalized, or parameterized, version can be used to return the product of *any* two numbers, whereas the specific version can be used to find only the product of the global variables **x** and **y**.

FUNCTION PARAMETERS AND ARGUMENTS — A CLOSER LOOK

The way in which data is passed to a function determines how that function can act on it. The ins and outs of function parameters are discussed here.

Call by Value, Call by Reference

In general, subroutines can be passed arguments in one of two ways. The first is called *call by value*. This method copies the value of an argument into the formal parameter of the subroutine. Therefore, changes made to the parameters of the subroutine have no effect on the variables used to call it.

Call by reference is the second way a subroutine can have arguments passed to it. In this method, the address of an argument is copied into the parameter. Inside the subroutine, the address is used to access the actual argument used in the call. Thus changes made to the parameter will affect the variable used to call the routine.

C uses call by value to pass arguments. In general, you cannot alter the variables used to call the function. (In the next section you will learn how to "force" a call by reference by using pointers to allow changes to the calling variables.) Consider the following function:

```
#include "stdio.h"

main()
{
  int t=10;

  printf("%d %d", sqr_it(t), t);
}

sqr_it(int x)
{
  x = x*x;
  return(x);
}
```

In this example, the value of the argument to **sqr_it( )**, 10, is copied into the parameter **x**. When the assignment **x = x*x** takes place, the only thing modified is the local variable **x**. The variable **t**, used to call **sqr_it( )**, will still have the value 10. Hence, the output will be 100 10.

Remember that it is a copy of the value of the argument that is passed into that function. What occurs inside the function will have no effect on the variable used in the call.

Creating a Call by Reference

Even though C's parameter passing convention is call by value, you can simulate a call by reference by passing a pointer to the argument. Since this will cause the address of the argument to be passed to the function, it will then be possible to change the value of the argument outside the function.

Pointers are passed to functions just like any other value. Of course, it is necessary to declare the parameters as pointer types. For example, consider the classic example of a call-by-reference function, **swap( )**. It exchanges the value of its two integer arguments, as shown here:

```
swap(int *x, int *y)
{
  int temp;

  temp = *x;   /* save the value at address x */
  *x = *y;     /* put y into x */
  *y = temp;   /* put x into y */
}
```

The * operator is used to access the variable pointed to by its operand. Thus the contents of the variables used to call the function will be swapped.

It is important to remember that **swap( )** (or any other function that uses pointer parameters) must be called with the *addresses* of the arguments. The following program shows the correct way to call **swap( )**:

```
#include "stdio.h"

main()
{
  int x, y;

  x = 10;
  y = 20;

  printf("initial values of x and y: %d %d \n", x, y);
  swap(&x, &y);
  printf("swapped values of x and y: %d %d \n", x, y);
}

swap(int *x, int *y)
{
  int temp;

  temp = *x;   /* save the value at address x */
```

```
     *x = *y;      /* put y into x */
     *y = temp;    /* put x into y */
  }
```

In this example, the variable **x** is assigned the value 10 and **y** the value 20. Then **swap( )** is called with the addresses of **x** and **y**. The unary operator **&** is used to produce the address of the variables. Therefore, the addresses of **x** and **y**, not their values, are passed into the function **swap( )**.

The **&** had to go in front of the arguments to **scanf( )** that were to receive values because, in actuality, you were passing their addresses so the calling variable could be modified. You can see now why pointers form such an integral part of the C language.

Calling Functions with Arrays

When an array is used as an argument to a function, only the address of the array is passed, not a copy of the entire array. When you call a function with an array name, a pointer to the first element in the array is passed into the function. (Remember, in C, an array name without an index is a pointer to the first element in the array.) This means the parameter declaration must be of a compatible pointer type.

There are three ways to declare a parameter that is to receive an array pointer. First, it may be declared as an array of the same type and size as that used to call the function, as shown here:

```
#include "stdio.h"

main()  /* print some numbers */
{
  int t[10],i;

  for(i=0; i<10; ++i) t[i]=i;
  display(t);
}


display(int num[10])
{
```

```
   int i;

   for(i=0; i<10; i++) printf("%d ", num[i]);
}
```

Even though the parameter **num** is declared to be an integer array of ten elements, the C compiler will automatically convert it to an integer pointer. This is necessary because no parameter can actually receive an entire array. Since only a pointer to the array will be passed, a pointer parameter must be there to receive it.

A second way to declare an array parameter is to specify it as an unsized array, as shown here:

```
display(int num[])
{
   int i;

   for(i=0; i<10; i++) printf("%d ", num[i]);
}
```

Here, **num** is declared to be an integer array of unknown size. Since C provides no array boundary checks, the actual size of the array is irrelevant to the parameter (but not to the program, of course). This method of declaration also defines **num** as an integer pointer.

The final way that **num** can be declared, and the most common form in professionally written C programs, is as a pointer, as shown here:

```
display(int *num)
{
   int i;

   for(i=0; i<10; i++) printf("%d ",num[i]);
}
```

This is allowed because any pointer may be indexed using [], as if it were an array.

Notice that all three methods of declaring an array parameter yield the same result: a pointer.

On the other hand, an array *element* used as an argument is treated like any other simple variable. For example, the same program just examined could have been written without passing the entire array, as shown here:

```c
#include "stdio.h"

main() /* print some numbers */
{
  int t[10],i;

  for(i=0; i<10; ++i) t[i]=i;
  for(i=0; i<10; i++) display(t[i]);
}

display(int num)
{
  printf("%d ", num);
}
```

As you can see, the parameter to **display( )** is of type **int**. It is not relevant that **display( )** is called using an array element, because only that one value of the array is used.

It is important to understand that when an array is used as a function argument, its address is passed to a function. This is an exception to C's call by value parameter-passing convention. It means that the code inside the function will be operating on, and potentially altering, the actual contents of the array used to call the function. For example, consider the function **cube( )**, which cubes each element in an array pointed to by the first argument:

```c
#include "stdio.h"

main()
{
  int i, nums[10];

  for(i=0; i<10; i++) nums[i] = i+1;
  cube(nums, 10);
  for(i=0; i<10; i++) printf("%d ", nums[i]);
}
```

```
cube(int *n, int num)
{
  while(num) {
    *n = *n * *n * *n;
    num--;
    n++;
  }
}
```

After the call to **cube( )**, the contents of array **nums** in **main( )** will be cubes of the original value.

argc AND argv — ARGUMENTS TO main( )

Sometimes it is useful to pass information into a program when you run it. The usual method is to pass information into the **main( )** function through the use of *command line arguments,* the information following the program's name on the command line of the operating system. For example, you probably compile C programs from the command line by typing something such as

    cc progname.c

where *progname* is the name of the program you want compiled. The name is passed into the C compiler as an argument.

ANSI defines two special built-in, but optional, arguments to **main( )**. They are **argc** and **argv**, which are used to receive command line arguments. These are the only parameters defined by ANSI for **main( )**. However, other arguments may be supported in your specific operating environment, so you will want to check your user manual. Let's look at **argc** and **argv** more closely.

The **argc** parameter holds the number of arguments on the command line and is an integer. It will always be at least 1 because the name of the program qualifies as an argument.

The **argv** parameter is a pointer to an array of character pointers. That is, **argv** is a pointer to an array of strings. Each element in this array points to a command line argument. The program's name is pointed to by **argv[0]**; **argv[1]** will point to the first argument, **argv[2]** to the second argument, and so on. All command line arguments are passed to the program as strings. Thus, numeric arguments will have to be converted by the program into their proper internal format.

It is important to declare **argv** properly. The most common method is

```
char *argv[];
```

The empty brackets indicate it is an array of undetermined length. You can now access the individual arguments by indexing **argv**. The simple program shown here illustrates the command line arguments. It prints "hello," followed by your name, which must be the second command line argument.

```
#include "stdio.h"

main(int argc, char *argv[])  /* name program */
{
  if(argc!=2) {
    printf("You forgot to type your name\n");
    exit(0);
  }
  printf("Hello %s", argv[1]);
}
```

If you titled this program **name** and your name was Tom, then to run the program you would type **name Tom**. The output from the program would be "Hello Tom." For example, if you were logged into drive A and running DOS, you would see

```
A>NAME Tom
  Hello Tom
A>
```

Although ANSI does not stipulate the exact nature of a command line argument because operating systems vary considerably on

this point, the most common convention is as follows. Each command line argument must be separated by a space or a tab. Commas, semicolons, and the like are not considered separators. For example,

```
one, two, and three
```

is made up of four strings, while

```
one,two,and three
```

is two strings—commas are not legal separators.

If you need to pass a command line argument that actually does contain spaces, you must place it between quotes. For example, this will be treated as a single command line argument:

```
"this is one argument"
```

Remember, the examples just given apply to a wide variety of environments, but not necessarily to yours.

To access an individual character in one of the command strings, you need to add a second index to **argv**. For example, the following program will show all the arguments with which it was called and display them on the screen one character at a time:

```
/* The program prints all command line arguments it is
   called with. */
#include "stdio.h"

main(int argc, char *argv[])
{
  int t, i;

  for(t=0; t<argc; ++t) {
    i = 0;
    while(argv[t][i]) {
      printf("%c", argv[t][i]);
      ++i;
    }
    printf(" ");
  }
}
```

Remember, the first index accesses the string and the second index accesses a character of the string.

As mentioned, when you need to pass numeric data to a program, that data will be received in its string form. Your program will need to convert it into the proper internal format using one or another of C's standard library functions. For example, this program prints the sum of the two numbers that follow its name on the command line:

```
/* This program displays the sum of the two numeric
   command line arguments.
*/

#include "stdio.h"
#include "stdlib.h"

main(int argc, char *argv[])
{

  double a, b;

  if(argc!=3) {
    printf("Usage: add num num\n");
    exit(1);
  }

  a = atof(argv[1]);
  b = atof(argv[2]);

  printf("%lf", a + b);
}
```

The program uses the **atof( )** function to convert each argument into a **double**. To add two numbers, use this type of command line (assuming the program is called ADD):

ADD 100.2 231

This program also introduces a new **printf( )** format code, **%lf**. Here, the **l** is a modifier to the **f**, which tells **printf( )** that a **double** value,

as opposed to a **float**, is being passed. Because of the way C automatically "promotes" arguments, the **1** is not technically necessary if you are only printing numbers that are in the range of a **float**. However, it is always a good idea to use the proper format code to avoid future troubles.

Usually, you will use **argc** and **argv** to get initial commands into your program. In C, you can have as many command line arguments as the operating system will allow. For example, in DOS, a command line is limited to 128 characters, or a maximum of 63 arguments. You normally use these arguments to indicate a filename or an option. Using command line arguments will give your program a professional appearance and facilitate the program's use in batch files.

Note: Technically, the names of the command line arguments are arbitrary—you can use any names you like. However, the names **argc** and **argv** have been conventions since C's beginning and it is best to use them so anyone reading your program can quickly identify them as the command line parameters.

THE return STATEMENT

As you know, the **return** statement has two important uses. First, it will cause an immediate exit from the function it is in. That is, the **return** will cause program execution to return to the calling code as soon as it is encountered. Second, it may be used to return a value. Both of these uses are examined in detail here.

Returning from a Function

There are two ways a function terminates execution and returns to the caller. The first is when the last statement in the function has executed and, conceptually, the function's ending brace is encountered. (Of course, the brace isn't actually present in the object code, but you can think of it that way.)

The second way a function can return is through the use of the **return** statement. The **return** statement can be used with or without an associated value. For example, the following function will print the outcome of one number raised to a positive integer power. If the exponent is negative, the **return** statement causes the function to terminate before the final brace is reached, without returning a value .

```
power(int base, int exp)
{
  int i;

  if(exp<0) return; /* can't do negative exponents */

  i = 1;

  for( ; exp; exp--) i = base * i;
  printf("The answer is: %d: ", i);
}
```

A function may contain several **return** statements. The function returns as soon as one is encountered. Be careful, though; having too many **returns** can muddy the operation of a routine and confuse its meaning. It is best to use multiple **returns** only when they help clarify a function.

Return Values

All functions, except those declared to be of type **void** (which will be discussed in the next section), may return a value. This value is explicitly specified by the **return** statement, or unknown if no **return** statement is specified. Thus, as long as a function is not declared as **void**, it can be used as an operand in any valid C expression. Each of the following expressions is valid in C:

```
x = power(y);

if(max(x, y) > 100) printf("greater");

switch(abs(x)) {
```

However, a function cannot be the target of an assignment. A statement such as

```
swap(x, y) = 100;  /* incorrect statement */
```

is wrong. The compiler will flag it as an error and will not compile a program that contains such a statement.

When you write programs, your functions will generally be of three types. The first is simply computational. It is specifically designed to perform operations on its arguments and return a value based on those operations—in essence, it is a "pure" function. Two examples of this sort of function are the library functions **sqrt( )** and **sin( )** that return the square root of a number and its sine, respectively.

The second type of function manipulates information and returns a value indicating the success or failure of that manipulation. An example is **fwrite( )**, which is used to write information to a disk file. If the write operation is successful, **fwrite( )** returns the number of items you requested to be written; any other value indicates an error has occurred. (You will learn about file I/O in Chapter 9.)

The last type of function has no explicit return value. In essence, the function is strictly procedural and produces no value. Many times, functions produce results in which you probably are not interested. For example, **printf( )** returns the number of characters written—which is not generally useful. Although all functions, except those of type **void**, return values, you don't have to use them. A very common question concerning function return values is, "Don't I have to assign this value to some variable since a value is being returned?" The answer is no. If there is no assignment specified, then the return value is simply discarded. Consider the following program, which uses the standard library function **abs( )**:

```
#include "stdio.h"
#include "stdlib.h"

main()
{
  int i;

  i = abs(-10);              /* line 1 */
```

```
    printf("%d", abs(-23));  /* line 2 */
    abs(100);                /* line 3 */
}
```

The **abs()** function returns the absolute value of its integer argument. It uses the STDLIB.H header file. In line 1, the return value of **abs()** is assigned to **i**. In line 2, the return value is not actually assigned, but it is used by the **printf()** function as an argument. Finally, in line 3, the return value is lost because it is neither assigned to another variable nor used as part of an expression.

FUNCTIONS RETURNING NON-INTEGER VALUES

When the type of a function is not explicitly declared, it automatically defaults to **int**. For many C functions this default will be just fine. However, when it is necessary to return a different data type, a two-step process is required. First, the function must be given an explicit type specifier. Second, the type of the function must be identified before the first call is made to it. This is the only way C can generate correct code for functions returning non-integer values.

Functions may be declared to return any valid C data type. The method of declaration is similar to that for variables: the type specifier precedes the function name to tell the compiler what type of data the function is to return. This information is critical if the program is going to run correctly because different data types have different sizes and internal representations.

Before a function returning a non-integer type can be used, its type must be made known to the rest of the program. Unless directed otherwise, C will assume that a function is going to return an integer value. If your program calls a function that returns a different type before that function's declaration, then the compiler will generate the wrong code for the function call. To prevent this, you must use a special form of declaration statement near the top of your program to tell the compiler what value the function is really returning. To see how this is done, examine this short program,

which computes the area and circumference of a circle given its radius.

```
/* This program computes the circumference and
   area of a circle given its radius. */

#include "stdio.h"

/*function type definitions*/
double circum();
double area();

main()
{
  double radius;

  printf("enter radius: ");
  scanf("%lf", &radius);
  printf("circumference: %lf\n", circum(radius));
  printf("area: %lf\n", area(radius));
}

double circum(double rad)
{
  return rad*3.1416;
}

double area(double rad)
{
  return rad*rad*3.1416;
}
```

The function type declarations tell the compiler that **area( )** and **circum( )** will return a **double** floating-point data type. This allows the compiler to correctly generate code for calls to these functions. To see for yourself the importance of the function declarations, first compile the program as it is shown. It should compile with no errors. Now, remove the function declarations. As you can see, the compiler reports a type mismatch error.

One final point about the preceding program: notice that the **%lf** format code is also being used by **scanf( )** to input a **double** value.

For somewhat complex reasons, unlike **printf( )**, which is fairly forgiving of certain mismatches between the format code and the type
of the actual argument, for **scanf( )** to work properly, you must
exactly match the format code with the type of the argument.

A function type declaration statement has the general form

type _ specifier function _ name( );

Even if the function takes arguments, they need not be listed in its
type declaration.

Without the type declaration statement, a mismatch between the
type of data the function returns and the type of data the calling
routine expects will occur. This may result in bizarre and unpredict-
able results. If both functions are in the same file, the compiler will
catch the type mismatch and not compile the program. However, if
they are in different files, the compiler will not find the error. Type
checking is not done at link time or run time, only at compile time.
Therefore, you must be very careful to make sure the types are
compatible.

Note: When a character is returned from a function declared to
be of type integer, the character value is converted into an integer.
Because C handles the conversion from character to integer and
back cleanly, often the programmer will rely on this conversion
rather than declaring the function as returning a character value.
This sort of thing is found frequently in older C code and is not
technically considered an error.

Functions of Type void

One of **void**'s uses is to explicitly declare those functions that do not
return values. Doing so prevents their use in any expression and
helps head off accidental misuse. For example, the function
print _ vertical( ) prints its string argument vertically down the side
of the screen. Since it returns no value, it is declared as **void**.

```
void print_vertical(char *str)
{
```

```
    while(*str)
      printf("%c\n", *str++);
}
```

Before you can use this, or any other **void** function, you must declare it. If you don't, C will assume that it is returning an integer, and when the compiler actually reaches the function it will declare a type mismatch. This program shows a proper example. It prints a single command line argument vertically on the screen.

```
#include "stdio.h"

void print_vertical();   /* declare the return type */

main(int argc, char *argv[])
{
   if(argc) print_vertical(argv[1]);
}

void print_vertical(char *str)
{
   while(*str)
      printf("%c\n", *str++);
}
```

Earlier in this book, functions that did not return values were simply allowed to default to type **int**. However, you should declare all functions not returning values as **void** because it is good practice. Now that you know about **void** functions, from this point on the examples in this book will use **void** where needed.

FUNCTION PROTOTYPES

As you know, a function returning a value other than **int** must be declared prior to its use. In ANSI C, you can take this idea one step further by also declaring the number and types of the function's arguments. This expanded definition is called a *function prototype*. Function prototypes were not part of the original C language. They are, however, one of the most important additions made by the

ANSI committee. Prototypes enable C to provide strong type-checking, somewhat similar to that provided by languages such as Pascal. When prototypes are used, they allow C to find and report any illegal type conversions between the type of arguments used to call a function and the type definition of its parameters. Also, differences between the number of arguments used to call a function and the number of parameters in the function will be caught.

The general form of a function prototype definition is shown here:

$$type\ func\_name(type\ parm\_name1,\ type\ parm\_name2,\ldots,$$
$$type\ parm\_nameN);$$

The use of parameter names is optional. However, their use does let the compiler identify any type mismatches by name when an error occurs, so it is a good idea to include them.

For example, this program will cause an error message to be issued because there is an attempt to call **sqr_it( )** with an integer argument instead of the integer pointer required. (It is illegal to transform an integer into a pointer.)

```
/* This program uses a function prototype to
   enforce strong type checking.
*/

void sqr_it(int *i); /* prototype */

main()
{
  int x;

  x = 10;
  sqr_it(x);   /* type mismatch */
}

void sqr_it(int *i)
{
  *i = *i * *i;
}
```

Because of the need to maintain compatibility with the older, UNIX version of C, some special rules apply to function prototypes. First, when a function's return type is declared, but no prototype information is included, the compiler simply assumes that no information about the parameters is given. As far as the compiler is concerned, the function could have several parameters or no parameters. How do you prototype a function that does not have any parameters? When a function has no parameters, its prototype uses **void** inside the parentheses. For example, if a function called **f( )** returns a **float** and has no parameters, its prototype looks like this:

```
float f(void);
```

This tells the compiler that the function has no parameters and any call to that function that has parameters is an error.

Another important point about prototyping is the way it affects C's automatic type promotions. In C, when a non-prototyped function is called, all characters are converted to integers and all **floats** into **doubles**. This somewhat odd type promotion has to do with the characteristics of the original environment in which C was developed. However, if you prototype a function, the types specified in the prototype are maintained and no type promotions will occur.

Not only does the use of function prototypes for your functions help you avoid bugs, but it also helps assure that your program is working correctly by not allowing functions to be called with mismatched arguments. Now that you have learned about prototypes, this book will use them in subsequent examples. Also, from this point forward, when new library functions are introduced, they will be shown in their prototype form.

Your code should, in general, include full prototyping information. But remember, even though the ANSI standard strongly recommends the use of function prototypes, it is not an error if no prototype for a function exists. This is necessary to support old C code developed before prototypes were invented.

HEADER FILES—A CLOSER LOOK

Early in this book you were told about the standard C header files. However, you were only told that they contained information needed

by certain C library functions. While this partial explanation is true, it does not tell the whole story. C's header files contain two main types of information: certain definitions used by the functions and the prototypes for the standard functions related to the header file. For example, the reason that STDIO.H has been included in almost all programs in this book is that it contains the prototype for the **printf( )** function. By including the appropriate header file for each library function used in your program, it is possible for C to catch any errors you make when using them.

CLASSIC VERSUS MODERN FUNCTION PARAMETER DECLARATIONS

When C was first invented a different parameter declaration method was used. This older method is sometimes called the "classic" form. The declaration approach used so far in this book is called the "modern" form. The proposed ANSI standard for C supports both forms. But the standard strongly recommends the modern form. You should know the classic form because there are literally millions of lines of existing C code that use it. Also, many programs published in books and magazines use this form because it will work with all compilers—even old ones. Let's see how the classic form differs from the modern one.

The classic function parameter declaration consists of two parts: a parameter list, which goes inside the parentheses that follow the function name; and the actual parameter declarations, which go between the closing parenthesis and the function's opening brace. The general form of the classic parameter definition is shown here:

```
type func _ name(parm1, parm2, . . . parmN)
type parm1;
type parm2;
    .
    .
    .
type parmN;
{
```

function code
```
}
```

For example, this modern declaration

```
float f(int a, int b, char ch)
{
    .
    .
    .
}
```

would look like this in its classic form:

```
float f(a, b, ch)
int a, b;
char ch;
{
    .
    .
    .
}
```

Notice that in classic form more than one parameter can be in a list after the type name.

Keep in mind that there are some very subtle reasons why the modern form is slightly better than the classic form, which is why it is used in this book. However, if you see a program that uses the classic form, remember that your compiler can compile it with no trouble.

RECURSION

In C, functions can call themselves. A function is *recursive* if a statement in the body of the function calls itself. Sometimes called *circular definition*, recursion is the process of defining something in terms of itself.

Examples of recursion abound. A recursive way to define an unsigned integer number is as the digits 0, 1, 2, 3, 4, 5, 6, 7, 8, 9 plus or minus an integer number. For example, the number 15 is the number 7 plus the number 8, 21 is 9 plus 12, and 12 is 9 plus 3.

For a computer language to be recursive, a function must be able to call itself. The classic example of recursion is the function **factr( )**, which computes the factorial of an integer. The factorial of a number n is the product of all the whole numbers between 1 and n. For example, 3 factorial is $1 \times 2 \times 3$, or 6. Both **factr( )** and its iterative equivalent are shown here:

```
factr(int n)   /* recursive */
{
  int answer;

  if(n==1) return(1);
  answer = factr(n-1)*n;
  return(answer);
}


fact(int n)     /* non-recursive */
{
  int t, answer;

  answer = 1;
  for(t=1; t<=n; t++) answer = answer*(t);
  return(answer);
}
```

The operation of the non-recursive version, **fact( )**, should be clear. It uses a loop starting at 1 and ending at the number, and progressively multiplies each number times the moving product.

The operation of the recursive **factr( )** is a little more complex. When **factr( )** is called with an argument of 1, the function returns 1; otherwise it returns the product of **factr(n−) 1*n**. To evaluate this expression, **factr( )** is called with n − 1. This happens until n equals 1 and the calls to the function begin returning.

Computing the factorial of 2, the first call to **factr( )** will cause a second call to be made with the argument of 1. This call will return

1, which is then multiplied by 2 (the original n value). The answer is then 2. You might find it interesting to insert **printf( )** statements into **factr( )**, which will show at what level each call is and what the intermediate answers are.

When a function calls itself, new local variables and parameters are allocated storage on the stack, and the function code is executed with these new variables from the start. A recursive call does not make a new copy of the function. Only the arguments are new. As each recursive call returns, the old local variables and parameters are removed from the stack and execution resumes at the point of the function call inside the function. Recursive functions could be said to "telescope" out and back.

Recursion has some minor disadvantages. Most recursive routines do not significantly save code size or variable storage. Also, the recursive versions of most routines may execute a bit more slowly than the iterative equivalent because of the added overhead of the function calls; but this will usually not be significant. Many recursive calls to a function could cause a stack overrun, but this is unlikely. Because storage for function parameters and local variables is on the stack and each new call creates a new copy of these variables, it is possible that the stack could "walk on" some other data or program memory. However, you probably will not have to worry about this unless a recursive function runs wild.

The main advantage to recursive functions is that they can be used to create clearer and simpler versions of several algorithms than their iterative brothers. For example, the QuickSort sorting algorithm is quite difficult to implement in an iterative way. Also, some problems, particularly ones related to artificial intelligence, seem to lend themselves to recursive solutions. Finally, some people seem to think recursively more easily than iteratively.

When writing recursive functions, you must have an **if** statement somewhere to force the function to return without the recursive call being executed. If you don't do this, once you call the function, it will never return. This is a very common error when writing recursive functions. Use **printf( )** liberally during development so that you can watch what is going on and abort execution if you see you have made a mistake.

Another example of a recursive function is **reverse( )**, shown here. It will print its string argument backwards on the screen.

```
/* Print a string backwards using recursion. */
#include "stdio.h"

void reverse(char *s);

main()
{
  char str[] = "this is a test";

  reverse(str);
}

void reverse(char *s)
{
  if(*s)
    reverse(s+1);

  printf("%c", *s);
}
```

The **reverse( )** function first checks to see if it is passed a null pointer, which signals the end of the string. If it isn't a null, then **reverse( )** calls itself with the next pointer position. When the null is found, the calls begin unraveling and the characters are displayed in reverse order.

The creation of recursive functions can be difficult for beginners. However, over time, you will find yourself using them frequently.

IMPLEMENTATION ISSUES

There are a few important things to remember when you create C functions that affect their efficiency and usability. These issues are the subject of this section.

Parameters and General-Purpose Functions

A general-purpose function is one that will be used in a variety of situations, perhaps by many different programmers. Typically, you

should not base general-purpose functions on global data. It is best if all of the information a function needs is passed to it by its parameters. Besides making your functions general purpose, parameters keep your code readable and less susceptible to bugs resulting from side effects.

Efficiency

Functions are the building blocks of C and crucial to the creation of all but the simplest programs. However, in certain specialized applications, you may need to eliminate a function and replace it with *in-line code* instead. In-line code is the equivalent of the function's statements used without a call to that function. It is used instead of function calls only when execution time is critical.

There are two reasons why in-line code is faster than a function call. First, a call instruction takes time to execute. Second, if there are arguments to pass, these have to be placed on the stack, which also takes time. For almost all applications, this very slight increase in execution time is of no significance. But it could be very important for time-critical tasks. Each function call uses time that would be saved if the code in the function were placed in line. For example, following are two versions of a program that prints the squares of the numbers from 1 to 10. The in-line version will run faster than the other because the function call takes time.

```
in line

#include "stdio.h"


main()
{
  int x;

  for(x=1; x<11; ++x)
  printf("%d", x*x);
}
```

```
function call

#include "stdio.h"

int sqr(int a);

main()
{
  int x;

  for(x=1; x<11; ++x)
  printf("%d", sqr(x));
}
```

```
sqr(int a)
{
            return a*a;
}
```

EXERCISES

1. Create your own version of the standard library functions **strcpy( )** and **strcat( )**.

2. Find and correct the problem with the following function.

```
f(float n, i, h)
{
  .
  .
  .
}
```

3. Write a function called **power( )** that will accept two integer arguments. The first argument is the base and the second is the exponent. Write **power( )** so that the first argument contains the answer after the function returns. Use the return value of the function to indicate math overflow: that is, to return a 1 if the operation was a success, or a 0 if an overflow occurred. Assume both arguments are positive. Hint: If math overflow occurs, the number will become negative.

4. Write two functions, **code( )** and **decode( )**, that both accept a string for an argument. The **code( )** function should modify the argument string by adding 1 to all characters in it, except the null terminator. The **decode( )** function restores the coded string to its original form.

5. Using the functions **code( )** and **decode( )** from exercise 4, write a short program that will accept a string on the command line, print the string coded, and then print it decoded. If no string is specified on the command line, prompt for one.

6. Write a recursive function called **print_num**( ) that has one integer argument. It will print the numbers from 1 to *n* on the screen, where *n* is the value of the argument.

7. Show the classic declaration form for this function's declaration.

```
f(char ch, char ch2, float balance)
```

8. Create your own program similar to the Add program that displays the difference, the product, and the dividend of its command line arguments.

Answers

1.
```
strcat(char *sl, char *s2)
{
    /* first, find the end of sl */
    while(*sl) sl++;

    /* add s2 */
    while(*s2) {
        *sl = *s2;
        sl++;
        s2++;
    }
    *sl = '\0';   /* add the null terminator */
}

strcpy(char *to, char *from)
{
    while(*from) *to++ = *from++;
    *to = '\0';   /* null terminate the string */
}
```

2. The modern form of parameter declaration requires that a type be associated with each parameter name. The declaration should look like this:

```
       f(float n, float i, float h)


3.     power(int *x, int *y)
       {
         int temp;

         temp = *x;

         if(*y==0) {
           *x=1;   /* anything to power of 0 is 1 */
           return 1;
         }

         (*y)--;

         for(; *y; (*y)--) {
           *x=(*x) * temp;
           if(*x<0) return 0;
         }
         return 1;
       }


4.     void code(char *s)
       {
         while(*s) {
           *s = *s + 1;
           s++;
         }
       }

       void decode(char *s)
       {
         while(*s) {
           *s = *s - 1;
           s++;
         }
       }
```

5.
```
#include "stdio.h"
#include "string.h"

void code(char *s), decode(char *s);

main(int argc, char *argv[])
{
  char s[80];

  if(argc!=2) {
    printf("enter your message: ");
    gets(s);
  }
  else strcpy(s, argv[1]);
  code(s);
  printf(s);
  printf("\n");
  decode(s);
  printf(s);
}

void code(char *s)
{
  while(*s) {
    *s = *s+1;
    s++;
  }
}

void decode(char *s)
{
  while(*s) {
    *s = *s - 1;
    s++;
  }
}
```

6.
```
void print_num(int n)
{
  if(n==1) printf("%d ",n);
  else {
    print_num(n-1);
```

```
     printf("%d ",n);
  }
}
```

CONSOLE I/O

Up until now, most of the ANSI C features you have learned about have been similar to (if more powerful than) other structured programming languages. However, C is practically unique in its approach to input/output (I/O) operations in that the C language does not define any keywords that perform I/O. Instead, input and output are accomplished through library functions. As you will see in this and the next chapter, C's I/O system is an elegant piece of engineering that offers the programmer a flexible and cohesive way to transfer data between devices. You will also see that C's I/O system is quite large and involves several different functions.

The C I/O system can be thought of as having two major categories: console I/O and file I/O. As you will see later on, C makes little distinction between console and disk I/O. However, to a beginning C programmer, they represent two very different worlds. Consequently the subject has been divided into two convenient pieces. This chapter examines in detail the console I/O functions—many of which have already been introduced to you. The next chapter presents the file I/O system and describes how the two systems relate to each other.

READING AND WRITING CHARACTERS

The simplest of the console I/O functions are **getchar( )**, which reads a character from the keyboard, and **putchar( )**, which prints a character to the screen. The **getchar( )** function waits until a key is pressed and then returns its value. The key pressed is also "echoed" to the screen automatically. The **putchar( )** function will write its character argument to the screen at the current cursor position. The prototypes for **getchar( )** and **putchar( )** are shown here:

```
int getchar(void);
int putchar(int c);
```

Don't be disturbed by the fact that **getchar( )** returns an integer; the low-order byte contains the character. Also, you can call **putchar( )** with a character argument. Even though **putchar( )** is declared as using an integer parameter, only the low-order byte is actually output to the screen. The use of integers is for compatibility with the original UNIX C compiler. The header file for these functions is in STDIO.H.

The program shown here displays each character typed as one greater; that is, A displays as B, and so on.

```
#include "stdio.h"

main()
{
    char ch;
```

```
printf("Enter some text (type a period to quit).\n");
do {
  ch = getchar();
  putchar(ch+1);
} while (ch!='.');
}
```

One point to keep firmly in mind when using **getchar( )** is that any key represents a valid return value. Thus keys such as RETURN, TAB, and ESC may be returned by **getchar( )**.

A Problem with getchar( )

There is a potential difficulty with **getchar( )** that you must be aware of. ANSI has defined **getchar( )** so it can be implemented in a way compatible with the original, UNIX-based version. The trouble is that in its original form under UNIX, **getchar( )** buffers input until a carriage return is entered, because in the original UNIX system you had to hit a carriage return to send anything to the computer. This means that there are one or more characters waiting in the input queue after **getchar( )** returns, which can be quite annoying in today's interactive environments. Even though the standard specifies that **getchar( )** can be implemented as an interactive function, it seldom is. Thus the preceding program may not have behaved as you expected.

Alternatives to getchar( )

As indicated in the preceding section, the way **getchar( )** is implemented by your compiler may not be useful in an interactive environment. Therefore, you may want to use a different function to read characters from the keyboard. Although the ANSI standard does not define any function that is guaranteed to provide interactive input, many C compilers include alternative keyboard input functions. Although these functions are not defined by ANSI, their

use can be recommended on the grounds that **getchar( )** does not fill the needs of the majority of programmers.

Two of the most common alternative functions are called **getch( )** and **getche( )**, which have these prototypes:

```
int getch(void);
int getche(void);
```

For most compilers, the prototypes for these functions are found in CONIO.H. The **getch( )** function waits for a key press and returns immediately when one is received. It does not echo the character to the screen. The **getche( )** function is the same as **getch( )** with the exception that the key is echoed.

For the remainder of this book, when a character needs to be read from the keyboard in an interactive program, **getche( )** will be used instead of **getchar( )**. However, if your compiler does not support this alternative function, or if **getchar( )** is implemented as an interactive function by your compiler, substitute **getchar( )** when necessary. For example, the preceding program is shown here using **getch( )** instead of **getchar( )**.

```c
#include "stdio.h"
#include "conio.h"

main()
{
  char ch;

  printf("Enter some text (type a period to quit).\n");
  do {
    ch = getch();
    putchar(ch+1);
  } while (ch!='.');
}
```

READING AND WRITING STRINGS

The next step up in console I/O in terms of complexity and power are the functions **gets( )** and **puts( )**. They enable you to read and

write strings of characters at the console. You have already been introduced to **gets( )**, but a more formal discussion follows.

The **gets( )** function reads a string of characters entered at the keyboard and places them at the address pointed to by its character pointer argument. You type characters at the keyboard, then press RETURN to place a null terminator at the end; **gets( )** then returns. The carriage return does not become part of the string. In fact, it is impossible to use **gets( )** to return a carriage return, although **getchar( )** can do so. Typing mistakes can be corrected by using BACKSPACE before pressing RETURN.

The prototype for **gets( )** is

```
char *gets(char *str);
```

where *str* is a character array that receives the characters input by the user. It also returns a pointer to **str**. Its prototype is found in STDIO.H. The following program reads a string into the array **str** and reprints it.

```
#include "stdio.h"
#include "string.h"

main()
{
  char str[80];

  gets(str);
  printf(str);
}
```

The **puts( )** function writes its string argument to the screen followed by a new line. Its prototype is

```
int puts(char *s);
```

It recognizes the same backslash codes as **printf( )**, such as "\t" for TAB. A call to **puts( )** requires far less "overhead" than the same call to **printf( )**, because **puts( )** can only output a string of characters—it

cannot output numbers or do format conversions. Therefore, **puts( )** takes up less space and runs faster than **printf( )**, since formatting and conversions take considerable time. Thus, the **puts( )** function is often used when it is important to have highly optimized code.

The following statement writes "hello" on the screen:

```
puts("hello");
```

The simplest functions that perform console I/O operations are summarized in Table 8-1.

The following program demonstrates several of these basic functions. The program is a synonym finder. It first prompts the user to enter a word, and then checks its built-in database to see if there is a match for the word. If a match is found, the program prints two synonyms. Pay special attention to the indirection used in this program. If you have any trouble understanding it, remember that the **syn** array is an array of pointers to strings.

Function	Operation
getchar( )	Reads a character from the keyboard; waits for carriage return
getche( )	Reads a character with echo; does not wait for carriage return; not defined by ANSI, but a common extension
getch( )	Reads a character without echo; does not wait for carriage return; not defined by ANSI, but a common extension
putchar( )	Writes a character to the screen
gets( )	Reads a string from the keyboard
puts( )	Writes a string to the screen

TABLE 8-1 Simple Console I/O Functions

```
/* A synonym finder program. */

#include "stdio.h"
#include "conio.h"
#include "string.h"
#include "ctype.h"

/* list of synonyms */
char  *syn[][40] = {
  "good", "great", "wonderful",
  "bad", "unfortunate", "terrible",
  "method", "approach", "program",
  "house", "dwelling", "abode",
  "car", "automobile", "transporter",
  "gun", "weapon", "rifle",
  "computer", "machine", "system",
  "quickly", "rapidly", "fast",
  "", "", ""    /* null terminate the list */
};

main()
{
  char word[80], ch;
  char **p;

  do {
    puts("\nEnter word: ");
    gets(word);

    p = syn;

    /* find matching word and print synomyms */
    do {
      if(!strcmp(*p, word)) {
        puts("synonyms are:");
        puts(*(p+1));
        puts(*(p+2));
        break;
      }
      if(!strcmp(*p, word)) break;
      p = p + 3;  /* advance through the list */
    } while(*p);
```

```
    if(!*p) puts("no synonyms found");
    printf("another? (y/n): ");
    ch = getche();
  } while(toupper(ch) != 'N');
}
```

FORMATTED CONSOLE I/O

Although you have been using **printf( )** and **scanf( )** since the beginning of this book, they will be examined in detail here. These functions perform formatted input and output. The term *formatted* means that these functions can read and write data in various formats that are under your control. The **printf( )** function is used to write data to the console; **scanf( )**, its complement, reads data from the keyboard. Both **printf( )** and **scanf( )** can operate on any of the built-in data types, including characters, strings, and numbers.

The printf( ) Function

Let's review what you already have learned about **printf( )**. The prototype for **printf( )** is

int printf(char *control _ string, *argument list*);

The prototype for **printf( )** is in STDIO.H. The **printf( )** function returns the number of characters written.

The control string consists of two types of items. The first type is made up of characters that will be printed on the screen. The second type contains format commands that define the way the arguments are displayed. A format command begins with a percent sign (%) and is followed by the format code. There must be exactly the same number of arguments as there are format commands, and the format commands and the arguments are matched in order. For example, this **printf( )** call

```
printf("I like %c %s", 'C', "very much!");
```

displays

```
I like C very much!
```

The **printf( )** function accepts a wide variety of format codes, as shown in Table 8-2. Let's take a closer look at the format commands you have not yet learned.

Code	Format
%c	Character
%d	Signed decimal integers
%i	Signed decimal integers
%e	Scientific notation (lowercase)
%E	Scientific notation (uppercase)
%f	Decimal floating point
%g	Uses %e or %f, whichever is shorter
%G	Uses %E or %f, whichever is shorter
%o	Unsigned octal
%s	String of characters
%u	Unsigned decimal integers
%x	Unsigned hexadecimal (lowercase)
%X	Unsigned hexadecimal (uppercase)
%p	Displays a pointer
%n	The associated argument will be an integer pointer into which is placed the number of characters written so far
%%	Prints a percent sign

TABLE 8-2   **printf( )** Format Commands

PRINTING NUMBERS   Although you have been using **%d** to indicate a signed decimal number, you may also use **%i**. These format commands are equivalent and both have a large degree of support.

The **%e** and **%E** formats tell **printf( )** to display a **double** argument in scientific notation. Numbers represented in scientific notation take the general form

x.dddddE+/−yy

If you want the "E" to be displayed in uppercase, use the **%E** format; otherwise use **%e**.

You can tell **printf( )** to use either **%f** or **%e** with the **%g** or **%G** format code. This causes **printf( )** to make the selection that will produce the shortest output. When it applies, if you want the "E" shown in uppercase use **%G**; for lowercase use **%g**. The following program demonstrates the effect of the **%g** format code:

```
#include "stdio.h"

main()
{
  double f;

  for(f=1.0; f<1.0e+10; f=f*10)
    printf("%g ", f);
}
```

The program produces the following output.

```
1 10 100 1000 10000 100000 1000000 1e+007 1e+008 1e+009
```

You can display unsigned integers in octal or hexadecimal format using **%o** and **%x** respectively. Since the hexadecimal number system uses the letters "A" through "F" to represent the numbers 10 through 15, you can have these letters displayed in either upper- or lowercase. For uppercase, use the **%X** format code; for lowercase use **%x**. The following program illustrates these format codes.

```
#include "stdio.h"

main()
{
  unsigned num;

  for(num=0; num<255; num++) {
    printf("%o ", num);
    printf("%x ", num);
    printf("%X\n", num);
  }
}
```

DISPLAYING AN ADDRESS   If you wish to display an address, use **%p**. This format specifier causes **printf( )** to display a machine address in a format compatible with the type of addressing used by the computer. The following program displays the address of **sample**:

```
#include "stdio.h"

int sample;

main()
{
  printf("%p", &sample);
}
```

THE %n SPECIFIER   The **%n** format code is different from the others. Instead of telling **printf( )** to display something, **%n** causes **printf( )** to load the variable pointed to by its corresponding argument with a value equal to the number of characters that have been output. In other words, the value that corresponds to the **%n** format command must be a pointer to a variable. After the call to **printf( )** has returned, this variable will hold the number of characters output up to the point at which the **%n** was encountered. To better understand this somewhat unusual format code, try this program:

```
#include "stdio.h"

main()
{
```

```
    int count;

    printf("this%nis a test\n", &count);
    printf("%d", count);
}
```

The program displays "this is a test" followed by the number 4. The main application of the **%n** format code is to enable your program to perform dynamic formatting.

Format Code Modifiers

Many format commands can take modifiers that alter their meaning slightly. For example, it is possible to specify a minimum field width, the number of decimal places, and left justification. The format modifier goes between the percent sign and the actual code. Let's take a look at these now.

THE MINIMUM FIELD WIDTH SPECIFIER   An integer placed between the percent sign and the format code acts as a *minimum field width specifier*. This pads the output to ensure that it reaches a certain minimum length. If the string or number is greater than that minimum, it will be printed in full even if it overruns the minimum. The default padding is done with spaces. If you wish to pad with zeros, place a 0 before the field width specifier. For example, %05d will pad a number of less than five digits with zeros so its total length is 5. The following program demonstrates the minimum field width specifier.

```
#include "stdio.h"

main()
{
    double item;

    item = 10.12304;

    printf("%f\n", item);
```

```
    printf("%10f\n", item);
    printf("%012f\n", item);
}
```

The program produces the following output:

```
10.123040
 10.123040
00010.123040
```

Perhaps the most common use of the minimum field width specifier is in the production of tables with aligned columns. For example, the following program produces a table of squares and cubes for the numbers between 1 and 19.

```
#include "stdio.h"

main()
{
    int i;

    /* display a table of squares and cubes */
    for(i=1; i<20; i++)
      printf("%8d %8d %8d\n", i, i*i, i*i*i);
}
```

A sample of its output is shown here:

```
 1        1        1
 2        4        8
 3        9       27
 4       16       64
 5       25      125
 6       36      216
 7       49      343
 8       64      512
 9       81      729
10      100     1000
11      121     1331
12      144     1728
13      169     2197
14      196     2744
```

15	225	3375
16	256	4096
17	289	4913
18	324	5832
19	361	6859

THE PRECISION SPECIFIER The *precision specifier* follows the minimum field width specifier, if one is present. It consists of a period followed by an integer. Its exact meaning depends on the type of data it is applied to.

When the precision specifier is applied to floating-point data, it determines the number of decimal places displayed. For example, %10.4f will display a number at least ten characters wide with four decimal places.

When the precision specifier is applied to strings, it specifies the maximum field length. For example, %5.7s will display a string between five and seven characters long. If the string is longer than the maximum field width, the excess characters will be left off.

When the precision specifier is applied to integer types, it specifies the minimum number of digits that will appear for each number. Leading zeros are added to achieve the minimum number of digits required.

The following program illustrates the precision specifier:

```
#include "stdio.h"

main()
{
  printf("%.4f\n", 123.1234567);
  printf("%3.8d\n", 1000);
  printf("%10.15s\n", "This is a simple test.");
}
```

The program produces the following output:

```
123.1234
00001000
This is a simpl
```

JUSTIFYING OUTPUT   By default, all output is *right-justified:* if the field width is larger than the data printed, the data will be placed on the right edge of the field. You can force the information to be *left-justified* by placing a minus sign directly after the percent sign. For example, % − 10.2f will left justify a floating-point number with two decimal places in a ten-character field.

The following program illustrates left justification:

```
#include "stdio.h"

main()
{
  printf("right-justified:%8d\n", 100);
  printf(" left-justified:%-8d\n", 100);
}
```

Handling Other Data Types

There are two format command modifiers that allow **printf( )** to display **short** and **long** integers. These modifiers may be applied to the **d, i, o, u,** and **x** type specifiers. The **l** modifier tells **printf( )** that a **long** data type follows. For example, **%ld** means that a **long int** is to be displayed. The **h** modifier instructs **printf( )** to display a **short int.** Thus, **%hu** indicates that the data is of type **short unsigned int.**

The **L** modifier may also prefix the floating-point commands of **e, f,** and **g** and indicates that a **long double** follows.

The scanf( ) Function

The general-purpose console input routine is **scanf( ).** It can read all the built-in data types and automatically convert numbers into the proper internal format. It is much like the reverse of **printf( ).** The prototype for **scanf( )** is

```
int scanf(char *control_string, argument list);
```

The prototype for **scanf( )** is in STDIO.H. The **scanf( )** function returns the number of data items successfully assigned a value.

The control string consists of three classifications of characters.

- Format specifiers
- White-space characters
- Non-white-space characters

Let's look at each of these in turn.

FORMAT SPECIFIERS   The input format specifiers are preceded by a percent sign and tell **scanf( )** what type of data is to be read next. These codes are listed in Table 8-3. Some of these you have already been using; the rest will be examined here.

Code	Meaning
%c	Read a single character
%d	Read a decimal integer
%i	Read a decimal integer
%e	Read a floating-point number
%f	Read a floating-point number
%g	Read a floating-point number
%o	Read an octal number
%s	Read a string
%x	Read a hexadecimal number
%p	Read a pointer
%n	Receive an integer value equal to the number of characters read so far
%u	Read an unsigned integer
%[]	Scan for a set of characters

TABLE 8-3   scanf( ) Format Codes

Inputting Octal and Hexadecimal Integers   You can use **scanf( )** to read integers in either octal or hexadecimal form using the **%o** and **%x** format commands, respectively. The **%x** may be either upper- or lowercase. Either way, you may enter the letters "A" through "Z" when entering hexadecimal numbers. The following program reads an octal and a hexadecimal number:

```
#include "stdio.h"

main()
{
  int i, j;

  scanf("%o%x", &i, &j);
  printf("%o %x", i, j);
}
```

Inputting Unsigned Integers   To input an unsigned integer, use the **%u** format specifier.

Reading Individual Characters Using scanf( )   As you learned earlier in this chapter, you can read individual characters using **getchar( )** or a derivative function. You can also use **scanf( )** for this purpose using the **%c** format command. However, like most implementations of **getchar( )**, **scanf( )** buffers a line of input when the **%c** specifier is used. This can be a little troublesome in an interactive environment.

Although spaces, tabs, and newlines are used as field separators when reading other types of data, when reading a single character, these white-space characters are read like any other character. For example, with an input stream of "x y",

```
scanf("%c%c%c", &a, &b, &c);
```

will return with the x in **a**, a space in **b**, and the y in **c**.

Reading Strings   The **scanf( )** function can be used to read a string from the input stream using the **%s** format specifier. Using the

%s causes **scanf( )** to read characters until a white-space character is encountered. The characters read are put into the character array pointed to by the %s format specifier's corresponding argument and the result is null terminated. As it applies to **scanf( )**, a white-space character is either a space, a carriage return, or a tab. Unlike **gets( )**, which reads a string until a carriage return is typed, **scanf( )** reads a string up to the first white-space character. This means you cannot use **scanf( )** to read a string such as "this is a test," because the first space terminates the reading process. To see the effect of the %s command, try this program using the string "hello there."

```
#include "stdio.h"

main()
{
  char str[80];

  printf("enter a string: ");
  scanf("%s", str);
  printf("here's your string: %s", str);
}
```

As you can see, the program responds with only the "hello" portion of the string.

Inputting an Address   To input a memory address (pointer), use the %p format code. Do not try to use an unsigned integer or any other format specifier because the %p makes **scanf( )** read the address in the format used by the CPU. For example, this program inputs a pointer and then displays what is at that memory address:

```
#include "stdio.h"

main()
{
  char *p;

  printf("enter an address: ");
  scanf("%p", &p);
  printf("at location %p is %c\n", p, *p);
}
```

THE %n SPECIFIER The %n specifier instructs **scanf( )** to assign to the variable pointed to by the corresponding argument, the number of characters read from the input stream at the point at which the %n was encountered.

USING A SCANSET The ANSI standard has added a feature to **scanf( )** called a scanset; this was not part of the original UNIX version. A *scanset* defines a set of characters that may be read by **scanf( )** and assigned to the corresponding character array. A scanset is defined by putting a string of the characters you want to scan for inside brackets ([]). The beginning bracket must be prefixed by a percent sign. For example, this scanset tells **scanf( )** to read only the characters X, Y, and Z.

```
%["XYZ"]
```

When a scanset is used, **scanf( )** continues to read characters and put them into the corresponding character array until a character that is not in the scanset is encountered. The corresponding variable must be a pointer to a character array. Upon return from **scanf( )**, the array will contain a null-terminated string composed of the characters read. To see how this works, try this program:

```
#include "stdio.h"

main()
{

   int i;
   char str[80], str2[80];

   scanf("%d%[abcdefg]%s", &i, str, str2);
   printf("%d %s %s", i, str, str2);
}
```

Try the program using this input: **123abcdtye**, followed by a carriage return. The program will then display "123 abcd tye." Because the "t" is not part of the scanset, **scanf( )** stops reading characters into **str** when it is encountered.

You can specify an inverted set if the first character in the set is a caret (^). When the ^ is present, it instructs **scanf( )** to accept any character that is *not* defined by the scanset.

You can specify a range using a hyphen. For example, this tells **scanf( )** to accept the characters A through Z.

```
%["A-Z"]
```

One important point to remember is that the scanset is case sensitive. Therefore, if you want to scan for upper- and lowercase letters, they must both be specified.

DISCARDING UNWANTED WHITE-SPACE CHARACTERS A white-space character in the control string causes **scanf( )** to skip over one or more white-space characters in the input stream. In essence, one white-space character in the control string will cause **scanf( )** to read, but not store, any number (including zero) of white-space characters up to the first non-white-space character.

NON-WHITE-SPACE CHARACTERS IN THE CONTROL STRING A non-white-space character in the control string causes **scanf( )** to read and discard a matching character in the input stream. For example, "%d,%d" causes **scanf( )** to first read an integer, then read and discard a comma, and finally read another integer. If the specified character is not found, **scanf( )** will terminate. If you wish to read and discard a percent sign, use %% in the control string.

YOU MUST PASS scanf( ) ADDRESSES   All the variables used to receive values through **scanf( )** must be passed by their addresses. This means that all arguments must be pointers to the variables used as arguments. If you remember, this is C's way of creating a call by reference and it allows a function to alter the contents of an argument. For example, if you wish to read an integer into the variable **count**, you would use the following **scanf( )** call:

```
scanf("%d", &count);
```

Strings will be read into character arrays, and the array name, without any index, is the address of the first element of the array. So, to read a string into the character array **str**, you would use

```
scanf("%s", str);
```

In this case, **str** is already a pointer and need not be preceded by the & operator.

FORMAT MODIFIERS   As with **printf( )**, **scanf( )** allows a number of its format specifiers to be modified. The format commands can specify a maximum field length modifier. This is an integer number placed between the percent sign and the format command code that limits the number of characters read for that field. For example, if you wish to read no more than 20 characters into **str**, then you would write

```
scanf("%20s", str);
```

If the input stream is greater than 20 characters, then a subsequent call to input begins where this call leaves off. For example, if

ABCDEFGHIJKLMNOPQRSTUVWXYZ

is entered as the response to the **scanf( )** call in this example, only the first 20 characters, or up to the "T," are placed into **str** because of the maximum size specifier. This means that the remaining characters, "UVWXYZ" have not yet been used. If another **scanf( )** call is made, such as

```
scanf("%s", str);
```

then the characters "UVWXYZ" are placed into **str**. Input for a field may terminate before the maximum field length is reached if a white-space character is encountered. In this case, **scanf( )** moves on to the next field.

To read a long integer, put an **l** in front of the format specifier. And to read a short integer, put an **h** in before the format specifier. These modifiers can be used with **d**, **i**, **o**, and **x** formats.

By default, the **%f**, **%e**, and **%g** specifiers instruct **scanf( )** to assign data to a **float**. If you put an l in front of one of these, **scanf( )** will assign the data to a **double**. Using an **L** tells **scanf( )** that the variable receiving the data is a **long double**.

EXERCISES

1. Create your own version of the standard library function **gets( )** and demonstrate its use in a program. Call the function **mygets( )**.

2. What is wrong with this call to **scanf( )**?

       scanf("Please enter an integer: %d", &x);

3. Write a program that reads a string, a **double**, and a hexadecimal integer from the keyboard.

4. How do the **printf( )** commands **%f** and **%e** differ?

5. Write a program that displays a table of 20 random numbers organized in four columns. (Use **rand( )** to generate the random numbers.)

6. Expand the synonym finder program.

Answers

1.
```
    #include "stdio.h"
    #include "conio.h"

    char *mygets(char *s);

    main()
    {
        char str[80];

        mygets(str);
```

```
  printf("\n%s", str);
}

char *mygets(char *s)
{
  char *p;

  p = s;

  for(;;) {
    *s = getche();
    if(*s=='\b') { /* user pressed backspace */
      s--;
      printf(" \b");
    }
    else if(*s=='\r') { /* user pressed RETURN */
      *s = '\0'; /* null terminate the string */
      break;
    }
    else s++;
  }
  return p;
}
```

2. You cannot use **scanf( )** to display a prompting message.

3.
```
  #include "stdio.h"

main()
{
  char str[80];
  double d;
  int x;

  printf("enter a string, a double and a hex number: ");
  scanf("%s%lf%x", str, &d, &x);
}
```

4. The **%f** command outputs numbers in normal decimal notation. The **%e** command outputs numbers in scientific notation.

5.
```c
#include "stdio.h"
#include "stdlib.h"

main()
{
  int i, j, k, 1;
  int x;

  for(x=0; x<20; x++) {
    i = rand();
    j = rand();
    k = rand();
    1 = rand();
    printf("%10d%10d%10d%10d\n", i, j, k, 1);
  }
}
```

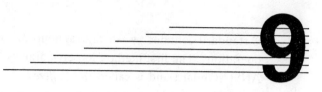

FILE I/O

The ANSI C file I/O system is both powerful and flexible. It lets you easily read or write any type of data. One thing that makes C's I/O system unique is that data may be transferred either in its internal binary representation or in a text format readable by human beings. This makes it easy to create files to fit any need.

Before beginning your examination of C's file system, a short historical note is necessary.

ANSI C I/O VERSUS UNIX I/O

The ANSI standard defines a complete set of I/O functions that can be used to read and write any type of data. However, the old UNIX

C standard contains two distinct systems of routines that handle I/O operations. The first method loosely parallels the one defined by the ANSI standard and is called the *buffered file system* (sometimes the terms "formatted" or "high level" are used instead). The second is the *UNIX-like file system* (sometimes called either "unformatted" or "unbuffered") and is defined only under the old UNIX de facto standard. The ANSI standard does not define the unbuffered file system. There are several reasons for this, including the fact that the two file systems are largely redundant. Also, the UNIX-like file system may not be relevant to some environments that could otherwise support C. The fact that ANSI has not defined the UNIX-like I/O system suggests its use will decline. And, in fact, it would be hard to justify its use on any new project. Since this book is about ANSI C, it covers only the ANSI-defined I/O system. If you wish to learn about the old UNIX-like I/O system, read *C: The Complete Reference* by Herbert Schildt (Berkeley, Ca.: Osborne/McGraw-Hill, 1987).

THE #define DIRECTIVE

It is possible to include various instructions to the C compiler in the source code of a C program. These are called *preprocessor directives* and, although not actually part of the C language, they expand the scope of the C programming environment. All preprocessor directives begin with the # sign. You have already used one preprocessor directive, **#include**, to include header files in your program. Most of the other preprocessor directives will be covered later in this book; however, you will need to understand **#define** to use C's file system.

The **#define** directive defines an identifier and a string that will be substituted for the identifier each time it is encountered in the source file. The identifier is called the *macro name* (or "macro" for short) and the replacement process is called *macro substitution*. The general form of the directive is

#define *identifier string*

Notice there is no semicolon in the statement. There may be any number of spaces between the identifier and the string, but once the string begins, it is only terminated by a newline character.

For example, if you want to use the word TRUE for the value 1 and the word FALSE for the value 0, then you would declare two macro **#define**s

```
#define TRUE 1
#define FALSE 0
```

This will cause C to substitute a 1 or a 0 each time the name TRUE or FALSE is encountered in your source file. For example, the following will print "0 1 2" on the screen:

```
printf("%d %d %d",FALSE, TRUE, TRUE+1);
```

It is important to understand that macro substitution is simply the replacement of an identifier with its associated string. Therefore, if you wished to define a copyright message, you might write something like this:

```
#define CPYRT "Copyright (c) 1988, Herbert Schildt"
  .
  .
  .
printf(CPYRT);
```

The compiler will substitute the string "Copyright © 1988, Herbert Schildt" when the identifier **CPYRT** is encountered. To the compiler, the **printf( )** statement will appear to be

```
printf("Copyright (c) 1988, Herbert Schildt");
```

No text substitutions will occur if the identifier occurs within a quoted string. For example,

```
printf("CPYRT is a macro");
```

will not print the copyright message, but rather "CPYRT is a macro."

A common usage of **#define** is to define the size of things that might change over the evolution of a program, for example, an array dimension. In this simple program, the macro **MAX_SIZE** is used both to dimension an integer array and to control the loop condition of the **for** loop that initializes it.

```
#include "stdio.h"

#define MAX_SIZE 16

unsigned int  pwrs_of_two[MAX_SIZE];

/* Display powers of 2. */
main()
{
    int i;

    pwrs_of_two[0] = 1; /* start the sequence */

    for(i=1; i<MAX_SIZE; i++)
      pwrs_of_two[i] = pwrs_of_two[i-1] * 2;

    printf("The first 16 powers of 2: \n");
    for(i=0; i<MAX_SIZE; i++)
        printf("%u ", pwrs_of_two[i]);
}
```

The reason **#define** is important in understanding and using the C file system is that the header file STDIO.H defines several macros your programs will need to use. These macros will be described as the need arises.

STREAMS AND FILES

Before beginning the discussion of ANSI C's file system, it is important to understand the difference between the terms "stream" and

"file." The C I/O system supplies a consistent interface to the C programmer, independent of the actual device being accessed — that is, the C I/O system provides a level of abstraction between the programmer and the device being used. This abstraction is called a *stream* and the actual device a *file*. It is important to understand how they interact.

Streams

The C file system is designed to work with a wide variety of devices, including terminals, disk drives, and tape drives. Even though each device is very different, the buffered file system transforms each into a logical device called a stream. All streams are similar in their behavior. Because streams are largely device independent, the same functions that write to a disk file can also write to another device, such as the console. There are two types of streams: text and binary.

TEXT STREAMS   A *text stream* is a sequence of characters organized in lines and terminated by a newline character. The ANSI standard states that the newline character is optional on the last line and is determined by the implementation. In a text stream, certain character translations may occur as required by the host environment. For example, a newline character may be converted to a carriage return-linefeed pair. Therefore, there may not be a one-to-one correspondence between the characters that are written (or read) and those in the external device. Similarly, because of possible translations, the number of characters written (or read) may not be the same as that in the external device.

BINARY STREAMS   A *binary stream* is a sequence of bytes that has a one-to-one correspondence to that found in the external device — that is, no character translations will occur. Thus, the number of bytes written (or read) will be the same as that found in the external device. The standard does specify, however, that a binary stream may have an implementation-defined number of null bytes appended to its end. These null bytes might be used, for example, to pad the information so that it fills a sector on a disk.

Files

In C, a file is a logical concept that may be applied to everything from disk files to terminals. A stream is associated with a specific file by performing an *open* operation. Once a file is open, information may be exchanged between it and your program.

Not all files have the same capabilities. For example, a disk file can support random access but a terminal cannot. This illustrates an important point about the C I/O system: all streams are the same but all files are not.

If the file can support random access (sometimes referred to as "position requests"), opening that file also initializes the *file position indicator* to the beginning of the file. As each character is read from or written to the file, the position indicator is incremented, thus ensuring progression through the file.

A file is disassociated from a specific stream through a *close* operation. On streams opened for output, closing a stream causes the contents, if any, of its associated stream to be written to the external device. This process, generally referred to as "flushing" the stream, guarantees that no information is accidentally left in the disk buffer. When your program terminates normally all files are closed automatically by **main( )**'s return to the operating system or by a call to **exit( )**. Files are not closed when a program terminates by crashing.

Each stream that is associated with a file has a file control structure of type **FILE**. This structure is defined in the header STDIO.H. You must not make modifications to this file control block. (You will learn about structures in the next chapter, but briefly, a structure is simply a group of variables accessed under one name. This is similar to a "record" in Pascal. However, you do not need to know about structures to learn and use C's I/O routines.)

If C's separation of streams and files seems unnecessary or strange, keep in mind its main purpose: consistency of interface. In C's approach, you, the programmer, need only think in terms of streams and need use only one file system to accomplish all I/O operations. The C compiler takes care of converting the raw input or output into an easily managed stream.

Now that you have the theory of C's file system, it's time to see how it actually works.

FILE SYSTEM BASICS

The ANSI C file system is composed of several interrelated functions. The most common are shown in Table 9-1. These functions require the header file STDIO.H to be included in any program that uses them. You'll notice that most of the functions begin with the letter "f."

Name	Function
fopen( )	Opens a stream
fclose( )	Closes a stream
putc( )	Writes a character to a stream
fputc( )	Same as putc( )
getc( )	Reads a character from a stream
fgetc( )	Same as getc( )
fseek( )	Seeks to specified byte in a stream
fprintf( )	Is to a stream what printf( ) is to the console
fscanf( )	Is to a stream what scanf( ) is to the console
feof( )	Returns true if end-of-file is reached
ferror( )	Returns true if an error has occurred
rewind( )	Resets the file position locator to the beginning of the file
remove( )	Erases a file
fflush( )	Flushes a file

TABLE 9-1   The Most Common Buffered File System Functions

This is a vestige of the old UNIX C standard, which defined two file systems. In the UNIX version, the UNIX I/O functions did not begin with a prefix and most of the formatted I/O system functions were prefixed with an "f." The ANSI committee elected to maintain this naming convention.

The File Pointer

The thread that ties the buffered I/O system together is the file pointer. A *file pointer* is a pointer that points to information that defines various things about the file, including its name, status, and the current position of the file. In essence, the file pointer identifies a specific disk file and is used by the stream associated with it to direct the operation of the buffered I/O functions. A file pointer is a pointer variable of type **FILE** that is defined in STDIO.H. In order to read or write files, your program will need to use file pointers. To obtain a file pointer variable, use a statement such as this:

```
FILE *fp;
```

Opening a File

The **fopen( )** function serves two purposes: (1) it opens a stream for use and links a file to that stream; (2) it returns the file pointer associated with that file. Most often, and for the rest of this discussion, the file is a disk file. The **fopen( )** function has the prototype

FILE *fopen(char *filename, char *mode);

where *filename* is a pointer to a string of characters that comprise a valid filename for the operating system and may include a path specification. The string pointed to by *mode* determines how the file will be opened. The legal values for *mode* are shown in Table 9-2. Strings such as **r+b** may also be represented as **rb+**.

Mode	Meaning
"r"	Open a text file for reading
"w"	Create a text file for writing
"a"	Append to a text file
"rb"	Open a binary file for reading
"wb"	Create a binary file for writing
"ab"	Append to a binary file
"r+"	Open a text file for read/write
"w+"	Create a text file for read/write
"a+"	Append a text file for read/write
"r+b"	Open a binary file for read/write
"w+b"	Create a binary file for read/write
"a+b"	Append a binary file for read/write

TABLE 9-2   The Legal Values for Mode

As stated, the **fopen( )** function returns a file pointer. Your program should never alter the value of this pointer. If an error occurs when you try to open the file, **fopen( )** returns a null pointer.

As Table 9-2 shows, a file may be opened in either text or binary mode. For most implementations in text mode, carriage return-linefeed sequences are translated to newline characters on input. On output, the reverse occurs. No translations occur on binary files.

If you wanted to open a file for writing with the name **test** you would write

```
FILE *fp;

fp = fopen("test", "w");
```

However, you will usually see it written as

```
FILE *fp;

if ((fp = fopen("test","w"))==NULL) {
  printf("cannot open file\n");
  exit(1);
}
```

The macro **NULL** is defined in STDIO.H as "\0". Using this method to open a file detects errors such as a write-protected or full disk before writing to the file. A null is used because a file pointer will never have that value.

If you use **fopen( )** to open a file for writing, any preexisting file by that name will be erased and a new file started. If no file by that name exists then one will be created. If you want to add to the end of the file you must use mode "a." Opening a file for read operations requires that the file exist. If it does not, an error will be returned. Finally, if a file is opened for read/write operations, it will not be erased if it already exists, but if the file does not exist, it will be created.

The ANSI standard specifies that at least eight files can be open at any one time. Most C compilers and environments allow more than this.

Writing a Character

The ANSI standard defines two equivalent functions that output a character: **putc( )** and **fputc( )**. (Technically, **putc( )** is implemented as a macro—you will see how this is accomplished later in this book—but for all intents and purposes, the two functions are the same.) The reason for having two identical functions is to preserve compatibility with older versions of C. This book uses **putc( )**, but you can use **fputc( )** if you like.

The **putc( )** function is used to write characters to a stream that was previously opened for writing with the **fopen( )** function. The function is declared as

int putc(int *ch*, FILE *fp*);

where *fp* is the file pointer returned by **fopen( )** and *ch* is the character to be output. The file pointer tells **putc( )** which disk file to write to. For historical reasons, *ch* is defined as an **int** but only the low-order byte is used.

If a **putc( )** operation is a success, it will return the character written. Upon failure, an **EOF** is returned. **EOF** (for "end of file") is a macro defined in STDIO.H.

Reading a Character

Like **putc( )** and **fputc( )**, the ANSI standard defines two equivalent functions that input a character: **getc( )** and **fgetc( )**. (Technically, **getc( )** is implemented as a macro.) Again, the reason for having two identical functions is to preserve compatibility with older versions of C. This book uses **getc( )**, but you can use **fgetc( )** if you want.

The **getc( )** function is used to read characters from a stream opened in read mode by **fopen( )**. The function is declared as

    int getc(FILE *fp);

where *fp* is a file pointer of type **FILE** returned by **fopen( )**. For historical reasons **getc( )** returns an integer, but the high-order byte is 0.

The **getc( )** function will return an **EOF** mark when the end of the file has been reached. Therefore, to read a text file until the end-of-file mark is read, you could use the following code:

```
do {
  ch = getc(fp);
} while(ch!=EOF);
```


Closing a File

The **fclose( )** function is used to close a stream opened by a call to **fopen( )**. It writes any data still remaining in the disk buffer to the file and does a formal operating system-level close on the file.

Failure to close a stream invites all kinds of trouble, including lost data, destroyed files, and intermittent errors in your program. An **fclose( )** also frees the file control block associated with the stream and makes it available for reuse. In most cases there is an operating system limit to the number of open files you may have at any one time, so you may need to close one file before opening another.

The **fclose( )** function has this prototype

```
int fclose(FILE *fp);
```

where *fp* is the file pointer returned by the call to **fopen( )**. A return value of 0 signifies a successful close operation; any other value indicates an error. You can use the standard function **ferror( )** (discussed in the section "**ferror( )**") to determine and report any problems. Generally, the only time **fclose( )** will fail is when a diskette has been prematurely removed from the drive or when there is no more space on the diskette.

Using fopen( ), getc( ), putc( ), and fclose( )

The functions **fopen( )**, **getc( )**, **putc( )**, and **fclose( )** comprise the minimal set of file routines. A simple example of using **putc( )**, **fopen( )**, and **fclose( )** is the program KTOD below. It simply reads characters from the keyboard and writes them to a disk file until a dollar sign is typed. The filename is specified from the command line. For example, if you call this program KTOD, then typing "KTOD TEST" will allow you to enter lines of text into the file called TEST.

```
/* KTOD: A key to disk program. */

#include "stdio.h"
#include "stdlib.h"

main(int argc, char *argv[])
{
  FILE *fp;
  char ch;
```

```
   if(argc!=2) {
     printf("You forgot to enter the filename\n");
     exit(1);
   }

   if((fp=fopen(argv[1], "w"))==NULL) {
     printf("cannot open file\n");
     exit(1);
   }

   do {
     ch = getchar();
     putc(ch, fp);
   } while (ch!='$');

   fclose(fp);
}
```

The complementary program DTOS will read any ASCII file and display the contents on the screen.

```
/* DTOS: A program that reads files and displays them
         on the screen.
*/

#include "stdio.h"
#include "stdlib.h"

main(int argc, char *argv[])
{
  FILE *fp;
  char ch;

  if(argc!=2) {
    printf("You forgot to enter the filename\n");
    exit(1);
  }

  if((fp=fopen(argv[1], "r"))==NULL) {
    printf("cannot open file\n");
    exit(1);
  }
```

```
  ch = getc(fp);    /* read one character */

  while (ch!=EOF) {
    putchar(ch);   /* print on screen */
    ch = getc(fp);
  }

  fclose(fp);
}
```

You should try these two programs now. First use KTOD to create a text file. Then read its contents using DTOS.

Using feof( )

As stated earlier, the buffered file system can also operate on binary data. When a file is opened for binary input, it is possible that an integer value equal to the **EOF** mark may be read. This would cause the input routine to indicate an end-of-file condition, even though the physical end of the file had not been reached. To solve this problem, C includes the function **feof( )**, which is used to determine the end of the file when reading binary data. The **feof( )** function has this prototype:

int feof(FILE *fp);

The prototype is in STDIO.H. It returns TRUE if the end of the file has been reached; otherwise 0 is returned. Therefore, the following routine reads a binary file until end of file is encountered.

```
while(!feof(fp)) ch = getc(fp);
```

Of course, this same method may be applied to text files as well as to binary files.

An example of using **feof( )** is found in the following program, which copies text or binary files. The files are opened in binary mode

and the **feof( )** is used to check for the end of the file. (No error-checking on output is performed; however, in a real-world situation it would be a good idea. The addition of error-checking is left as an exercise.)

```c
/* Copy a file. */

#include "stdio.h"
#include "stdlib.h"

main(int argc, char *argv[])
{
  FILE *in, *out;
  char ch;

  if(argc!=3) {
    printf("You forgot to enter a filename\n");
    exit(1);
  }

  if((in=fopen(argv[1], "rb"))==NULL) {
    printf("cannot open source file\n");
    exit(1);
  }
  if((out=fopen(argv[2], "wb")) == NULL) {
    printf("cannot open destination file\n");
    exit(1);
  }

  /* this code acutally copies the file */
  while(!feof(in)) {
    ch = getc(in);
    if(!feof(in)) putc(ch, out);
  }

  fclose(in);
  fclose(out);

}
```

Working with Strings: fputs( ) and fgets( )

In addition to **getc( )** and **putc( )**, C supports two related functions: **fputs( )** and **fgets( )**. They are used to write and read character strings to and from a disk file. These functions work exactly the same as **putc( )** and **getc( )** except that instead of single characters they write or read strings. They have the following prototypes:

  int fputs(char *str, FILE *fp);
  int fgets(char *str, int length, FILE *fp);

The prototypes for **fgets( )** and **fputs( )** are in STDIO.H.
  The function **fputs( )** works like **puts( )** except that it writes a string to the specified stream. The **fgets( )** function reads a string from the specified stream until either a newline character or *length − 1* characters have been read. Unlike **getc( )**, if a newline character is read, it will be part of the string. The resulting string will be null-terminated.
  The **fputs( )** function is demonstrated by the following program. It reads strings from the keyboard and writes them to the file called TEST. To terminate the program, enter a blank line. Since **fgets( )** does not store the newline character, one is added before the string is written to the file so it can be read more easily.

```
#include "stdio.h"
#include "stdlib.h"
#include "string.h"

main()
{
  char str[80];
  FILE *fp;

  if((fp = fopen("TEST", "w"))==NULL) {
    printf("cannot open file\n");
    exit(1);
  }
  do {
    printf("enter a string (CR to quit):\n");
    gets(str);
```

```
    strcat(str, "\n");   /* add a newline */
    fputs(str, fp);
  } while(*str!='\n');
fclose(fp);
}
```

rewind( )

The **rewind( )** function resets the file position indicator to the begin-ning of the file specified as its argument. That is, it "rewinds" the file. Its prototype is

   void rewind(FILE *fp)

where *fp* is a valid file pointer. The prototype for **rewind( )** is in STDIO.H.

   To see an example of **rewind( )**, modify the program shown in the previous section so it displays the contents of the file just created. To accomplish this, the program rewinds the file after input is complete and then uses **fgets( )** to read back the file. Notice that the file must now be opened in read/write mode using **w+** for the mode parameter.

```
#include "stdio.h"
#include "stdlib.h"
#include "string.h"

main()
{
  char str[80];
  FILE *fp;

  if((fp = fopen("TEST", "w+"))==NULL) {
    printf("cannot open file\n");
    exit(1);
  }
  do {
    printf("enter a string (CR to quit):\n");
    gets(str);
```

```
    strcat(str, "\n");  /* add a newline */
    fputs(str, fp);
} while(*str!='\n');

/* now, read and display the file */
rewind(fp);  /* reset file position indicator to
                 start of the file. */
while(!feof(fp)) {
  fgets(str, 79, fp);
  printf(str);
}
fclose(fp);
}
```

ferror( )

The **ferror( )** function is used to determine if a file operation has produced an error. It has the following prototype.

int ferror(FILE *fp)

where *fp* is a valid file pointer. It returns true if an error has occurred during the last file operation; it returns false otherwise. Because each file operation sets the error condition, **ferror( )** should be called immediately after each file operation or an error may be lost. The prototype for **ferror( )** is in STDIO.H.

Erasing Files

The **remove( )** function erases the specified file. Its prototype is

int remove(char *filename);

It returns 0 upon success, non-zero if it fails.

Flushing a Stream

To flush the contents of an output stream, use the **fflush( )** function. Its prototype is shown here:

int fflush(FILE *fp);

This function will write the contents of any buffered data to the file associated with *fp*. If you call **fflush( )** with a null, all files opened for output are flushed.

The **fflush( )** function returns 0 if successful, **EOF** upon failure.

fread( ) AND fwrite( )

So far, the C file system probably appears to be largely byte oriented. At this point you may be wondering how to read and write data types that are longer than 1 byte. To accomplish these goals, the ANSI C file system provides two functions, **fread( )** and **fwrite( )**, that allow the reading and writing of blocks of any data type. Their prototypes are

unsigned fread(void *buffer*, unsigned *num_bytes*,
          unsigned *count*, FILE *fp*)
unsigned fwrite(void *buffer*, unsigned *num_bytes*,
          unsigned *count*, FILE *fp*);

In the case of **fread( )**, *buffer* is a pointer to a region of memory that will receive the data read from the file. For **fwrite( )**, *buffer* is a pointer to the information that will be written to the file. The number of bytes to be read or written is specified by *num_bytes*. The argument *count* determines how many items (each *num_bytes* long) will be read or written. Finally, *fp* is a file pointer to a previously opened stream. Both functions have their prototypes defined in STDIO.H.

Before you can correctly use **fread( )** or **fwrite( )**, you will need to learn about a special C compile-time operator: **sizeof.**

The sizeof Operator

In C, a character is defined to be equivalent to 1 byte. However, all of the other built-in data types, including **int**, **float**, and **double**, do not have defined lengths. In some implementations a **float**, for example, might be 4 bytes long, in others, 6 bytes. As stated, the **fread( )** and **fwrite( )** functions operate on a buffer of data of some particular length. In order to determine the length of the buffer for non-character data you need to know the exact length of the basic data type or types you are operating on. To accomplish this, C provides the **sizeof** compile time operator. The **sizeof** operator returns the size, in bytes, of the variable or type of its operand. This value is unsigned. The general form of **sizeof** is shown here:

sizeof *var-name*
sizeof(*type-name*)

When you use **sizeof** with a variable name, the name of the variable does not need to be enclosed in parentheses (although you can, if you like). However, when **sizeof** is applied to a type, the type must be contained in parentheses. For example, this program displays the size of an integer and a **float** for your compiler.

```
#include "stdio.h"

main()
{
  int i;
  float f;

  printf("%d %d %d %d", sizeof i, sizeof f,
         sizeof(int), sizeof(float));
}
```

When **sizeof** is used with an array, the length of the entire array is returned.

In addition to being useful with **fread( )** and **fwrite( )**, the **sizeof** operator aids in the construction of portable code and is used with C's dynamic allocation routines (discussed in Chapter 11).

Using fread( ) and fwrite( )

As long as the file has been opened for binary data, **fread( )** and **fwrite( )** can read and write any type of information. For example, this program writes and then reads back a **double**, an **int**, and a **long** to and from a disk file. Notice how it uses **sizeof** to determine the length of each data type.

```c
/* Write some non-character data to a disk file
   and read it back.
 */
#include "stdio.h"
#include "stdlib.h"

main()
{
  FILE *fp;
  double d = 12.23;
  int i = 101;
  long l = 123023L;

  if((fp=fopen("test","wb+"))==NULL) {
    printf("cannot open file\n");
    exit(1);
  }

  fwrite(&d, sizeof(double), 1, fp);
  fwrite(&i, sizeof(int), 1, fp);
  fwrite(&l, sizeof(long), 1, fp);

  rewind(fp);

  fread(&d, sizeof(double), 1, fp);
  fread(&i, sizeof(int), 1, fp);
  fread(&l, sizeof(long), 1, fp);

  printf("%f %d %ld", d, i, l);
  fclose(fp);
}
```

As this program illustrates, the buffer can be, and often is, simply the memory used to hold a variable.

One of the most useful applications of **fread( )** and **fwrite( )** involves the reading and writing of arrays (or, as you will see in the next chapter, structures). For example, this fragment writes the contents of the floating-point array **sample** to the file SAMPLE using a single **fwrite( )** statement:

```
#include "stdio.h"
#include "stdlib.h"

main()
{
  FILE *fp;
  float sample[100];
  int i;

  if((fp=fopen("sample","wb"))==NULL) {
    printf("cannot open file\n");
    exit(1);
  }

  for(i=0; i<100; i++) sample[i] = (float) i;

  /* this saves the entire array in one step */
  fwrite(sample, sizeof(sample), 1, fp);

  fclose(fp);
}
```

The next program uses **fread( )** to read the information written by the previous program. It displays the numbers on the screen for verification.

```
#include "stdio.h"
#include "stdlib.h"

main()
{
  FILE *fp;
  float sample[100];
  int i;

  if((fp=fopen("sample","rb"))==NULL) {
```

```
        printf("cannot open file\n");
        exit(1);
    }

    /* this reads the entire array in one step */
    fread(sample, sizeof(sample), 1, fp);

    for(i=0; i<100; i++) printf("%f ", sample[i]);

    fclose(fp);
}
```

Later in this book you will see other more complex examples of how these functions can be used.

fseek( ) AND RANDOM ACCESS I/O

You can perform random read and write operations using the buffered I/O system with the help of **fseek( )**, which sets the file position locator. Its prototype is shown here:

int fseek(FILE *fp, long num_bytes, int origin);

Here, fp is a file pointer returned by a call to **fopen( )**; num_bytes, a long integer, is the number of bytes from origin to the current position. Origin is one of the following macros defined in STDIO.H.

Origin	Macro Name
Beginning of file	SEEK_SET
Current position	SEEK_CUR
End of file	SEEK_END

Therefore, to seek num_bytes from the start of the file, origin should be **SEEK_SET**. To seek from the current position use **SEEK_CUR**, and from the end of the file use **SEEK_END**.

It is important to remember that *num_bytes* must be a **long**. This is necessary to support files larger than 64K bytes. The following fragment illustrates the use of **fseek( )**. It will seek and display the specified byte in the named file. Both the filename and the byte you are seeking are specified on the command line, with the filename followed by the byte number.

```c
#include "stdio.h"
#include "stdlib.h"

main(int argc, char *argv[])
{

  FILE *fp;

  if(argc!=3) {
    printf("Usage: SEEK filename byte\n");
    exit(1);
  }

  if((fp = fopen(argv[1], "r"))==NULL) {
    printf("cannot open file\n");
    exit(1);
  }

  if(fseek(fp, atol(argv[2]), SEEK_SET)) {
    printf("seek error\n");
    exit(1);
  }
  printf("Byte at %ld is %c\n",atol(argv[2]),getc(fp));
  fclose(fp);
}
```

Notice that the string form of the number specifying which byte to seek to is transferred into a **long** by the standard library function **atol( )**. (See Appendix A for details on **atol( )**.)

A return value of 0 means that **fseek( )** succeeded. A non-zero value indicates failure.

You can use **fseek( )** to seek in multiples of any type of data by simply multiplying the size of the data by the number of the one you want to reach. For example, if you have a file of floating-point numbers, this code fragment will seek to the tenth number.

```
fseek(fp, 9*sizeof(float), SEEK_SET);
```

fprintf( ) AND fscanf( )

In addition to the basic I/O functions previously discussed, the buffered I/O system includes **fprintf( )** and **fscanf( )**. These functions behave exactly like **printf( )** and **scanf( )**, except that they operate with disk files. The prototypes of **fprintf( )** and **fscanf( )** are

> int fprintf(FILE *fp, char *control _ string, argument list);
> int fscanf(FILE *fp, char *control _ string, argument list);

where *fp* is a file pointer returned by a call to **fopen( )**. Except for directing their I/O operations to the file defined by *fp*, these functions operate exactly like **printf( )** and **scanf( )**.

To illustrate how useful these functions can be, the following program maintains a simple accounts payable database. You can enter an account name and current balance or look up an account and balance.

```
/* A simple accounts payable database using fscanf()
   and fprintf(). */

#include "stdio.h"
#include "conio.h"
#include "string.h"
#include "stdlib.h"
#include "ctype.h"

void add_acct(void), lookup(void);
int menu(void);

main()
{
 char choice;

  do {
    choice = menu();
    switch(choice) {
```

```
      case 'a': add_acct();
        break;
      case 'l': lookup();
        break;
    }
  } while (choice!='q');

}

/* Display menu and get request. */
menu(void)
{
  char ch;

  do {
    printf("(A)dd, (L)ookup, or (Q)uit: ");
    ch = tolower(getche());
    printf("\n");
  } while(ch != 'q' && ch != 'a' && ch != 'l');

  return ch;
}

/* Add an account and balance to the database. */
void add_acct(void)
{
  FILE *fp;
  char name[80];
  double balance;

  /* open it for append */
  if((fp=fopen("acct.dat","a"))==NULL) {
    printf("cannot open file\n");
    exit(1);
  }

  printf("enter name and balance: ");
  fscanf(stdin, "%s%lf", name, &balance);
  fscanf(stdin, "%*c"); /* remove CR from input stream */

  /* write to file */
  fprintf(fp,"%s %lf\n", name, balance);
```

```
    fclose(fp);
}


/* Report balance given name. */
void lookup(void)
{
  FILE *fp;
  char name[80], name2[80];
  double balance;

  /* open it for read */
  if((fp=fopen("acct.dat","r"))==NULL) {
    printf("cannot open file\n");
    exit(1);
  }

  printf("name? ");
  gets(name);

  /* look for account and balance */
  while(!feof(fp)) {
    fscanf(fp,"%s%lf", name2, &balance);
    if(!strcmp(name, name2)) {
      printf("%s: $%7.2lf\n", name, balance);
      break;
    }
  }
  fclose(fp);
}
```

The program first displays a short menu from which you can choose to add an account, look up an account, or quit. When you add an account, the **add_acct( )** function is called. When you look up an account, **lookup( )** is called. Enter the program and run it now. After you have entered a couple of names and numbers, examine the file ACCT.DAT. As you would expect, it appears just as it would if the information had been displayed on the screen using **printf( )**.

Note: Although **fprintf( )** and **fscanf( )** are often the easiest ways to write and read assorted data to disk files, they are not always the most efficient. Because formatted ASCII data is being written just as it would appear on the screen, rather than in binary, extra overhead

is incurred with each call. So if speed or file size is a concern, you should probably use **fread( )** and **fwrite( )** instead.

THE STANDARD STREAMS

Whenever a C program starts execution three streams are opened automatically. They are standard input (**stdin**), standard output (**stdout**), and standard error (**stderr**). Normally these refer to the console, but they may be redirected by the operating system to some other device in environments that support redirectable I/O. (Redirectable I/O is supported by UNIX, OS/2, and DOS, for instance.)

Because the standard streams are file pointers they may be used by the buffered I/O system to perform I/O operations on the console. For example, **putchar( )** could be defined as

```
putchar(char c)
{
    putc(c, stdout);
}
```

In general, **stdin** is used to read from the console and **stdout** and **stderr** are used to write to the console. You may use **stdin**, **stdout**, and **stderr** as file pointers in any function that uses a variable of type **FILE**. For example, you can use **fputs( )** to output a string to the console using a call such as this one:

```
fputs("hello there", stdout);
```

Keep in mind that **stdin**, **stdout**, and **stderr** are not variables in the normal sense and may not be assigned a value using **fopen( )**. Also, just as these file pointers are created automatically at the start of your program, they are closed automatically at the end; you should not try to close them.

The Console I/O Connection

As stated at the beginning of Chapter 8, C makes little distinction between console and file I/O. As the preceding section describes, it

is possible to perform console I/O using any of C's file system functions. However, what may surprise you is that you can perform disk file I/O using what you have come to think of as console I/O functions, such as **printf( )**.

This is because the functions described in Chapter 8, which were temporarily called "console I/O functions," are not precisely that. Instead, these functions operate on **stdin** and **stdout**. Therefore, in environments that allow redirection of I/O, **stdin** and **stdout** could refer to a device other than the keyboard and screen. For example, consider this program:

```
#include "stdio.h"

main()
{
  char str[80];

  printf("enter a string: ");
  gets(str);
  printf(str);
}
```

Assume this program is called TEST. If you execute TEST normally, it displays its prompt on the screen, reads a string from the keyboard, and displays that string on the display. However, in an environment that supports redirection of I/O, either **stdin**, **stdout**, or both could be redirected to a file. For example, in a DOS, OS/2, or UNIX environment, executing TEST this way

```
TEST > OUTPUT
```

causes the output of TEST to be written to a file called OUTPUT. Executing TEST this way

```
TEST < INPUT > OUTPUT
```

causes **stdin** to be directed to the file called INPUT and output to be sent to the file called OUTPUT.

When a C program terminates, any redirected streams are reset to their default status.

Using freopen( ) to Redirect the Standard Streams

It is possible to redirect the standard streams using the **freopen( )** function. This function associates an existing stream with a new file. Thus, you can use it to associate a standard stream with a new file. Its prototype is

FILE *freopen(char *_filename_, char *_mode_, FILE *_stream_)

where _filename_ is a pointer to the filename you want associated with the stream pointed to by _stream_. The file is opened using the value of _mode_ which is the same as the one used with **fopen( )**.

The following program uses **freopen( )** to redirect **stdout** to a file called OUTPUT.

```
#include "stdio.h"

main()
{
  char str[80];

  freopen("OUTPUT", "w", stdout);

  printf("enter a string: ");
  gets(str);
  printf(str);
}
```

The string is written to the file output, not to the console.

In general, redirecting the standard streams using **freopen( )** is useful in special situations, such as debugging. However, performing disk I/O using redirected **stdin** and **stdout** is not as efficient as using functions like **fread( )** or **fwrite( )**.

EXERCISES

1. Write a program that counts the number of spaces in a text file.

2. Add full error checking to the file copy program.

3. What is wrong with the following fragment?

```
FILE *fp;
if((fopen("myfile", 'rb+'))==NULL)....
```

4. Will this code work?

```
stdin = fopen("myfile", "r");
```

5. How do **printf( )**, **scanf( )**, and the other console I/O functions relate to C's file system?

6. Write a program that compares two files for equality.

Answers

```
1.      /* This program counts the number of spaces
            in the text file specified as the first command
            line argument.
        */

        #include "stdio.h"
        #include "stdlib.h"

        main(int argc, char *argv[])
        {
          int spaces = 0;
          FILE *fp;

          if(argc!=2) {
```

```
      printf("usage: COUNT filename\n");
      exit(1);
    }

    if((fp=fopen(argv[1], "r"))==NULL) {
      printf("cannot open file");
      exit(1);
    }

    while(!feof(fp))
      if(getc(fp)==' ') spaces++;

    fclose(fp);

    printf("%d spaces\n", spaces);
}
```

2.   /* Copy a file. */

```
#include "stdio.h"
#include "stdlib.h"

main(int argc, char *argv[])
{
  FILE *in, *out;
  char ch;

  if(argc!=3) {
    printf("You forgot to enter a filename\n");
    exit(1);
  }

  if((in=fopen(argv[1], "rb"))==NULL) {
    printf("cannot open source file\n");
    exit(1);
  }
  if((out=fopen(argv[2], "wb")) == NULL) {
    printf("cannot open destination file\n");
    exit(1);
  }
  /* this code acutally copies the file */
```

```
        while(!feof(in)) {
          ch = getc(in);
          if(ferror(in))
            printf(""error in reading file\n");

          if(!feof(in)) putc(ch, out);
          if(ferror(out))
            printf("error in writing file\n");
        }

        fclose(in);
        fclose(out);

      }
```

3. The *mode* parameter of **fopen( )** must be a string. In the question, the mode is enclosed in single quotes, which won't work.

4. No, you cannot use a standard stream as a target of **fopen( )**. You can, however, redirect a standard stream using **freopen( )**.

5. The console I/O functions are special cases that work with the standard streams **stdin**, **stdout**, and **stderr**. Any of the other file system functions can be used with the standard streams, thus allowing the console I/O functions to be bypassed if desired.

6.
```
      /* A file comparison program. */

      #include "stdio.h"
      #include "stdlib.h"

      main(int argc, char *argv[])
      {

        FILE *fp1, *fp2;
        char ch1, ch2;

        if(argc!=3) {
          printf("Usage: CMP filename filename\n");
```

```
    exit(1);
}

if((fp1 = fopen(argv[1], "rb"))==NULL) {
  printf("cannot open first file\n");
  exit(1);
}
if((fp2 = fopen(argv[2], "rb"))==NULL) {
  printf("cannot open second file\n");
  exit(1);
}

while(!feof(fp1) && !feof(fp2)) {
  ch1 = getc(fp1);
  ch2 = getc(fp2);
  if(ch1!=ch2) break;
}

/* The files will be equal if both have been
   read to the end.
*/
if(feof(fp1) && feof(fp2))
  printf("files are equal");
else
  printf("files differ");

fclose(fp1);
fclose(fp2);
}
```

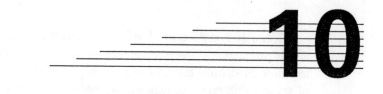

STRUCTURES AND UNIONS

C supports two types of conglomerate data types: the structure and the union. Although they fulfill different needs, both the structure and the union provide convenient means of managing groups of different yet related variables. Another important aspect is that in creating structures and unions you also define custom or *programmer-defined* data types. As you will see, the ability to create your own data types is a very powerful feature of C.

Let's begin our discussion with a look at structures.

STRUCTURES

Of the programmer-defined data types, perhaps the most important one is the structure, because of its broad range of applications. In C,

a *structure* is a collection of variables referenced under one name, which provides a convenient means of keeping related information together. Structures are *conglomerate* data types because they consist of several different, yet logically connected, variables. For example, the **FILE** structure defined in STDIO.H is a grouping of variables related to a disk file. A *structure definition* forms a template that may be used to create structure variables. The variables that comprise the structure are called *structure elements*. (If you are familiar with Pascal, structures in C are the equivalent of RECORDs in Pascal.)

Generally, all the elements in the structure will be logically related to each other. For example, information on a company's inventory would normally be represented in a structure. The code fragment that follows declares a structure template that defines the item name, cost and retail prices, number on hand, and resupply time for maintaining an inventory. The keyword **struct** tells the compiler that a structure template is being defined.

```
struct inv_type {
   char item[40];    /* name of item */
   double cost;      /* cost */
   double retail;    /* retail price */
   int on_hand;      /* amount on hand */
   int lead_time;    /* number of days before resupply */
} ;
```

Notice that the definition is terminated by a semicolon. This is because a structure definition is a statement. Also, the structure tag **inv_type** identifies this particular data structure and is its type specifier.

At this point in the code, no variable has actually been declared. Only the form of the data has been defined. To declare an actual variable with this structure, you would write something similar to the following:

```
struct inv_type inv_var;
```

This declares a structure variable of type **inv_type** called **inv_var**. When you define a structure, you are in essence defining a complex

item	40 bytes	
cost	8 bytes	
retail	8 bytes	inv_var
on_hand	2 bytes	
lead_time	2 bytes	

FIGURE 10-1   The **inv_var** structure as it appears in memory

variable type made up of the structure elements. It is not until you declare a variable of that type that one actually exists.

C automatically allocates sufficient memory to accommodate all the variables that comprise a structure variable. Figure 10-1 shows how **inv_var** would appear in memory (assuming 8-byte **doubles** and 2-byte **ints**).

You may also declare one or more variables at the same time that you define a structure. For example,

```
struct inv_type {
  char item[40];  /* name of item */
  double cost;    /* cost */
  double retail;  /* retail price */
  int on_hand;    /* amount on hand */
  int lead_time;  /* number of days before resupply */
} inv_varA, inv_varB, inv_varC;
```

will define a structure type called **inv_var** and declare variables **inv_varA**, **inv_varB**, and **inv_varC** of that type.

If you only need one structure variable, the structure type name is unnecessary. For example,

```
struct {
  char item[40];  /* name of item */
  double cost;    /* cost */
  double retail;  /* retail price */
```

```
    int on_hand;    /* amount on hand */
    int lead_time;  /* number of days before resupply */
} temp;
```

declares one variable named **temp** as defined by the structure preceding it.

The general form of a structure definition is

```
struct struct-type-name {
type element _ name1;
type element _ name2;
type element _ name3;
    .

    .

    .

type element _ nameM;
} structure-variables;
```

where either the structure type name or the structure variable name
may be omitted, but not both.

Referencing Structure Elements

Individual structure elements are referenced through the use of a
period (sometimes called the "dot operator"). For example, the
following code will assign the value 10.39 to the **cost** field of the
structure variable **inv _ var** declared earlier.

```
inv_var.cost = 10.39;
```

The structure variable name followed by a period and the element name will reference that individual structure element. All
structure elements are accessed in the same way. The general form
follows:

```
structure _ varname.element _ name
```

So, to print the **cost** field to the screen, write the following.

```
printf("%lf", inv_var.cost);
```

In the same fashion, the character array **inv_var.item** can be used to call **gets( )**, as in the following example:

```
gets(inv_var.item);
```

This will pass a character pointer to the start of element **item**.

If you wanted to access the individual elements of **inv_var.item**, you could index **item**. For example, you could print the contents of **inv_var.item** one character at a time by using this code:

```
int t;

for(t=0; addr_info.name[t]; ++t)
  putchar(inv_var.item[t]);
```

ARRAYS OF STRUCTURES

Often structures are used when constructing databases. This implies that a collection of variables of the same type will be needed. One common way to obtain several structures is to create an array of structures. To declare an array of structures you must first define a structure, then declare an array variable of that type. For example, to declare a 100-element array of structures of type **inv_type** (defined earlier), you would write

```
struct inv_type invtry[100];
```

To access a specific structure, the structure name is indexed. For example, to print the **on_hand** field of the third structure, you would write

```
printf("%d", invtry[2].on_hand);
```

Like all array variables, arrays of structures begin their indexing at zero.

A Simple Inventory Example

To help illustrate how structures and arrays of structures are used, a simple inventory management program will be developed that uses an array of structures to hold the inventory information. The functions in this program interact with structures and their elements to illustrate structure usage. The inventory will be held in the array called **invtry**, as shown here:

```
#define SIZE 100

struct inv_type {
  char item[40];   /* name of item */
  double cost;     /* cost */
  double retail;   /* retail price */
  int on_hand;     /* amount on hand */
  int lead_time;   /* number of days before resupply */
}  invtry[SIZE];
```

The value for **SIZE** is arbitrary. Feel free to change it if you desire.
   The program will provide five basic functions:

- Entry of inventory information
- Display of inventory information
- Modification of any item
- Saving inventory information to disk
- Loading inventory information from disk

The first function needed for the program is **main( )**, shown here:

```
main()
{
  char choice;

  init_list();

  for(;;) {
    choice = menu();
    switch(choice) {
      case 'e': enter();
```

```
        break;
      case 'd': display();
        break;
      case 'u': update();
        break;
      case 's': save();
        break;
      case 'l': load();
        break;
      case 'q': exit(1);
    }
  }
}
```

First, the function **init_list( )** prepares the structure array for use by putting a null character into the first byte of the **item** field. The program assumes that a structure variable is not in use if the **item** field is empty. The **init_list( )** function is shown here:

```
/* Initialize the invtry array. */
void init_list(void)
{
  int t;

  for(t=0; t<SIZE; t++) *invtry[t].item = '\0';
  /* a zero-length name signifies empty */
}
```

The **menu_select( )** function displays the options and returns the user's selection:

```
/* Get a menu selection. */
menu(void)
{
  char s[80];

  do {
    printf("(E)nter\n");
    printf("(D)isplay\n");
    printf("(L)oad\n");
    printf("(U)pdate\n");
    printf("(S)ave\n");
```

```
      printf("(Q)uit\n\n");
      printf("choose one: ");
      gets(s);
    } while(!strchr("edlsuq", tolower(*s)));
    return tolower(*s);
}
```

This function makes use of another of C's library functions, **strchr( )**, which has this prototype:

char *strchr(char *str, char ch);

The function searches the string pointed to by str for an occurrence of the character specified in ch. If the character is found, a pointer to that character is returned. This is by definition a true value. However, if no match is found, a null is returned, which is by definition false. **strchr( )** is used in this program to see whether the user made a proper selection or not.

The **enter( )** function sets up the call to **input( )**, which prompts the user for information. The **enter( )** function first finds an empty structure. To do this, **enter( )** starts with the first element in **invtry** and advances through the array, checking the **item** field. If it finds an **item** field that is null, it knows that structure is unused. If the routine reaches the end of the array without finding a free structure, the loop control variable **i** will be equal to **SIZE**. If the array is full, then the message "list full" is printed on the screen. The actual entry of the data is performed by **input( )**. This code is not part of **enter( )** because **input( )** is also used by the **update( )** function, which you will see next.

```
/* Input items into the list */
void enter(void)
{
  int i;

  /* find the first free structure */
  for(i=0; i<SIZE; i++)
    if(!*invtry[i].item) break;

  /* i will equal SIZE if the list is full */
```

```
  if(i==SIZE) {
    printf("invtry full\n");
    return;
  }

  input(i);
}

/* Actually input the information. */
void input(int i)
{
  char str[80];

  /* enter the information */
  printf("item: ");
  gets(invtry[i].item);

  printf("cost: ");
  gets(str);
  invtry[i].cost = atof(str);

  printf("retail price: ");
  gets(str);
  invtry[i].retail = atof(str);

  printf("on hand: ");
  gets(str);
  invtry[i].on_hand = atoi(str);

  printf("lead time to resupply (in days): ");
  gets(str);
  invtry[i].lead_time = atoi(str);
}
```

Since inventory information changes, the program lets you
change the information about any item. To accomplish this the
update( ) function is called. This function prompts the user for the
name of the item that needs to be changed. It then looks in the list
to see if it is there. If it is, **input( )** is called.

```
void update(void)
{
  int i;
```

```
  char name[80];

  printf("enter item: ");
  gets(name);

  for(i=0; i<SIZE; i++)
    if(!strcmp(name, invtry[i].item)) break;

  if(i==SIZE) {
    printf("item not found\n");
    return;
  }

  printf("Enter new information.\n");
  input(i);
}
```

The routines **save( )** and **load( )**, shown here, are used to save and load the database. Note how little code each routine contains because of the power of the **fread( )** and **fwrite( )** functions. Instead of each field being handled separately, an entire structure is written or read with each call. Notice also that **sizeof** is used to compute the size of the structure. Never try to add up the fields that comprise a structure yourself. The C compiler may need to pad one or more fields to efficiently construct it; thus the size of the structure may be greater than the sum of its parts.

```
/* Save the list. */
void save(void)
{
  FILE  *fp;
  int i;

  if((fp=fopen("invtry.dat","wb"))==NULL) {
    printf("cannot open file\n");
    return;
  }

  for(i=0; i<SIZE; i++)
    if(*invtry[i].item)
      if(fwrite(&invtry[i],
          sizeof(struct inv_type), 1, fp)!=1)
```

```
          printf("file write error\n");
     fclose(fp);
}

/* Load the file. */
void load(void)
{
   FILE  *fp;
   int i;

   if((fp=fopen("invtry.dat","rb"))==NULL) {
     printf("cannot open file\n");
     return;
   }

   init_list();
   for(i=0; i<SIZE; i++)
      if(fread(&invtry[i],
         sizeof(struct inv_type), 1, fp)!=1) {
        if(feof(fp)) {
          fclose(fp);
          return;
        }
        printf("file read error\n");
      }
}
```

Both routines confirm a successful file operation by checking the
return value of **fread( )** or **fwrite( )**. Also, **load( )** must explicitly
check for end of file through the use of **feof( )**, because **fread( )**
returns the same value whether end of file has been reached or an
error has occurred.

The final function the program needs is **display( )**. It prints the
entire inventory list on the screen.

```
/* Display the list. */
void display(void)
{
   int t;

   for(t=0; t<SIZE; t++) {
     if(*invtry[t].item) {
        printf("%s\n", invtry[t].item);
```

```
        printf("cost: $%5.2lf - retail: $%5.2lf\n",
                invtry[t].cost, invtry[t].retail);
        printf("on hand: %d\n", invtry[t].on_hand);
        printf("resupply time: %d\n\n",
                invtry[t].lead_time);

    }
  }
}
```

The complete inventory program is shown here. If you have any doubts about structures, enter this program into your computer and study its execution, making changes and watching their effects. Also try adding functions that search the list, remove an item from the list, and send the list to the printer.

```
/* A simple inventory program that uses an array
   of structures. */

#include "stdio.h"
#include "ctype.h"
#include "string.h"
#include "stdlib.h"

#define SIZE 100

struct inv_type {
  char item[40];      /* name of item */
  double cost;        /* cost */
  double retail;      /* retail price */
  int on_hand;        /* amount on hand */
  int lead_time;      /* number of days before resupply */
} invtry[SIZE];

void enter(void), init_list(void), display(void);
void save(void),load(void),update(void),input(int i);
int menu(void);

main()
{
  char choice;

  init_list();
```

```
    for(;;) {
      choice = menu();
      switch(choice) {
        case 'e': enter();
          break;
        case 'd': display();
          break;
        case 'u': update();
          break;
        case 's': save();
          break;
        case 'l': load();
          break;
        case 'q': exit(1);
      }
    }
}

/* Initialize the invtry array. */
void init_list(void)
{
  int t;

  for(t=0; t<SIZE; t++) *invtry[t].item = '\0';
  /* a zero length name signifies empty */
}

/* Get a menu selection. */
menu(void)
{
  char s[80];

  do {
    printf("(E)nter\n");
    printf("(D)isplay\n");
    printf("(L)oad\n");
    printf("(U)pdate\n");
    printf("(S)ave\n");
    printf("(Q)uit\n\n");
    printf("choose one: ");
    gets(s);
  } while(!strchr("edlsuq", tolower(*s)));
```

```
    return tolower(*s);
}

/* Input items into the list */
void enter(void)
{
  int i;

  /* find the first free structure */
  for(i=0; i<SIZE; i++)
    if(!*invtry[i].item) break;

  /* i will equal SIZE if the list is full */
  if(i==SIZE) {
    printf("invtry full\n");
    return;
  }

  input(i);
}

/* Actually input the information. */
void input(int i)
{
  char str[80];

  /* enter the information */
  printf("item: ");
  gets(invtry[i].item);

  printf("cost: ");
  gets(str);
  invtry[i].cost = atof(str);

  printf("retail price: ");
  gets(str);
  invtry[i].retail = atof(str);

  printf("on hand: ");
  gets(str);
  invtry[i].on_hand = atoi(str);

  printf("lead time to resupply (in days): ");
```

```
    gets(str);
    invtry[i].lead_time = atoi(str);
}

/* Modify an existing item. */
void update(void)
{
  int i;
  char name[80];

  printf("enter item: ");
  gets(name);

  for(i=0; i<SIZE; i++)
    if(!strcmp(name, invtry[i].item)) break;

  if(i==SIZE) {
    printf("item not found\n");
    return;
  }

  printf("Enter new information.\n");
  input(i);
}

/* Display the list. */
void display(void)
{
  int t;

  for(t=0; t<SIZE; t++) {
    if(*invtry[t].item) {
      printf("%s\n", invtry[t].item);
      printf("cost: $%5.2lf - retail: $%5.2lf\n",
             invtry[t].cost, invtry[t].retail);
      printf("on hand: %d\n", invtry[t].on_hand);
      printf("resupply time: %d\n\n",
             invtry[t].lead_time);
    }
  }
}

/* Save the list. */
void save(void)
```

```
{
  FILE  *fp;
  int i;

  if((fp=fopen("invtry.dat","wb"))==NULL) {
    printf("cannot open file\n");
    return;
  }

  for(i=0; i<SIZE; i++)
    if(*invtry[i].item)
      if(fwrite(&invtry[i],
          sizeof(struct inv_type), 1, fp)!=1)
          printf("file write error\n");
  fclose(fp);
}

/* Load the file. */
void load(void)
{
  FILE  *fp;
  int i;

  if((fp=fopen("invtry.dat","rb"))==NULL) {
    printf("cannot open file\n");
    return;
  }

  init_list();
  for(i=0; i<SIZE; i++)
    if(fread(&invtry[i],
        sizeof(struct inv_type), 1, fp)!=1) {
      if(feof(fp)) {
        fclose(fp);
        return;
      }
      printf("file read error\n");
    }
}
```

PASSING STRUCTURES TO FUNCTIONS

When a structure is used as an argument to a function, the entire structure is passed using the standard call-by-value method. This, of

course, means that any changes made to the contents of the structure inside the function to which it is passed do not affect the structure used as an argument.

Note: In the original version of C, structures could *not* be passed to functions. Instead, they were treated like arrays and only a pointer to the structure was passed. If you sometime need to use an old C compiler, keep this in mind.

The most important consideration to remember when using a structure as a parameter is that the type of the argument must match the type of the parameter. For example, here the argument **arg** and the parameter **parm** are declared to be of the same type of structure.

```
#include "stdio.h"

main()
{
  struct {
    int a, b;
    char ch;
  } arg;

  arg.a = 1000;

  fl(arg);
}

fl(struct {
    int x,y;
    char ch;
  } parm)
{
  printf("%d", parm.x);
}
```

This program will, as you can see, print the number 1000 on the screen. Although it is not wrong to use parallel structure declarations of this type, a more common approach—and one that requires less work—is to define a structure globally and then use its name to declare structure variables and parameters as needed. Using this method, the same program is written as follows.

```
#include "stdio.h"

/* define a structure type */
struct sample {
  int a, b;
  char ch;
} ;

main()
{
  struct sample arg;   /* declare arg */

  arg.a = 1000;

  f1(arg);
}

f1(struct sample parm)
{
  printf("%d", parm.a);
}
```

Not only does this method save programming effort, but, more importantly, it helps ensure that the arguments and the parameters match. It also establishes in the minds of other people who read your program the fact that **parm** and **arg** are of the same type.

POINTERS TO STRUCTURES

C allows pointers to structures the same way that it allows pointers to any other type of variable. However, there are some special aspects of using structure pointers that you must be aware of.

Structure Pointers

Structure pointers are declared by placing an asterisk (∗) in front of a structure variable's name. For example, assuming the previously

defined structure **inv_type**, the following declares **inv_pointer** to be a pointer to data of that type:

```
struct inv_type *inv_pointer;
```

Using Pointers

There are two primary uses for structure pointers. The first is to achieve a call-by-reference call to a function. The second is to create linked lists and other dynamic data structures using C's allocation system. This chapter will only be concerned with the first use. The second is covered in *Advanced C* by Herbert Schildt (Berkeley, Ca.: Osborne/McGraw-Hill, 1988).

The one major drawback to passing all but the simplest structures to functions is the overhead needed to pass all the fields that make up a structure. As you may know, virtually all C compilers use the computer's stack to pass arguments to functions. Thus the time it takes to push and pop all the structure elements onto the stack can be considerable. In structures with few elements this overhead is not too significant, but if several elements are used, or if some of the elements are arrays, then run-time performance may be unacceptable. The solution is to pass only a pointer to the structure.

When a pointer to a structure is passed to a function, only the address of the structure is pushed and popped on the stack. This means a very fast function call can be executed. Also, because the function will reference the actual structure and not a copy, it will be able to modify the contents of the elements of the structure used in the call.

To find the address of a structure variable, the **&** operator is placed before the structure variable's name. For example, given the following fragment,

```
struct bal {
  float balance;
  char name[80];
} person;
struct bal *p;  /* declare a structure pointer */
```

this

```
p = &person;
```

will place the address of **person** into the pointer **p**. To access the elements of a structure using a pointer to that structure, you must use the −> operator. For example, this references the **balance** field:

```
p->balance
```

The −> is called by most C programmers the *arrow operator*. It is formed by using the minus sign followed by a greater than sign. The arrow is used in place of the dot operator when accessing a structure element, given a pointer to the structure variable.

Using Pointers with Time and Date Functions

An interesting use of structure pointers is found in ANSI C's time and date functions. The time and date functions require the header file TIME.H. This header supplies two data types needed by the time and date functions. The first type is **time_t**. It is capable of representing the system time and date as a long integer. This is referred to as the *calendar time*. The second type is a structure called **tm** that holds the date and time broken down into its elements. This is called the *broken-down time*. The **tm** structure is defined as shown in the following:

```
struct tm {
    int tm_sec;   /* seconds, 0-59 */
    int tm_min;   /* minutes, 0-59 */
    int tm_hour;  /* hours, 0-23 */
    int tm_mday;  /* day of the month, 1-31 */
    int tm_mon;   /* months since Jan, 0-11 */
    int tm_year;  /* years from 1900 */
    int tm_wday;  /* days since Sunday, 0-6 */
    int tm_yday;  /* days since Jan 1, 0-365 */
    int tm_isdst; /* Daylight Saving Time indicator */
}
```

The value of **tm_isdst** will be positive if daylight saving time is in effect, 0 if it is not in effect, and negative if there is no information available.

The foundation for C's time and date functions is **time( )**, which has this prototype:

time_t time(time_t *time);

The **time( )** function returns the calendar time. It can be called either with a null pointer or with a pointer to a variable of type **time_t**. If the latter is used, then the variable pointed to by *time* will also be assigned the calendar time.

To convert the calendar time into broken-down time, use **localtime( )**, which has this prototype:

struct tm *localtime(time_t *time);

The **localtime( )** function returns a pointer to the broken-down form of *time* in the form of a **tm** structure. The time is represented in local time. (Another time function called **gmtime( )** returns the Greenwich mean time.) The *time* value is generally obtained through a call to **time( )**.

The structure used by **localtime( )** to hold the broken-down time is internally allocated by the **localtime( )** function and is overwritten each time the function is called. If you want to save the contents of the structure, you need to copy it elsewhere.

This program demonstrates **time( )** and **localtime( )** by displaying the current time of the system.

```
/* This program displays the current system time. */

#include "stdio.h"
#include "time.h"

main()
{
  struct tm *ptr;
  time_t lt;
```

```
lt = time(''\0');
ptr = localtime(&lt);

printf("%d:%d:%d\n", ptr->tm_hour, ptr->tm_min,
       ptr->tm_sec);
}
```

Although your programs can use the broken-down form of the time and date, the easiest way to generate a time and date string is to use **asctime( )**, whose prototype is shown here:

char *asctime(struct tm *ptr);

The **asctime( )** function returns a pointer to a string that is the information stored in the structure pointed to by *ptr*, converted into the following form:

day month hours:minutes:seconds year\n\0

The structure pointer passed to **asctime( )** is the one obtained from **localtime( )**.

The buffer used by **asctime( )** to hold the formatted output string is an internally allocated character array and is overwritten each time the function is called. If you want to save the contents of the string, you need to copy it elsewhere.

The following program uses the time functions just described to print the system time and date on the screen:

```
/* This program displays the current system time. */

#include "stdio.h"
#include "time.h"

main()
{
  struct tm *ptr;
  time_t lt;

  lt = time('\0');
```

```
  ptr = localtime(&lt);
  printf(asctime(ptr));
}
```

C contains several other time and date functions, so you will want to check the manuals that came with your compiler.

Remember: Use the dot operator to access structure elements when operating on the structure itself. When you have a pointer to a structure, the arrow operator should be used.

ARRAYS AND STRUCTURES WITHIN STRUCTURES

A structure element may be either simple or complex. A simple element is any of the built-in data types, such as an integer or character. You have already seen one complex element: the character array used in **inv_type**. Other complex data types are single- and multidimensional arrays of the other data types and structures.

A structure element that is an array is treated as you might expect from earlier examples. For example, consider this structure:

```
struct x {
  int a[10][10]; /* 10 x 10 array of ints */
  float b;
} y;
```

To reference integer 3,7 in **a** of structure **y**, you would write

```
y.a[3][7]
```

When a structure is an element of another structure, it is called a *nested structure.* For example, here the structure **addr** is nested inside **emp**.

```
struct addr {
  char name[40];
  char street[40];
  char city[40];
```

```
    long zip;
}

struct emp {
  struct addr address;
  float wage;
} worker;
```

Structure **emp** has been defined as having two elements. The first element is the structure of type **addr**. This structure will contain an employee's address. The second is **wage**, which holds the employee's wage. The following code fragment will assign the ZIP code 98765 to the **zip** field of **address** of **worker**.

```
worker.address.zip = 98765;
```

As you can see, the elements of each structure are referenced left to right from the outermost to the innermost.

BITFIELDS

Unlike most other computer languages, C has a built-in method of accessing a single bit within a byte. This can be useful for a number of reasons: (1) if storage is limited you can store several *Boolean* (true/false) values in 1 byte, (2) certain device interfaces transmit information encoded into bits within 1 byte, and (3) certain encryption routines need to access the bits within a byte. Although all these functions can be performed using some of the C operators you will learn about later in this book, a bitfield can add more structure and readability to your code. It could also make it more portable.

The method C uses to access bits is based on the structure. A bitfield is really just a special type of structure that defines how long, in bits, each element is to be. The general form of a bitfield definition is

```
struct struc-type-name {
  type name1 : length;
  type name2 : length;.
```

.
.
.

type nameN : *length*;
}

A bitfield must be declared as either **int, unsigned,** or **signed.** Bitfields of length 1 should be declared as **unsigned** because a single bit cannot have a sign.

Bitfields are commonly used when analyzing input from a hardware device. For example, the status port of a serial communications adapter might return a status byte organized this way:

Bit	Meaning When Set
0	Change in clear-to-send line
1	Change in data-set-ready
2	Trailing edge detected
3	Change in receive line
4	Clear-to-send
5	Data-set-ready
6	Telephone ringing
7	Received signal

You can represent the information in a status byte using the following bit field:

```
struct status_type {
  unsigned delta_cts: 1;
  unsigned delta_dsr: 1;
  unsigned tr_edge:   1;
  unsigned delta_rec: 1;
  unsigned cts:       1;
  unsigned dsr:       1;
  unsigned ring:      1;
  unsigned rec_line:  1;
} status;
```

You might use a routine similar to that shown here to enable a program to determine when it can send or receive data.

```
status = get_port_status();

if(status.cts) printf("clear to send");
if(status.dsr) printf("data ready");
```

To assign a value to a bitfield, simply use the same form as you would for any other type of structure element. For example, this clears the **ring** field:

```
status.ring = 0;
```

As you can see from these examples, each bitfield is accessed using the dot operator. However, if the structure is referenced through a pointer, you must use the —> operator.

You do not have to name each bitfield. This makes it easy to reach the bit you want, passing up unused ones. For example, if you only care about the **cts** and **dsr** bits, you could declare the **status _ type** structure this way:

```
struct status_type {
  unsigned :        4;
  unsigned cts:     1;
  unsigned dsr:     1;
} status;
```

Also, notice that the bits after **dsr** do not need to be mentioned in any way.

Bitfield variables have certain restrictions. You cannot take the address of a bitfield variable. Bitfield variables cannot be arrayed. You cannot overlap integer boundaries. You cannot know, from machine to machine, whether the fields will run from right to left or from left to right; thus code that uses bitfields may have machine dependencies.

It is valid to mix normal structure elements with bitfield elements. For example:

```
struct emp {
  struct addr address;
  float pay;
  unsigned lay_off:1;   /* lay off or active */
  unsigned hourly:1;    /* hourly pay or wage */
  unsigned deductions:3; /* IRS deductions */
};
```

This structure defines an employee record that uses only 1 byte to hold three pieces of information: the employee's status, whether the employee is salaried, and the number of deductions. Without the use of the bitfield, this information would have taken 3 bytes.

The next section presents a program that uses a bitfield to display the ASCII character codes in binary.

UNIONS

In C, a *union* is a memory location that is shared by several different types of variables at different times. The union definition is similar to that of a structure, as shown in this example:

```
union union_type {
  int i;
  char ch;
} ;
```

Note: It is not possible to have this union hold both an integer and a character at the same time, because **i** and **ch** overlay each other. (But your program is free to treat the information in the union as an integer or a character at any time.)

As with structures, this definition does not declare any variables. You may declare a variable either by placing its name at the end of the definition or by using a separate declaration statement. To declare a union variable **u_var** of type **union_type** using the definition just given, you would write

```
union union_type u_var;
```

In **u‿var**, both integer **i** and character **ch** share the same memory location. (Of course, **i** occupies 2 bytes and **ch** uses only 1.) Figure 10-2 shows how **i** and **ch** share the same address.

When a union is declared, the compiler automatically creates a variable large enough to hold the largest variable type in the union.

To access a union element you use the same syntax as you would for structures: the dot and arrow operators. If you are operating on the union directly, use the dot operator. If the union variable is accessed through a pointer, use the arrow operator. For example, to assign the letter "A" to element **ch** of **u‿var**, you would write

```
u_var.ch = 'A';
```

In this next example, a pointer to **u‿var** is passed to a function.

```
void func1(union union_type *un)
{
  un->i = 10; /* assign 10 to u_var using
               a pointer */
}
```

Using a union can help you produce machine-independent, or portable, code. Because the compiler keeps track of the actual sizes of the variables that make up the union, no machine dependencies are produced. You don't need to concern yourself with sizes.

Unions are used frequently when type conversions are needed.

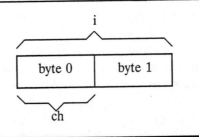

FIGURE 10-2   How **i** and **ch** utilize the union **u‿var**

For example, we can make use of a union to create our own version of **putw( )**, which will write the binary representation of an integer to a disk file. First, a union composed of one unsigned integer and a 2-byte character array is created.

```
union pw {
  unsigned i;
  char ch[2];
};
```

Now, **putw( )** can be written using this union.

```
void putw(union pw word, FILE *fp)
{
  putc(word.ch[0], fp); /* write first half */
  putc(word.ch[1], fp); /* write second half */
}
```

Although called with an integer, **putw( )** can still use the standard function **putc( )** to write an integer to a disk file.

a:	0	1	1	0	0	0	0	1
b:	0	1	1	0	0	0	1	0
c:	0	1	1	0	0	0	1	1
d:	0	1	1	0	0	1	0	0
e:	0	1	1	0	0	1	0	1
f:	0	1	1	0	0	1	1	0
g:	0	1	1	0	0	1	1	1
h:	0	1	1	0	1	0	0	0
i:	0	1	1	0	1	0	0	1
j:	0	1	1	0	1	0	1	0
k:	0	1	1	0	1	0	1	1
l:	0	1	1	0	1	1	0	0
m:	0	1	1	0	1	1	0	1
n:	0	1	1	0	1	1	1	0
o:	0	1	1	0	1	1	1	1
p:	0	1	1	1	0	0	0	0
q:	0	1	1	1	0	0	0	1

FIGURE 10-3   A sample run of the ASCII program

Here is a program that combines unions with bitfields to display the ASCII code, in binary, for a key you press. The union allows **getche( )** to assign the pressed key's value to a character variable, while the bitfield is used to display the individual bits. Study this program to make sure you fully understand its operation. Figure 10-3 shows a sample run.

```c
/* Display the ASCII code in binary for characters. */

#include "stdio.h"
#include "conio.h"

/* a bitfield that will be decoded */
struct byte {
  unsigned a : 1;
  unsigned b : 1;
  unsigned c : 1;
  unsigned d : 1;
  unsigned e : 1;
  unsigned f : 1;
  unsigned g : 1;
  unsigned h : 1;
};

union bits {
  char ch;
  struct byte bit;
} ascii ;

void decode(union bits b);

main()
{
  do {
    ascii.ch = getche();
    printf(": ");
    decode(ascii);
  } while(ascii.ch!='q'); /* quit if q typed */
}
/* Display the bit pattern for each character. */
void decode(union bits b)
{
```

```
   if(b.bit.h) printf("1 ");
      else printf("0 ");
   if(b.bit.g) printf("1 ");
      else printf("0 ");
   if(b.bit.f) printf("1 ");
      else printf("0 ");
   if(b.bit.e) printf("1 ");
      else printf("0 ");
   if(b.bit.d) printf("1 ");
      else printf("0 ");
   if(b.bit.c) printf("1 ");
      else printf("0 ");
   if(b.bit.b) printf("1 ");
      else printf("0 ");
   if(b.bit.a) printf("1 ");
      else printf("0 ");
   printf("\n");
}
```

USING sizeof TO ENSURE PORTABILITY

You have seen that structures and unions can be used to create variables of varying sizes, and that the actual size of these variables may change from machine to machine. The **sizeof** unary operator is used to compute the size of any variable or type and can help eliminate machine-dependent code from your programs.

For example, many C compilers use the sizes for data types shown here:

Type	Size in Bytes
char	1
int	2
long int	4
float	4
double	8

Assuming these sizes, the code shown here will print the numbers "1," "2," and "8" on the screen.

```
char ch;
int i;
double f;

printf("%d", sizeof(ch));

printf("%d", sizeof(i));

printf("%d", sizeof(f));
```

sizeof is a compile time operator: all the information necessary to compute the size of any variable is known at compile time. For example, consider

```
union x {
  char ch;
  int i;
  float f;
} u_var;
```

The **sizeof(u_var)** will be 4. At run time, it does not matter what **u_var** is actually holding; all that matters is the size of the largest variable it can hold, because the union must be as large as its largest element.

EXERCISES

1. Create a structure called **player** that will store the following information about baseball players:

    - player's name

    - team name

    - batting average

2. Using **player** from exercise 1, declare a 100-element array of structures of this type. Call this array **p_info**.

3. Write a short function called **enter( )** that will input the player's name, team name, and batting average. Assume that **p _ info** is global.

4. Create a bitfield that will accommodate the following bits:

Bit	Meaning
0	Out of RAM
1	Disk failure
2	Port failure
3	Bad media
4	CPU instruction failure
5	Unused
6	Unused
7	Low power

5. Define a union that consists of the following:

```
int i[10];
char ch[20];
float f;
```

6. What's wrong with this code?

```
union x {
  int a;
  char c;
} example;

   .
   .
   .
if(sizeof(example)==2) printf("holding an integer");
else printf("holding a character");
```

7. Write a program that displays the day of the week by name. Hint: Use the broken-down form of the time.

Answers

1.
```
struct player {
  char name[40];
  char team[40];
  float bat_avg;
}
```

2.
```
struct player p_info[100];
```

3.
```
void enter(int rec)
{
  printf("enter name: ");
  gets(p_info[rec].name);
  printf("enter team: ");
  gets(p_info[rec].team);
  printf("enter batting average: ");
  scanf("%f", &p_info[rec].bat_avg);
}
```

4.
```
struct status {
  unsigned no_ram: 1;
  unsigned disk:   1;
  unsigned port:   1;
  unsigned media:  1;
  unsigned CPU:    1;
  unsigned         2;
  unsigned low_pwr:1;
} ;
```

5.
```
union u {
  int i[10];
  char ch[20];
  float f;
};
```

6. A union's contents do not affect the **sizeof** operator. The union will always be the same size regardless of what it contains.

7.
```
#include "stdio.h"
#include "time.h"

char days[][20] = {
  "Sunday",
  "Monday",
  "Tuesday",
  "Wednesday",
  "Thursday",
  "Friday",
  "Saturday"
};

main()
{
  struct tm *ptr;
  time_t lt;

  lt = time('\0');

  ptr = localtime(&lt);

  printf("Day is %s", days[ptr->tm_wday]);
}
```

ADVANCED
DATA TYPES

In addition to structures and unions, which you learned about in the previous chapter, C supports several other data types. Some of these advanced data types are created using modifiers to existing types. You have used some of these already, such as **long**. Other data types include enumerations, **typedef**s, and pointers to functions. Finally, C's dynamic allocation system lets you create storage for data as it is needed. This chapter looks at these topics in depth.

ACCESS MODIFIERS

C has two type modifiers that control the ways variables can be accessed or modified. These modifiers are called **const** and **volatile**. Like other type modifiers, the access modifiers precede the base type and the variable name.

const

Variables declared with the **const** modifier cannot be changed by your program during execution. You may give a variable declared as **const** an initial value, however. For example:

```
const float version =  3.20;
```

creates a **float** variable called **version** that cannot be modified by your program. It can, however, be used in other types of expressions. A **const** variable will receive its value either from an explicit initialization or by some hardware dependent means. Applying the **const** modifier to a variable's declaration ensures that the variable will not be modified by other parts of your program.

Variables of type **const** have one very important use — they can protect the arguments to a function from modification by that function. That is, when a pointer is passed to a function, that function can modify the actual variable pointed to by the pointer. However, if the pointer is specified as **const** in the paramenter declaration, it will not be possible for the function code to modify what it points to. For example, the **code( )** function in this short program shifts each letter in a message by one. Therefore an "A" becomes a "B," and so forth. The use of **const** in the parameter declaration ensures that the code inside the function cannot modify the object pointed to by the parameter.

```
#include "stdio.h"

void code(const char *str);

main()
{
  code("this is a test");
}

void code(const char *str)
{
  while(*str) printf("%c", (*str++)+1);
}
```

If, for some reason, you had written **code( )** in such a way that the argument to it would be modified, it could not be compiled. For example, if you had coded **code( )** in this way, an error would have resulted.

```
/* this is wrong */
void code(const char *str)
{
  while(*str) {
    *str = *str + 1;
    printf("%c", *str++);
  }
}
```

Many functions in the C standard library use **const** in their parameter declarations. For example, the **strlen( )** function has the following prototype:

   int strlen(const char *str);

By specifying **str** as **const**, the ANSI standard effectively says that no implementation of **strlen( )** can modify the string pointed to by **str**. In previous chapters the **const** was left off because you hadn't learned about it yet. However, in general, when a standard library function doesn't need to modify an object pointed to by a calling argument, it is declared as **const**.

The second use for **const** is to verify that your program does not modify a variable. Remember, a variable of type **const** can be modified by something outside your program; for example, a hardware device may set its value. However, by declaring a variable as **const** you can prove that any changes to that variable occur because of external events.

volatile

The modifier **volatile** tells the compiler that a variable's value may be changed in ways not explicitly specified by the program. For example, a global variable's address may be passed to the clock

routine of the operating system and used to hold the real time of the system. In this situation, the contents of the variable are altered without any explicit assignment statements in the program. The external alteration of a variable may be important because a C compiler is permitted to automatically optimize certain expressions by assuming the content of a variable is unchanged if it does not occur on the left side of an assignment statement. For example, assume that **clock** is being updated every tenth second by the computer's clock mechanism. If it is not declared as **volatile**, the following statements may not work properly.

```
int clock, timer;
   .
   .
   .
timer = clock;
/* do something */
printf("elapsed type is %d\n", clock-timer);
```

Because **clock** is not altered by the program and it is not declared as **volatile**, a C compiler may optimize the code so that the value of **clock** is not re-examined in the **printf( )** statement. However, if you declare **clock** as

```
volatile int clock;
```

no such optimization will take place and **clock**'s value will be examined each time it is referenced.

Although it may seem strange at first, it is possible to use **const** and **volatile** together. For example, if 0x30 is assumed to be the value of a port that is changed only by external conditions, then you would include the following declaration to prevent any side effects.

```
const volatile unsigned char *port=0x30;
```

STORAGE CLASS SPECIFIERS

There are four storage class specifiers supported by C:

- auto
- extern
- register
- static

These tell the compiler how the variable that follows should be stored. The storage specifier precedes the rest of the variable declaration. Its general form is

storage-class-specifier type-specifier variable-list;

Each specifier will be examined in turn.

auto

The **auto** specifier is used to declare local variables. It is rarely if ever used, however, because local variables are **auto** by default. It is extremely rare to see this keyword used in a program.

extern

All the programs you have worked with so far have been quite small—so small, in fact, that many fit within the 25 lines of the screen. However, in real programming tasks, programs tend to be much larger. As the file grows, the compilation time will eventually get long enough to be annoying. When this happens you should break your program into two or more separate files. This way small changes to one file do not require that the entire program be recompiled—a substantial time savings in large projects. C contains the **extern** keyword, which helps support the multiple-file approach.

Although your program may consist of two or more files, there must be some way of telling all the files about the global variables required by the program. Your program can only have one copy of each global variable. If you tried to declare two global variables with the same name inside the same file, either an error would be reported or the compiler would arbitrarily choose one. Likewise, if you try to declare the global variables needed by your program in each file of a multiple-file program, you will have trouble. Although the compiler does not issue any error messages at compile time, you are actually trying to create two or more copies of each variable. This will be found by the linker when it attempts to link your modules together. The linker will issue a warning message because it will not know which variable to use.

The solution is to declare all of your globals in one file and use **extern** declarations in the other, as shown in Figure 11-1. In file two, the global variable list is copied from file one and the **extern** specifier is added to the declarations. The **extern** specifier tells the

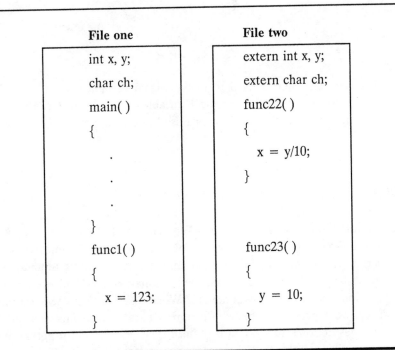

File one

```
int x, y;
char ch;
main( )
{
    .
    .
    .
}
func1( )
{
    x = 123;
}
```

File two

```
extern int x, y;
extern char ch;
func22( )
{
    x = y/10;
}




func23( )
{
    y = 10;
}
```

FIGURE 11-1   Using global variables in separately compiled modules

compiler the following variable types and names have already been declared elsewhere. In other words, **extern** lets the compiler know the types and names for these global variables without actually creating storage for them again. When the linker links the two modules together, all references to the external variables are resolved.

When you use a global variable inside a function that is in the same file as the declaration for the global variable, you may elect to use **extern**, (although it is rarely done). This program fragment shows the use of this option.

```
int first, last;  /* global definition of first
                      and last */

main()
{
   extern int first;  /* optional use of the
                          extern declaration */
}
```

Although **extern** variable declarations can occur inside the same file as the global declaration, they are not necessary. If C comes across an undeclared variable, the compiler will see if it matches any of the global variables. If it does, C will assume that the global variable is being referenced.

static Variables

Variables of type **static** are permanent variables within their own function or file. They differ from global variables in that they are not known outside their function or file, but they do maintain their values between calls. This feature can make them very useful when you write generalized functions and function libraries, which may be used by other programmers. Because **static** has different effects on local variables than on global ones, they will be examined separately.

static LOCAL VARIABLES   When the **static** modifier is applied to a local variable it causes C to create permanent storage for it in

much the same way that it does for a global variable. The key difference between a **static** local variable and a global variable is that the **static** local variable remains known only to the block in which it is declared. In simple terms, a **static** local variable is a local variable that retains its value between function calls.

It is important to the creation of stand-alone functions that **static** local variables are available because there are several types of routines that must preserve a value between calls. If **static** variables did not exist, globals would have to be used—opening the door to possible side effects.

To see an example of a **static** variable, try the following program:

```
/* Compute a running average of numbers entered by
   the user.
*/
#include "stdio.h"

int r_avg(int i);

main()
{
  int num;

  do {
    printf("enter numbers (-1 to quit): ");
    scanf("%d", &num);
    printf("running average is: %d\n", r_avg(num));
  } while(num>-1);
}

int r_avg(int i)
{
  static int sum=0, count=0;

  sum = sum + i;

  count++;

  return sum / count;
}
```

Here, the local variables **sum** and **count** are both declared as **static** and initialized to 0. When initializations are used with **static** variables, the initialization only occurs once—not each time the function is entered. The program uses **r_avg( )** to compute and report the current average of the numbers entered by the user. Because both **sum** and **count** are **static**, they will maintain their values between calls, making the program work properly. To prove that the **static** modifier is necessary, try removing it and running the program. As you can see, it doesn't accomplish the desired task.

static GLOBAL VARIABLES   When the specifier **static** is applied to a global variable it instructs the compiler to create a global variable known only to the file in which the **static** global variable is declared. Thus, even though the variable is global, other routines in other files have no knowledge of it and cannot alter its contents directly. Consequently, it is not subject to side effects. Therefore, for the few situations where a local **static** cannot do the job, you can create a small file containing only the functions that need the global **static** variable, separately compile that file, and use it without fear of side effects.

To see an example of this, create the two files shown here:

```
/* First file */

#include "stdio.h"

int r_avg(int i);
void reset(void);

main()
{
  int num;

  do {
    printf("enter numbers (-1 to quit, -2 to reset):");
    scanf("%d", &num);
    if(num==-2) {
      reset();
      continue;
    }
    printf("running average is: %d\n", r_avg(num));
```

```
  } while(num!=-1);
}

/* --------------------- Second File ---------------*/

static sum=0, count=0;

int r_avg(int i)
{
  sum = sum + i;

  count++;

  return sum / count;
}

void reset(void)
{
  sum = 0;
  count = 0;
}
```

Compile and link the two files. In this version of the program the variables **sum** and **count** are global **statics**. Thus, they may be accessed by both **r_avg( )** and **reset( )** in the second file. This allows them to be reset so that a second set of numbers can be averaged. However, no functions outside the second file can access those variables. When you run this program, you can reset the average by entering −2. Try it now. You might also try attempting to access either **sum** or **count** from the first file. You should receive an error message.

Let's review what you've learned about **static** variables. The names of local **static** variables are known only to the function or block of code in which they are declared, and the names of global **static** variables are known only to the file in which they reside. In essence, the **static** modifier allows variables to exist that are known only to the functions that need them, thereby controlling and limiting the possibility of side effects. Variables of type **static** enable you, the programmer, to hide portions of your program from other portions. This can be a tremendous advantage when trying to manage large and complex programs.

register Variables

Another important type modifier found in ANSI C is called **register**. It traditionally applies only to variables of type **int** and **char**. Originally, the **register** specifier was used to request that C keep the value of variables declared with it in the register of the CPU rather than in memory, where normal variables are stored. This means that operations on **register** variables can occur much faster than on other variables because no memory access is required to determine or modify their values. (A memory access takes much longer than a register access.)

However, the ANSI standardization committee elected to expand the definition of **register**. According to the proposed ANSI standard, the **register** modifier may be applied to any type of data. It simply tells the compiler to make access to a **register** type as fast as possible. For situations involving characters and integers this means putting them into a CPU register, so the traditional definition still holds. It's not yet known what C compiler manufacturers will come up with for situations where **register** is applied to types other than character and integer, since the standard does not require any specific action.

Also, traditionally **register** could only be applied to local variables or parameters. Although this restriction is not part of the proposed ANSI standard, it is best to assume that it still applies because in practice it will.

Because accessing **register** variables is faster than accessing normal variables, they are ideal for loop control. Here is an example that uses a **register** variable of type **int** to control a loop. This function computes the result of m^e for integers.

```
int_pwr(int m, register int e)
{
   register int temp;

   temp = 1;

   for( ;e ;e--) temp = temp * m;
   return temp;
}
```

In this example, both **e** and **temp** are declared to be **register** vari-

ables because both are used within the loop. In general practice, **register** variables are used where they will do the most good, which implies that they be used where many references will be made to the same variable. This is important because you cannot have an unlimited number of register variables in use at any one time.

The exact number of **register** variables allowed within any one function is determined by both the processor type and the specific implementation of C you are using; but you can generally count on two. You don't have to worry about declaring too many **register** variables, though, because C will automatically make register variables into nonregister variables when the limit is reached. (This is done to ensure the portability of C code across a broad range of processors.)

To illustrate the difference **register** variables make, the following program measures the execution time of two **for** loops that differ only in the type of variable that controls them. This program uses the **time( )** function found in C's standard library.

```
/* This program shows the difference a register
   variable can make to the speed of program
   execution.
*/

#include "stdio.h"
#include "time.h"

unsigned int i;  /* non-register */
unsigned int delay;

main()
{
  register unsigned int j;
  long t;

  t = time('\0');
  for(delay=0; delay<10; delay++)
    for(i=0; i<64000; i++);
  printf("time for non-register loop: %ld\n",
         time('\0')-t);
```

```
   t = time('\0');
   for(delay=0; delay<10; delay++)
     for(j=0; j<64000; j++) ;
   printf("time for register loop: %ld", time('\0')-t);
}
```

When you run this program you will find the register-controlled loop executes in about half the time of the non-register-controlled loop.

ENUMERATIONS

An *enumeration* is a type of data that consists of named integer constants and specifies all the legal values a variable of that type may have. Enumerations are defined much like structures, with the keyword **enum** used to signal the start of an enumeration type. The general form is shown here:

enum *enum-type-name* { *enumeration list* } *variable list*;

Here, the *enumeration list* is a comma-separated list of names that represents the values a variable of the enumeration type may have. Both the enumeration type name and the *variable list* are optional. As with structures, the enumeration type name is used to declare variables of its type. The following fragment defines an enumeration called **apple** and declares **fruit** to be of that type.

```
enum  apple {Jonathan, Golden_Del, Red_Del, Winesap,
       Cortland, McIntosh};

enum apple fruit;
```

Given this definition and declaration, the following types of statements are valid:

```
fruit = Winesap;

if(fruit==Red_Del) printf("Red Delicious\n");
```

The key point to understand about an enumeration is that each of the symbols stands for an integer value. As such, they may be used in any integer expression. Unless initialized otherwise, the value of the first enumeration symbol is 0, the value of the second symbol is 1, and so forth. Therefore,

```
printf("%d %d", Jonathan, Cortland);
```

displays "0 4" on the screen.

It is possible to specify the value of one or more of the symbols by using an initializer. You do this by following the symbol with an equal sign and an integer value. Whenever an initializer is used, symbols that appear after it are assigned values greater than the previous initialization value. For example, the following assigns the value of 10 to **Winesap**:

```
enum  apple {Jonathan, Golden_Del, Red_Del, Winesap=10,
        Cortland, McIntosh};
```

The values of these symbols are now

Jonathan	0
Golden _ Del	1
Red _ Del	2
Winesap	10
Cortland	11
McIntosh	12

One common, but erroneous, assumption made about enumerations is that the symbols can be input and output directly. This is not the case. For example, the following code fragment will not perform as desired.

```
/* this will not work */

fruit = McIntosh;

printf("%s", fruit);
```

Remember, the symbol **McIntosh** is simply a name for an integer; it is not a string.

Actually, to create code to input and output enumeration symbols is quite tedious (unless you are willing to settle for their integer values). For example, the following code is needed to display, in words, the kinds of apple that **fruit** contains:

```
switch(fruit) {
  case Jonathan: printf("Jonathan");
    break;
  case Golden_Del: printf("Golden Delicious");
    break;
  case Red_Del: printf("Red Delicious");
    break;
  case Winesap: printf("Winesap");
    break;
  case Cortland: printf("Cortland");
    break;
  case McIntosh: printf("McIntosh");
    break;
}
```

Sometimes it is possible to declare an array of strings and use the enumeration value as an index in order to translate an enumeration value into its corresponding string. For example, this program prints the names of the apples:

```
#include "stdio.h"

enum  apple {Jonathan, Golden_Del, Red_Del, Winesap,
      Cortland, McIntosh};

char name[][20] = {
  "Jonathan",
  "Golden Delicious",
  "Red Delicious",
  "Winesap",
  "Cortland",
  "McIntosh"
};
```

```
main()
{
  enum apple fruit;

  for(fruit=Jonathan; fruit<=McIntosh; fruit++)
    printf("%s\n", name[fruit]);
}
```

Given that enumeration values must be converted manually to their human-readable string values for console I/O, they are most useful in routines that do not make such conversions. It is common to see an enumeration used to define a compiler's symbol table, for example.

typedef

C allows you to explicitly define new data type names using the **typedef** keyword. You do not actually create a new data class, but define a new name for an existing type. This process can help make machine-dependent programs more portable; only the **typedef** statements have to be changed. It also can help you document your code, by allowing descriptive names for the standard data types. The general form of the **typedef** statement is

typedef *type name*;

where *type* is any allowable data type and *name* is the new name for this type. The new name you define is in addition to, not a replacement for, the existing type name.

For example, you could create a new name for **float** using

```
typedef float balance;
```

This statement tells the compiler to recognize **balance** as another name for **float**. Next, you could create a **float** variable using **balance**.

```
balance over_due;
```

Here, **over_due** is a floating-point variable of type **balance**, which is another word for **float**.

You can use **typedef** to create names for more complex types, as well. For example:

```
typedef struct client {
  float due;
  int over_due;
  char name[40];
};


client clist[NUM_CLIENTS]; /* define array of
             structures of type client */
```

Using **typedef** can help make your code easier to read and easier to port to a new machine. But remember, you are *not* creating any new data types.

POINTERS TO FUNCTIONS

A particularly confusing yet powerful feature of C is the *function pointer*. A function pointer is, in a way, a new type of data. Even though a function is not a variable, it still has a physical location in memory that can be assigned to a pointer. The address assigned to the pointer is the entry point of the function. This pointer can then be used in place of the function's name. It also allows functions to be passed as arguments to other functions.

To understand how function pointers work, you must understand a little about how a function is compiled and called in C. First, as each function is compiled, source code is transformed into object code and an entry point is established. When a call is made to a function while your program is running, a machine language call is made to this entry point. Therefore, a pointer to a function actually contains the memory address of the entry point of the function.

The address of a function is obtained by using the function's name without any parentheses or arguments. (This is similar to the way an array's address is obtained when only the array name, without indices, is used.) If you assign the address of a function to a

pointer, you can call that function using the pointer. As an example, study the following program. It contains two functions, **vline( )** and **hline( )**, which draw vertical and horizontal lines of a specified length on the screen.

```
#include "stdio.h"

void vline(int i), hline(int i);

main()
{
  void (*p)(int i);

  (*p) = vline;

  (*p)(4);

  (*p) = hline;

  (*p)(3);
}

void vline(int i)
{
    for( ;i; i--) printf("-");
    printf("\n");
}

void hline(int i)
{
    for( ; i; i--) printf("|\n");
}
```

Let's examine this program in detail. The first line after **main( )** declares a pointer to a function that takes one integer argument and returns no value. It does not in any way specify what the function is. All it does is create a pointer that can be used to point to a function of that type. Because of the C precedence rules, the parentheses around ***p** are necessary.

The next line assigns to ***p** the address of **vline( )**. The line after that actually calls **vline( )** with an argument of 4. Again, the paren-

theses are necessary. The program then assigns the address of **hline** to ***p** and calls **hline( )** using the pointer.

Function pointers have very important uses. One of these is the creation of generic functions that operate on a wide variety of data. An important example of this is the **qsort( )** function, which is found in C's standard library. The **qsort( )** function is a generic sorting function based upon the Quicksort algorithm. Its prototype follows.

> void qsort(void *start*, size _ t *length*, size _ t *size*,
>   int (*compare) (const void *, const void *));

The prototype for **qsort( )** is in STDLIB.H, which also defines the type **size _ t**, which is essentially an **unsigned int**. (Technically, the ANSI standard specifies the type **size _ t** as capable of holding any value returned by **sizeof**. In general, this is the same as an **unsigned int**.) To use **qsort( )** you must pass it a pointer to the start of the array of objects you wish sorted in *start,* the length of the array in *length,* the width of each element (in bytes) in *size,* and a pointer to a comparison function.

The comparison function used by **qsort( )** compares two elements. It must return less than zero if the first argument points to a value less than the second, zero if they are equal, and greater than zero if the second argument points to a value less than the first.

To see how **qsort( )** can be used, try this program:

```
#include "stdio.h"
#include "stdlib.h"

int comp(char *a, char *b);

main()
{
  char str[] = "this is a test";

  qsort(str, strlen(str), 1, comp);
  printf("sorted string: %s", str);
}

int comp(char *a, char *b)
{
  return *a - *b;
}
```

The program sorts the string **str** into ascending order. Since **qsort( )** is generic, it can be used to sort any type of data. For example, this program sorts an array of integers. To ensure portability, it finds the width of an integer using **sizeof**.

```c
#include "stdio.h"
#include "stdlib.h"
int comp(int *a, int *b);

main()
{
  int num[] = {10, 4, 3, 6, 5 ,7 ,8};
  int i;

  qsort(num, 7, sizeof(int), comp);

  for(i=0; i<7; i++)
    printf("%d ", num[i]);
}

int comp(int *a, int *b)
{
  return *a - *b;
}
```

Although function pointers may still be somewhat confusing to you, with a little practice and thought, you should have no trouble using them.

DYNAMIC ALLOCATION

Before leaving the subject of advanced data types it is necessary to discuss C's dynamic allocation system, which allows the dynamic creation of variables during program execution.

There are two primary ways a C program can store information in the main memory of the computer. The first uses global and local variables, which are defined by the C language. As you know, in the case of global variables, the storage is fixed throughout the run time

of your program. For local variables, storage is allocated from the stack space of the computer. Although these variables are efficiently implemented in C, they require the programmer to know, in advance, the amount of storage needed for every situation.

The second way information can be stored is through the use of C's *dynamic allocation* system. In this method, storage for information is allocated from the free memory area that lies between your program and its permanent storage area and the stack. This region is called the *heap*. Figure 11-2 shows conceptually a C program in memory. The stack grows downward as it is used, so the amount of memory it needs is determined by your program design. For example, a program with many recursive functions will make much greater demands on stack memory than one without recursive functions. (Remember, because local variables are stored on the stack, each recursive call to a function requires additional stack space.) The memory required for the program and global data is fixed during the execution of the program. Memory to satisfy a dynamic allocation request is taken from the heap. As you might guess, it is possible under fairly extreme cases to exhaust free memory.

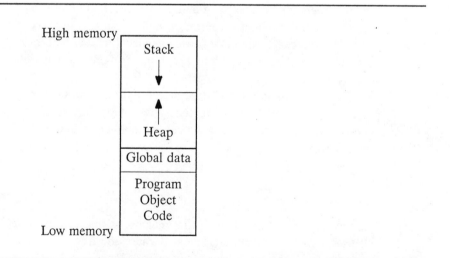

FIGURE 11-2   Conceptual view of a C program's memory usage

Allocating and Freeing Memory

The core of C's allocation system are the functions **malloc( )** and **free( )**. (ANSI C has several other dynamic allocation functions that add flexibility, but these are the most important.) They work together using the free memory region to establish and maintain a list of available storage. The **malloc( )** function allocates memory and the **free( )** function releases it. That is, each time a **malloc( )** memory request is made, a portion of the remaining free memory is allocated. Each time a **free( )** call is made, memory is returned to the system. Any program that uses these functions should include the header file STDLIB.H.

The **malloc( )** function has this prototype:

void *malloc(size _ t *number _ of _ bytes*);

Here, *number _ of _ bytes* is the number of bytes of memory you wish to allocate. Remember, **size _ t** is defined by ANSI as, more or less, an **unsigned** integer. The **malloc( )** function returns a pointer of type **void**, which means you can assign it to any type of pointer. After a successful call, **malloc( )** will return a pointer to the first byte of the region of memory allocated from the heap. If there is not enough available memory to satisfy the **malloc( )** request, an allocation failure occurs and **malloc( )** returns a null. You can use **sizeof** to determine the exact number of bytes needed for each type of data. In this way you can make your programs portable to a variety of systems.

The **free( )** function is the opposite of **malloc( )** in that it returns previously allocated memory to the system. Once the memory has been freed, it may be reused by a subsequent call to **malloc( )**. The function **free( )** has the prototype

void free(void *p);

The only really important thing to remember is that you must *never* call **free( )** with an invalid argument because the free list would be destroyed.

The following short program will allocate enough storage for several types of variables, including a structure.

```c
#include "stdio.h"
#include "stdlib.h"
#include "math.h"

main()
{
  int *i;
  float *j;

  struct s_type {
    int i;
    double d;
  } *s_var;

  i = malloc(sizeof(int));
  if(!i) {
    printf("allocation failure");
    exit(1);
  }
  j = malloc(sizeof(float));
  if(!j) {
    printf("allocation failure");
    exit(1);
  }
  s_var = malloc(sizeof(struct s_type));
  if(!s_var) {
    printf("allocation failure");
    exit(1);
  }

  *i = 10;
  *j = 100.123;

  s_var->i = *i;
  s_var->d = sqrt(100.0);

  printf("%d %f %d %lf", *i, *j, s_var->i, s_var->d);
}
```

Remember: Before using the pointer returned by **malloc( )**, always make sure that your allocation request succeeds by testing the return value against zero. Do not try to use a pointer of value zero because it will probably crash your system.

Dynamic allocation is very useful when you don't know in advance how many items of data you will be dealing with. Although meaningful examples of dynamic allocation tend to be fairly long and complex, the following example gives you the flavor of its use. The program first asks the user how many numbers are to be averaged. It then allocates an array large enough to hold them, inputs the numbers, averages them, and finally frees the array.

```
/* This program averages an arbitrary
   number of integers. */
#include "stdlib.h"
#include "stdio.h"

main()
{
  int *p;
  int num, i, avg;

  printf("enter number of integers to average: ");
  scanf("%d", &num);

  /* allocate space */
  if((p = malloc(sizeof(int)*num))==NULL) {
    printf("allocation error");
    exit(1);
  }

  for(i=0; i<num; i++) {
    printf("%d: ", i+1);
    scanf("%d",&p[i]);
  }

  avg = 0;
  for(i=0; i<num; i++) avg = avg + p[i];

  printf("average is: %d", avg/num);

  free(p);
}
```

For an in-depth look at dynamic allocation, refer to *Advanced C* by Herbert Schildt (Berkeley, Ca.: Osborne/McGraw-Hill, 1988).

EXERCISES

1. What is wrong with this code?

```
#include "stdio.h"
#include "ctype.h"

void uppercase(char const *s);

main()
{
  char str[] = "this is a test";

  uppercase(str);

  printf("string in uppercase: %s", str);
}

void uppercase(char const *s)
{
  while(*s) {
    *s = toupper(*s);
    s++;
  }
}
```

2. Which variables would be best modified by **register** in this program?

```
main()
{
  int i;
  int j;
  int k;

  printf("how many times: ");
  scanf("%d", &j);
  for(i=0; i<j; i++) {

    .

    .

    .

  }
```

```
       .
       .
       .
    k = 100;
}
```

3. Use **typedef** to make **counter** a new name for **int**.

4. Create an enumeration that defines the notes do, re, mi, fa, sol, la, ti.

5. Show how to allocate memory to hold this structure.

```
struct s_type {
  char str[80];
  double balance;
  int i;
};
```

6. Write a program that sorts an array of strings using **qsort( )**.

Answers

1. The function defines **s** as **const**, which means that the string it points to cannot be changed as the program source code would have you believe.

2. The **i** and **j** variables will benefit the most from the **register** modifier because they are used to control the loop.

3.   `type counter int;`

4.   `enum notes {do, re, mi, fa, sol, la, ti};`

5.
```
struct s_type *p;

p = malloc(sizeof(struct s_type));

if(!p) {
  printf("Allocation error");
  exit(1);
}
```

6.
```
#include "stdio.h"
#include "stdlib.h"
#include "string.h"

int comp(char *a, char *b);

main()
{
  register int i;

  char strs[][20] = {
    "this",
    "that",
    "one",
    "alpha"
  };

  qsort(strs, 4, 20, comp);

  for(i=0; i<4; i++) printf("%s\n", strs[i]);
}

int comp(char *a, char *b)
{
  return strcmp(a, b);
}
```

ADVANCED
OPERATORS

In Chapter 3 you learned about the more commonplace C operators. Unlike many computer languages, C contains several special operators that greatly increase its power and flexibility—especially for system level programming. These operators are the subject of this chapter.

BITWISE OPERATORS

Since C was designed to take the place of assembly language for most programming tasks, it was important for it to have the ability to operate directly on the bits within a byte or word. *Bitwise operations* refer to the testing, setting, or shifting of the actual bits in a byte or word that correspond to C's character and integer types. Bitwise operations may not be used on **float, double, long double, void,** or

Operator	Action
&	AND
|	OR
^	exclusive OR (XOR)
~	one's complement (NOT)
>>	shift right
<<	shift left

TABLE 12-1 The Bitwise Operators

other more complex types. Bitwise operations are important in a wide variety of system level programming, in which status information from a device must be interrogated or constructed. Table 12-1 lists the bitwise operators. Let's take a look at these operators now.

AND, OR, XOR, and NOT

The bitwise AND, OR, and one's complement (NOT) are governed by the same truth table as their logical equivalents, except that they work on a bit-by-bit level. The exclusive OR (XOR, ^) has the truth table shown here:

p	q	p ^ q
0	0	0
1	0	1
1	1	0
0	1	1

As the table indicates, the outcome of an XOR is true only if exactly one of the operands is true; it is false otherwise.

Bitwise operations most often find application in device drivers, modem programs, disk file routines, printer routines, and the like, because the bitwise operations can be used to mask off certain bits, such as parity. (The parity bit is used to confirm that the rest of the bits in the byte are unchanged. It is usually the high-order bit in each byte.)

In terms of its most common usage, you can think of the bitwise AND as a way to turn bits off. That is, any bit that is 0 in either operand will cause the corresponding bit in the outcome to be set to 0. For example, the following program reads characters from the keyboard and turns any lowercase letters into uppercase by resetting the sixth bit to 0. As the ASCII character set is defined, the lowercase letters are the same as the uppercase ones, except that they are greater in value by 32. Thus, to capitalize a lowercase letter you need to turn off the sixth bit, as this program illustrates:

```
#include "stdio.h"
#include "conio.h"

main()
{
  char ch;

  do {
    ch = getche();

    /* this statement turns off the 6th bit */
    ch = ch & 223;

    printf("%c", ch);
  } while(ch!='Q');
}
```

The value 223 used in the AND statement is the decimal representation of 1101 1111. Thus, the AND operation leaves all bits in **ch** unchanged except the sixth one, which is set to 0.

The AND operator is also useful when you want to check to see if a bit is on or off. For example, this statement checks to see if bit 4 in **status** is set.

```
if(status & 8) printf("bit 4 is on");
```

The reason 8 is used is that in binary it is represented as 0000 1000. That is, the number 8 in binary has only the fourth bit on. Thus, the **if** statement can only succeed when bit 4 of **status** is also on. An interesting use of this procedure is the new version of the **disp_binary( )** function shown here. It displays, in binary format, the bit pattern of its argument. You will use it later in this chapter to see the effects of other bitwise operations.

```
/* display the bits within a byte */
void disp_binary(unsigned u)
{
  register int t;

  for(t=128; t>0; t = t/2)
    if(u & t) printf("1 ");
    else printf("0 ");
  printf("\n");
}
```

The **disp_binary( )** function works by successively testing each bit in the byte, using the bitwise AND to determine if it is on or off. If it is on, the digit "1" is displayed; otherwise "0" is displayed.

The bitwise OR, as the reverse of AND, can be used to turn bits on. Any bit that is set to 1 in either operand will cause the corresponding bit in the variable to be set to 1. For example,

```
        1 0 0 0 0 0 0 1
        0 0 0 0 0 1 0 1
      | — — — — — — — —   bitwise OR result
        1 0 0 0 0 1 0 1
```

The OR can be used to change the capitalization program from the previous example into a program that converts to lowercase, as shown here:

```
#include "stdio.h"
#include "conio.h"
```

```
main()
{
  char ch;

  do {
    ch = getche();

    /* this lowercases the letter by turning
       on bit 6
    */
    ch = ch | 32;

    printf("%c", ch);
  } while(ch!='q');
}
```

By setting the sixth bit, all uppercase letters are changed to their lowercase equivalents.

An exclusive OR, usually abbreviated XOR, will set a bit on if—and only if—the bits being compared are different. For example:

```
  0 1 1 1 1 1 1 1
  1 0 1 1 1 0 0 1
^ _ _ _ _ _ _ _ _  bitwise XOR result
  0 0 0 0 0 1 1 1
```

The following program demonstrates the NOT operator by displaying a number and its complement in binary using the **disp_binary**( ) function developed earlier.

The unary one's complement (NOT) operator reverses the state of all the bits of the operand. For example, if some integer called **A** has the bit pattern 1001 0110, then ~**A** produces a result with the bit pattern 0110 1001.

```
#include "stdio.h"

void disp_binary(unsigned u);

main()
```

```
{
  unsigned u;

  printf("enter a number: ");
  scanf("%u", &u);

  printf("Here's the number in binary: ");
  disp_binary(u);

  printf("Here's the complement of the number: ");
  disp_binary(~u);
}

/* display the bits within a byte */
void disp_binary(unsigned u)
{
  register int t;

  for(t=128; t>0; t = t/2)
    if(u & t) printf("1 ");
    else printf("0 ");
  printf("\n");
}
```

In general, bitwise ANDs, ORs, NOTs, and XORs apply their operations directly to each bit in the variable individually. For this and other reasons, bitwise operations are usually not used in conditional statements the way the relational and logical operators are. For example, if X equals 7, then X **&&** 8 evaluates to true (1), whereas X **&** 8 evaluates to false (0).

Remember: Relational and logical operators always produce a result that is either 0 or 1, whereas the similar bitwise operations may produce any arbitrary value depending on the specific operation. In other words, bitwise operations may have values other than 0 or 1, while the logical operators will always evaluate to 0 or 1.

The Shift Operators

The shift operators, >> and <<, move all bits in a variable to the right or left, as indicated. The general form of the shift right statement follows.

variable >> number of bit positions

and the shift left statement is

variable << number of bit positions

As bits are shifted off one end, zeros are brought in at the other end. A shift is not the same as a rotate operation. (Creating a rotate operation is one of this chapter's exercises.) That is, the bits shifted off one end do not come back around to the other. Instead, the bits shifted off are lost, and zeros are brought in.

Bit-shift operations can be very useful when decoding external device input, like D/A convertors, and reading status information. The bitwise shift operators can also be used to perform very fast multiplication and division of integers. A shift right will effectively multiply a number by 2 and a shift left will divide it by 2.

The following program shows the effect of the shift operators. It produces the output shown in Figure 12-1.

```c
/* Example of bit shifting. */

#include "stdio.h"

void disp_binary(unsigned u);

main()
{
  int i=1, t;

  for(t=0; t<8; t++) {
    disp_binary(i);
    i = i << 1;
  }

  printf("\n");

  for(t=0; t<8; t++) {
    i = i >> 1;
    disp_binary(i);
  }
}
```

```
/* Display the bits within a byte. */
void disp_binary(unsigned u)
{
  register int t;

  for(t=128; t>0; t=t/2)
    if(u & t) printf("1 ");
    else printf("0 ");
  printf("\n");
}
```

THE ? OPERATOR

The ? operator can be used to replace **if/else** statements of the general form, as shown on the next page.

```
0 0 0 0 0 0 0 1
0 0 0 0 0 0 1 0
0 0 0 0 0 1 0 0
0 0 0 0 1 0 0 0
0 0 0 1 0 0 0 0
0 0 1 0 0 0 0 0
0 1 0 0 0 0 0 0
1 0 0 0 0 0 0 0

1 0 0 0 0 0 0 0
0 1 0 0 0 0 0 0
0 0 1 0 0 0 0 0
0 0 0 1 0 0 0 0
0 0 0 0 1 0 0 0
0 0 0 0 0 1 0 0
0 0 0 0 0 0 1 0
0 0 0 0 0 0 0 1
```

FIGURE 12-1 The output from the bit-shift program

if(*condition*)
   expression
else
   expression

The key restriction is that the target of both the **if** and the **else** must be a single expression—not another C statement.

The **?** is called a *ternary operator* because it requires three operands and takes the general form

   Exp1 ? *Exp2* : *Exp3*

where *Exp1, Exp2,* and *Exp3* are expressions. Notice the use and placement of the colon.

The value of a **?** expression is determined as follows. *Exp1* is evaluated; if it is true, *Exp2* is evaluated and becomes the value of the entire **?** expression. If *Exp1* is false, *Exp3* is evaluated and its value becomes the value of the expression. For example, consider:

```
while(something) {
  count = 20 ;

  done = count>0 ? 0 : 1;
  .
  .
  .

  if(done) break;

}
```

In this example, **done** will be assigned the value 0 until **count** is less than or equal to 0. The same code written using the **if/else** statement would be

```
while(something) {
  count = 20;

  if(count>0) done = 0;
  else done = 1;
  .
  .
  .
```

```
    if(done) break;
}
```

Here's an example of the ? operator in action. This program divides two numbers, but will not allow a division by zero.

```
/* This program uses the ? operator to prevent
   a division by zero. */

#include "stdio.h"
int div_zero(void);

main()
{
  int i, j, result;

  printf("Enter dividend and divisor: ");
  scanf("%d%d", &i, &j);

  /* this statement prevents a divide by zero error */
  result = j ? i/j : div_zero();

  printf("Result: %d", result);
}

div_zero(void)
{
  printf("cannot divide by zero\n");
  return 0;
}
```

C SHORTHAND

C has a special shorthand that simplifies the coding of a certain type of assignment statement. For example,

```
x = x+10;
```

can be written, in C shorthand, as the following illustrates.

```
x += 10;
```

The operator pair **+ =** tells the compiler to assign to **x** the value of **x** plus 10.

This shorthand will work for all the binary operators in C (that is, those that require two operands). The general form of the shorthand is

var op = *expression*;

For another example,

```
x = x-100;
```

is the same as

```
x -= 100;
```

You will see shorthand notation used widely in professionally written C programs and you should become familiar with it.

THE COMMA OPERATOR

You can see some examples of the comma operator in the **for** loop when it is used to allow multiple initialization or incrementation statements. However, the comma can be used as a part of any expression. It is used to string together several expressions. The value of a comma-separated list of expressions is the value of the rightmost expression. The value of the other expressions will be discarded. This means that the expression on the right side will become the value of the total comma-separated expression.

For example,

```
var = (count=19, incr=10, count+1);
```

first assigns **count** the value 19, assigns **incr** the value 10, and finally assigns **var** the value 20 (19+1) — the value produced by the entire comma expression. (The parentheses are necessary because the comma operator has a lower precedence than does the assignment operator.)

To actually see the effects of the comma operator, try this program:

```
#include "stdio.h"

main()
{
  int i, j;

  j = 10;

  i = (j++, j+100, 999);

  printf("%d", i);
}
```

It will print 999 on the screen.

Essentially, the comma's effect is to cause a sequence of operations to be performed. When it is used on the right side of an assignment statement, the value assigned is the value of the last expression of the comma-separated list. You can, in some ways, think of the comma operator as having the same meaning that the word "and" has in English as used in the phrase "do this and this and this."

A CLOSER LOOK AT
THE ASSIGNMENT OPERATOR

For most situations, assignments in C are intuitively understandable. However, there are a few special cases you should know about. First, the assignment operator may be successfully applied to both structures and unions. That is, it is possible to assign the contents of one

structure or union to another of the same type. You do not need to individually assign each field. For example, examine this program:

```c
#include "stdio.h"
#include "string.h"

main()
{
  struct s_type {
    int i;
    double d;
    char str[80];
  } s1, s2;

  union u_type {
    int i;
    double d;
  } u1, u2;

  s1.i = 10;
  s1.d = 100.123;
  strcpy(s1.str, "hello");

  u1.d = 123.0321;

  /* The next statement assigns one union to another. */
  u2 = u1;

  /* This statement assigns one structure to another. */
  s2 = s1;

  printf("%d %lf %s\n", s2.i, s2.d, s2.str);
  printf("%lf", u2.d);
}
```

The output from this program will confirm that the contents of **s1** and **u1** have been copied into **s2** and **u2**, respectively.

Note: Some older, non-ANSI standard compilers do not allow the assignment of a structure or union in the manner just shown. If you have reason to work with such a compiler you should keep this possibility in mind.

C allows a very convenient method of assigning many variables the same value using multiple assignments in a single statement. For example, this fragment assigns **count, incr,** and **index** the value 10.

```
count = incr = index = 10;
```

In professionally written programs, it is not uncommon to see variables assigned common values using this format.

PRECEDENCE SUMMARY

Table 12-2 lists the precedence of all C operators. Please note that all operators, except the unary operators and ?, associate from left to right. The unary operators, (*, &, −) and the ? operator associate from right to left.

EXERCISES

1. Although C supplies many bitwise operators, one important bit manipulation has been left out of C: the rotate. A rotate shifts the bits of a byte or word to the right or left and takes the bit shifted off the end and moves it to the other end. For example, 1101 0110 rotated one to the left becomes 1010 1101. Write a function that performs a left rotate operation on a byte. Hint: The easiest way to do this uses a union.

2. What is the outcome of the following bitwise operations?

    a. 1101 0110 & 0010 0101

    b. 0010 1100 ¦ 1010 0101

    c. 0011 1011 ˆ 0000 1111

3. Transform this fragment into its equivalent ? operator form.

```
if(x>100) y = 10;
else y = 20;
```

Highest	( ) [] –> .
	! ~ + + – – – (type cast) * & sizeof
	* / %
	+ –
	<< >>
	< <= > >=
	== !=
	&
	^
	|
	&&
	||
	?
	= += –= *= /=
Lowest	,

TABLE 12-2   Precedence of C Operators

4. What is the shorthand form of this statement?

```
x = x << 2;
```

5. What is **count** equal to after this assignment?

```
count = (10, 20, 30);
```

6. Will this fragment work?

```
struct A {
   int i;
   float f;
} al;
```

```
struct B {
  char str[80];
  double d;
} b1;

    .
    .
    .

a1 = b1;
```

Answers

1.
```
union rotate {
  char ch[2];
  unsigned int i;
} rot;

/* Rotate a byte. */
void rotate_it(union rotate *rot)
{
  rot->ch[1] = 0;   /* clear the high-order byte */

  rot->i = rot->i << 1;   /* shift once to the left */

  /* See if a bit has been shifted out of ch[0] -
     if so, put it on the other end.
  */
  if(rot->ch[1]) rot->i = rot->i | 1;   /* OR it back in */
}
```

2. a.   0000 0101
   b.   1010 1101
   c.   0011 0100

3.   y = x>100 ? 10: 20;

4.   x <<= 2;

5. 30

6. No, you cannot assign a structure of one type to a structure of another type. To assign complete structures, both must be of the same type.

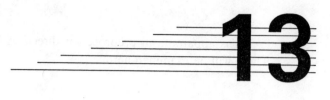

THE C
PREPROCESSOR

It is possible to include various instructions to the C compiler in the source code of a program. These are called *preprocessor directives*. Although not actually part of the C language, they expand the scope of the C programming environment. In addition to these directives some of C's built-in macros are also examined in this chapter.

The C preprocessor contains the following directives:

#if
#ifdef
#ifndef
#else
#elif
#include
#define
#undef
#line
#error
#pragma

As is apparent, all preprocessor directives begin with a # sign. These will be examined here.

#define

Although you have already been introduced to **#define**, it will be examined more closely now. As you recall, in its simplest form, **#define** is used to define an identifier and a string that will be substituted for the identifier each time it is encountered in the source file. The identifier is called the macro name and the replacement process is called macro substitution. The general form of the directive is

#define *macro-name string*

Notice that there is no semicolon in this statement. There may be any number of spaces between the identifier and the string, but once the string begins, it is only terminated by a newline character.

For example, you can define the word **SIZE** as the value 100.

```
#define SIZE 100
```

This will cause C to substitute the value 100 each time the macro name **SIZE** is encountered in your source file.

You can also use a macro name in place of a string. For example, this code fragment prints the string "BETA Test Copy 12."

```
#define BETA "BETA Test Copy 12"

printf(BETA);
```

Remember, however, that no text substitutions will occur if the macro name occurs within a string. For example,

```
printf("This is BETA version 0.9");
```

will be displayed as shown, with no substitution of the word "BETA."

It is common practice among C programmers to use capital letters for defined identifiers. This convention helps anyone reading the program to know at a glance that a macro substitution will take place. Also, it is best to put all **#define**s at the start of the file, or perhaps, in a separate include file, rather than sprinkling them throughout the program.

The most common usage of macro substitutions is to define names for "magic numbers" that occur in a program. For example, you may have a program that defines an array and has several routines that access that array. Instead of "hard coding" the array's size with a constant, it is better to define a value and use that name whenever the size of the array is needed. In this way, a change in only one place, plus a recompilation, is required to alter the size of the array if it needs to be changed. For example:

```
#define MAX_SIZE 100

float balance[MAX_SIZE];
```

The **#define** directive has another powerful feature: the macro name can have arguments. Each time the macro name is encountered, the arguments associated with it are replaced by the actual arguments found in the program. For example:

```
#include "stdio.h"

#define MIN(a,b)  ((a)<(b)) ? (a) : (b)

main()
{
  int x, y;

  x = 10;
  y = 20;
  printf("the minimum is: %d", MIN(x,y));
}
```

When this program is compiled, the expression defined by **MIN(a,b)** will be substituted, except that **x** and **y** will be used as the operands. In other words, the **printf( )** statement will be substituted as in the following:

```
printf("the minimum is: %d",((x)<(y)) ? (x) : (y));
```

The reason for the parentheses around **a** and **b** in the macro definition is to ensure that whatever expressions are substituted for **a** and **b** are fully evaluated. In some instances, leaving the parentheses off will cause erroneous results.

The use of macro substitutions in place of real functions has the benefit of increasing the speed of the code, since no overhead for a function call is incurred. However, sometimes increased speed is paid for with an increase in the size of the program because of duplicated code.

The C standard library actually defines several functions as macros. For example, in actuality, **getc( )** is a macro. However, from the programmer's perspective it is largely irrelevant whether a function is really a function or a macro since it makes no difference in the way it works.

Predefined Macro Names

The proposed ANSI standard specifies five built-in macro names. They are

> _ _LINE_ _
> _ _FILE_ _
> _ _DATE_ _
> _ _TIME_ _
> _ _STDC_ _

The _ _LINE_ _ macro contains a decimal value that corresponds to the currently compiling source line in your program.

The $\_\_$**FILE**$\_\_$ macro is a pointer to a string that contains the name of the source file.

The $\_\_$**DATE**$\_\_$ macro contains a string of the form

month/day/year

that is the date of the translation of the source file into object code.

The time of the translation of the source code into object code is contained as a string in $\_\_$**TIME**$\_\_$. The form of the string is

hour:minute:second

The macro $\_\_$**STDC**$\_\_$ contains the decimal constant 1, which means that the compiler conforms to the ANSI standard.

For the most part, these built-in macros are used in fairly complex programming environments where several different versions of a program—perhaps running on different computers—are developed or maintained. As a beginning C programmer it is good to be aware that these macros are available, but you will probably not need to use one for some time. Your compiler may also contain other built-in macros.

#error

The **#error** directive forces the C compiler to stop compilation when it is encountered. It is used primarily for debugging. The general form of the directive is

#error *error message*

The *error message* is not enclosed in double quotation marks. When the **#error** directive is encountered the error message is displayed, along with other information if so defined by the creator of the compiler.

#include

The **#include** preprocessor directive instructs the compiler to include another source file with the one that has the **#include** directive in it. The source file to be read in must be enclosed in double quotation marks or angle brackets. For example,

```
#include "stdio.h"
#include <stdio.h>
```

both angle brackets and quotation marks instruct the C compiler to read and compile the header for the disk file library routines.

It is valid for include files to have **#include** directives in them. These are referred to as "nested **include**s." The number of levels of nesting is implementation-dependent, but the ANSI standard specifies that at least eight levels of nested **#include**s be supported.

If the filename is enclosed by angle brackets, the file is searched for in a manner defined by the creator of the compiler. Often, this means searching some special directory set aside for **include** files. If the filename is enclosed in quotes, the file is looked for in another implementation-defined manner. For many implementations, this means searching the current working directory. If the file is not found, then the search is repeated as if the filename had been enclosed in angle brackets.

CONDITIONAL COMPILATION DIRECTIVES

There are several directives that allow you to selectively compile portions of your program's source code. The process of using these directives is called *conditional compilation* and is used widely by commercial software houses that provide and maintain many customized versions of one program.

#if, #else, #elif, and #endif

The general idea behind the **#if** is that if the constant expression following the **#if** is true, then the code that is between it and an

#endif will be compiled. Otherwise it will be skipped over. **#endif** is used to mark the end of an **#if** block.

The general form of **#if** is

#if *constant expression*
     statement sequence
#endif

If the constant expression is true, the block of code will be compiled; otherwise it will be skipped.

The use of the **#if** is very helpful when debugging. For example, you can keep debug code in your program and have it included in the compiled version whenever you need it. This concept is illustrated by the following program:

```
#include "stdio.h"

#define DEBUG 1

main()
{
  int i, j;

  for(i=0; i<10; i++)
    for(j=0; j<10; j++) {
#if DEBUG
      printf("%d %d\n", i, j);
#endif
      /* do something */
    }
}
```

When **DEBUG** is set to any value other than 0, then the debug code is compiled. To remove the debug code, set **DEBUG** to 0.

This example shows another important point. The expression that follows the **#if** is evaluated at compile time. Therefore, it must contain only identifiers that have been previously defined and constants—no variables may be used.

You can use any of the relational and logical operators in an **#if** statement. For example, the previous program could be rewritten so that two different levels of debugging information could be conditionally displayed, as shown here:

```
#include "stdio.h"

#define DEBUG 1

main()
{
  int i, j;

  for(i=0; i<10; i++)
    for(j=0; j<10; j++) {
#if DEBUG == 1
      /* debug level 1 */
      printf("%d %d\n", i, j);
#endif
#if DEBUG == 2
      /* debug level 2 */
      printf("%d ", i*j);
#endif
      /* do something */
    }
}
```

The **#else** works in much the same way as the **else** that forms part of the C language: it establishes an alternative if the **#if** fails. The following program uses the value of **ANSI** to allow the program to be compiled by both ANSI-standard and non-ANSI-standard compilers. (Remember, non-standard compilers cannot process the modern function declaration form or prototypes.)

```
#include "stdio.h"

#define ANSI 1

#if ANSI
void mult(int a, int b);
#endif
```

```
main()
{
  mult(10, 20);
}

#if ANSI
void mult(int a, int b)
{
  printf("%d", a * b);
}

#else
mult(a, b)
int a, b;
{
  printf("%d", a * b);
}
#endif
```

As the program is shown, it can be compiled only by an ANSI-standard compiler. However, if you set the value of **ANSI** to 0, the program can be compiled by a non-standard compiler.

Notice that the **#else** is used to mark both the end of the **#if** block and the beginning of the **#else** block. This is necessary because there can be only one **#endif** associated with any **#if**.

The **#elif** means "else if" and is used to establish an "if/else/if" sequence for multiple compilation options. The **#elif** is followed by a constant expression. If the expression is true, that block of code is compiled and no other **#elif** expressions are tested. Otherwise, the next in the series is checked. The general form is

> #if *expression*
>   *statement sequence*
> #elif *expression 1*
>   *statement sequence*
> #elif *expression 2*
>   *statement sequence*
> #elif *expression 3*
>   *statement sequence*
> #elif *expression 4*

.

.

.

```
#elif expression N
  statement sequence
#endif
```

For example, this fragment uses the value of **TZONE** to tell the user what adjustments are needed in interpreting the time:

```
#include "stdio.h"

#define EST 0
#define CST 1
#define MNT 2
#define PAC 3

#define TZONE CST

main()
{
  printf("Times shown in the program are ");
#if TZONE == EST
  printf("normal\n");
#elif TZONE == CST
  printf("early by 1 hour\n");
#elif TZONE == MNT
  printf("early by 2 hours\n");
#else
  printf("early by 3 hours\n");
#endif
}
```

#ifdef and #ifndef

Another method of conditional compilation uses the directives **#ifdef** and **#ifndef**, which mean "if defined" and "if not defined," respectively.

The general form of **#ifdef** is

```
#ifdef macro name
    statement sequence
#endif
```

If the *macro name* has been previously defined in a **#define** statement, the statement sequence between the **#ifdef** and **#endif** will be compiled.

The general form of **#ifndef** is

```
#ifndef macro name
    statement sequence
#endif
```

If *macro name* is currently undefined by a **#define** statement, the block of code is compiled.

Both **#ifdef** and **#ifndef** can use an **#else** statement but not an **#elif**. For example,

```
#include "stdio.h"

#define FRANCE

main()
{
#ifdef US
  printf("compiled for U.S.A.\n");
#endif
#ifdef UK
  printf("compiled for U. K.\n");
#endif
#ifdef FRANCE
  printf("compiled for France\n");
#endif

#ifndef GERMAN
    printf("no German version\n");
#endif
}
```

will display

```
compiled for France
no German version
```

As this program shows, you do not have to give a defined macro a value if you simply want to use **#ifdef** or **#ifndef** with it.

You may nest **#ifdef**s and **#ifndef**s to at least eight levels.

#undef

The **#undef** directive is used to remove an earlier definition of the macro name that follows it. The general form is

#undef *macro name*

For example:

```
#define VERT 20
#define HORIZ 10

char matrix[VERT][HORIZ];

#undef VERT
#undef HORIZ
```

Both **VERT** and **HORIZ** are defined until the **#undef** statements are encountered.

The principal use of **#undef** is to allow macro names to be localized to only those sections of code that need them.

#line

The **#line** directive is used to change the values of _ _ **LINE** _ _ and _ _ **FILE** _ _. The basic form of the command is

#line *number* "*filename*"

where *number* is any positive integer and the optional *filename* is any valid file identifier. The line number is the number of the current source line and the filename is the name of the source file. **#line** is primarily used for debugging purposes and special applications.

For example, the following specifies that the line count will begin with 100. The **printf( )** statement displays the number 102 because it is the third line in the program after the **#line 100** statement.

```
#include "stdio.h"

#line 100    /* reset the line counter */
main()       /* line 100 */
{            /* line 101 */
  printf("%d\n",__LINE__);  /* line 102 */
}
```

#pragma

The **#pragma** directive is an implementation-defined directive that allows various instructions, defined by the compiler's designer, to be given to the compiler. The general form of the **#pragma** directive is

#pragma *name*

where *name* is the name of the **#pragma** you want. If a **#pragma** is encountered that the compiler does not recognize, it is ignored.

THE # AND ## PREPROCESSOR OPERATORS

ANSI C provides two preprocessor operators: **#** and **##**. These operators are used when a macro defines a function. As a beginner you may have little or no use for these operators, but the brief discussion that follows will give you the flavor of their usage.

The *#* operator causes the argument it precedes to be turned into a quoted string. For example, consider this program:

```
#include "stdio.h"

#define mkstr(s)   # s

main()
{
  printf(mkstr(hello));
}
```

The C preprocessor turns the line

```
printf(mkstr(hello));
```

into

```
printf("hello");
```

The *##* operator is used to concatenate two tokens, as in the following example:

```
#include "stdio.h"

#define concat(a, b)   a ## b

main()
{
  int xy = 10;

  printf("%d", concat(x, y));
}
```

Here the preprocessor transforms

```
printf("%d", concat(x, y));
```

into

```
printf("%d", xy);
```

If these operators seem strange to you, keep in mind that they are not needed or used in most C programs. They exist primarily to allow some special cases to be handled by the preprocessor.

EXERCISES

1. Define **COUNT** as having a value of 100, **STRING** as "This is a string," and **DEBUG** as having no value.

2. Show the macro equivalent of this function:

```
int abs(int i)
{
  if(i<0) return -i;
  else return i;
}
```

3. Write a program that prints the time and date when it was compiled.

4. What is wrong with this code?

```
#define COUNT 10
  .
  .
  .
#ifdef COUNT<100
  .
  .
  .
#endif
```

5. Is this valid code?

```
#define COUNT 100
#define MAX    COUNT+1
```

6. On your own, experiment with the various preprocessor directives.

Answers

1.
```
#define COUNT 100
#define STRING "This is a string"
#define DEBUG
```

2.
```
#define abs(i) (i) < 0 ? -(i) : (i)
```

3.
```
#include "stdio.h"

main()
{
   printf("%s %s", __TIME__, __DATE__);
}
```

4. The **#ifdef** directive cannot be used with a comparison—it only can be used to determine if a macro is defined or not.

5. Yes, once a macro has been defined, it can be used to define others.

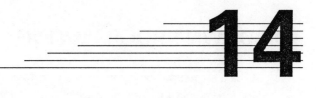

WRITING A C PROGRAM

So far, the examples in this book have, of necessity, been fairly short and simple. Now it's time to see a larger example. It is not enough to simply know the C syntax—you must also be able to effectively design your C programs. This chapter develops a mailing list program with an emphasis on design procedures and style.

There are three general approaches to writing a program: *top-down, bottom-up,* and *ad hoc.* In the top-down approach you start with the top-level routine and move down to the low-level routines. The bottom-up approach works in the opposite direction; you start with specific routines and build them progressively into more complex structures, ending at the top-level routine. The ad hoc approach has no predetermined method. The top-down approach is generally considered the best and it is the only method that will be used here.

TOP-DOWN PROGRAMMING

C as a structured language lends itself to a top-down approach. The top-down method can produce clean, readable code that is easily maintained. It also helps you clarify the overall structure and operation of the program before you code low-level functions. This can reduce time wasted by false starts.

The top-down approach to programming is similar to outlining. You start with the general idea and move progressively towards the more specific.

A good way to start to design any program is to determine exactly what the program is going to do at the top level. This corresponds loosely to determining the main headings of an outline. For example, the mailing list program developed in this chapter can perform the following tasks.

- Add a new address to the list.

- Delete an address from the list.

- Print the list.

- Search for an address.

- Save the list to a disk file.

- Load the list from a disk file.

- Quit the program.

These operations form the basis of the functions in the program.

After the work of the program has been defined, you can begin to design the *main loop* of the program. The main loop of a program is that portion of code that essentially drives the application. An easy way to sketch out the main loop is to use pseudo-code. For example, the main loop of the mailing list program can be outlined as in the following.

```
do {
   display menu
   get user selection
   process the selection
} while selection does not equal quit
```

The use of this type of algorithmic notation can help you clarify the general structure of your program even before you sit down at the computer. C-type syntax has been used because it is familiar, but any type of syntax is acceptable.

Once you have the main loop defined, you can begin to expand the definition of each element. For example, the "process the selection" element can be expanded this way:

```
switch(user-selection) {
   case 1: enter( ); /* enter a new entry */
     break;
   case 2: delete( ); /* delete an existing entry */
    break;
   case 3: show_list( ); /* display the list */
     break;
   case 4: search( ); /* find an entry */
     break;
   case 5: save( ); /* save list to disk */
     break;
   case 6: load( ); /* read list from disk */
     break;
   case 7: exit(0);
}
```

Once you have the main loop well defined (even if just in pseudo-code), you should sketch out each functional area using the same approach as with the main loop. For example, the function that saves the list to a disk file can be defined as

```
save {
  open disk file
  write data to disk
  close disk file
}
```

Notice that the definition does not mention data structure or variables. This is intentional. At this point you are only interested in defining what your program will do, not how it will actually do it. This definition process will help you decide on what the actual structure of data will be.

Once you have outlined how each major part of your program will work, it is time to choose its main data structures.

STRUCTURING DATA

The selection of both the data structure and its implementation is critical because they each help determine the design limits of your program. Generally, what the program does helps define the structure of the data it will use.

Consider the mailing list example. Since an address is a collection of several related objects, using a structure to hold each address immediately suggests itself. Further, since you will need a list of these structures, an array of structures seems a logical choice. Thus the following structure type and array are called for.

```
struct addr {
  char name[30];
  char street[40];
  char city[20];
  char state[3];
  char zip[10]; /* hold US and Canadian zips */
} list[MAX];
```

You can set the value of **MAX** according to the number of addresses you want to store.

Now that the general operation of the program and representation of data used by it have been defined, it is time to begin writing the program.

THE main( ) FUNCTION

You are now ready to create the **main( )** function. The **main( )** function is almost a direct translation from the outline. It is very easy for anyone reading the program to see exactly what the program does.

```
main()
{
  int choice;

  init_list();  /* initialize the list */

  for(;;) {
    choice = menu_select();  /* get user's selection */
    switch(choice) {
      case 1: enter();  /* enter a new entry */
        break;
      case 2: delete(); /* delete an existing entry */
        break;
      case 3: show_list();  /* display the list */
        break;
      case 4: search(); /* find an entry */
        break;
      case 5: save();  /* save list to disk */
        break;
      case 6: load();  /* read list from disk */
        break;
      case 7: exit(0);
    }
  }
}
```

Even though descriptive names were chosen for the main functions **enter( )**, **delete( )**, **show_list( )**, **search( )**, **save( )**, and **load( )**,

adding comments helps clarify what each case does. Anyone reading the program can easily find the correct function to examine in each program area.

The **init _ list( )** function initializes the **list** array. The mailing list program assumes that if the first character in the **name** field of a structure is null, the entire structure is unused. The **init_ list( )** function puts a null at the start of each **name** field, as shown here:

```
/* Initialize the list by putting a null into the
   first character of the name field.
*/
void init_list(void)
{
  register int i;

  for(i=0; i<MAX; i++) *list[i].name = '\0';
}
```

The **menu _ select( )** function looks like this:

```
/* Return user's menu selection. */
menu_select(void)
{
  char s[80];
  int c;

  printf("1. Enter a name\n");
  printf("2. Delete a name\n");
  printf("3. List the file\n");
  printf("4. Search\n");
  printf("5. Save the file\n");
  printf("6. Load the file\n");
  printf("7. Quit\n");

  do {
    printf("\nEnter your choice: ");
    gets(s);
    c = atoi(s);
  } while(c<0 || c>7);
  return c;
}
```

It will prompt and loop until a valid selection is made.

When you write programs, remember that someone has to use them. It is very important to trap invalid input. In this case, only a response between 1 and 7 is allowed. This helps prevent unpleasant surprises when using the program.

DEFINING enter( )

The **enter( )** function is used to input a new name and address into the list. It first calls a support function called **find _ free( )** to find an open structure in the array. It then calls **inputs( )** to prompt the user for input for each field. The **inputs( )** function performs three tasks: (1) it displays the specified prompting message, (2) it inputs the user's response, and (3) it checks the length of that response against the maximum specified in its **count** parameter. If the user's response is too long, the user is reprompted. The **enter( )** function continues to input addresses until the user enters a blank line when prompted for the name.

The **enter( )**, **find _ free( )**, and **inputs( )** functions are shown here:

```
/* Enter name and address. */
void enter(void)
{
  int i;
  for(;;) {
    i = find_free();  /* find a free structure */
    if(i<0) {
      printf("list full\n");
      return;
    }

    inputs("enter name: ", list[i].name, 30);
    if(!*list[i].name) break;  /* stop entering */
    inputs("enter street: ", list[i].street, 40);
    inputs("enter city: ", list[i].city, 20);
    inputs("enter state: ", list[i].state, 3);
    inputs("enter zip: ", list[i].zip, 10);
  }
}
```

```
/* Return the index of a free structure. If none
   are free, return -1. */
find_free(void)
{
  register int i;

  for(i=0; i<MAX; i++)
    if(!*list[i].name) return i;

  return -1;
}

/* This function will input a string up to
   the length in count.  This will prevent
   the string from overrunning its space and
   displaying a prompting message. */
void inputs(char *prompt, char *s, int count)
{
  char str[255];

  do {
    printf(prompt);
    gets(str);
    if(strlen(str)>=count) printf("\ntoo long\n");
  } while(strlen(str)>=count);
  strcpy(s, str);
}
```

DEFINING delete( )

The **delete( )** function is used to remove an entry from the mailing
list. To remove an entry, first enter the name. The **delete( )** function
will then call **find( )** with the name. The **find( )** function searches the
list until it either finds a match or reaches the end of the list. If a
match is found, its index is returned. Otherwise, a −1, indicating no
match, is returned. If **find( )** is successful, the entry is deleted by
putting a null value in the first character of the **name** field.

```
/* This function removes an address from the list. */
void delete(void)
{
  int i;
  char str[255];

  inputs("enter name: ", str ,30);
  i = find(str);
  if(i>=0) *list[i].name = '\0';
  else printf("not found\n");
}

/* Find a name and return its index.  Return -1
   if name not found.
*/
find(char *name)
{
  int i;

  for(i=0; i<MAX; i++)
    if(!strcmp(name, list[i].name)) break;

  if(i==MAX) return -1;  /* not found */
  else return i;
}
```

Notice that **inputs( )** was used to enter the name to be deleted. This is the advantage of a generalized function—it can be used over and over again.

PRINTING THE MAILING LIST

Most mailing lists generate mailing labels. However, the ANSI standard does not define any function that writes to the printer. Because the exact method of accessing the printer can vary widely (based on the operating system and C compiler used), this program will simply print the mailing list to the screen of your computer. However, you are encouraged to examine your C compiler's user manual for the library function that sends output to the printer.

The **show_list( )** function is used to print the mailing list. It checks the **name** field in each structure in the **list** array. If it does not begin with a null, then it must contain an address, in which case it is printed. The actual output of the information is done by **display( )**. As you will see, **display( )** is also used by the search routine, thus avoiding duplicate code.

```
/* Display the list. */
void show_list(void)
{
  int i;

  for(i=0; i<MAX; i++) {
   if(*list[i].name) {
    display(i);
    printf("\n\n");
   }
  }
  printf("\n\n");
}
/* Actually output the names and addresses. */
void display(int i)
{
  printf("%s\n", list[i].name);
  printf("%s\n", list[i].street);
  printf("%s %s %s", list[i].city, list[i].state,
list[i].zip);
}
```

FINDING A NAME IN THE MAILING LIST

A mailing list is often used to look up a person's address. The **search( )** function performs this task. To use **search( )**, enter the name you want to find. Again, **inputs( )** is used to input the name. The name is searched for by using **find( )**, described earlier. If a match is found, the address information is displayed using **display( )**.

```
/* Search the list. */
void search(void)
{
```

```
    int i;
    char name[30];

    inputs("enter name to find: ", name, 30);
    if((i=find(name))<0) printf("not found\n");
    else display(i);
}
```

SAVING AND LOADING THE LIST

To save the mailing list to disk, the function **save( )** is needed. In this simple version, the name "mlist" is permanently coded as the filename. The list is saved as a binary file in a single write operation using **fwrite( )**.

```
/* Save the list. */
void save(void)
{
  FILE *fp;

  if((fp=fopen("mlist", "wb"))==NULL) {
    printf("cannot open file\n");
    return;
  }

  printf("\nsaving file\n");
  fwrite(list, sizeof list, 1, fp);
  if(ferror(fp))
    printf("An error occurred while writing file.\n");
  fclose(fp);
}
```

This function actually writes the entire **list** array to disk, which means if most of **list** is not used, substantial disk space is wasted. You might find it interesting to change the function so that only elements of the array containing address information are saved. (If you try this, be sure to change **load( )**, which is shown next.)

The **load( )** function loads the **list** array using one **fread( )** call.

```
/* Load the list. */
void load(void)
{
  FILE *fp;

  if((fp=fopen("mlist", "rb"))==NULL) {
    printf("cannot open file\n");
    return;
  }

  printf("\nloading file\n");
  fread(list, sizeof list, 1, fp);
  if(ferror(fp))
    printf("An error occurred while reading file.\n");
  fclose(fp);
}
```

LIMITATIONS

Several limitations have been built into this program. Most keep the example simple, but some were specific design decisions. Either way, a good programmer must be aware of the limitations as well as the capabilities of a program.

One obvious limitation of the program is in the data structure itself. There is only room for one name and one street. This is fine for many addresses, but often businesses need two name and two street lines. A second name line can also allow a "To the attention of" line. You might want to try adding additional fields.

Because a statically allocated array is used, the number of addresses it holds is permanently fixed (unless you recompile the program, of course). This is fine for a simple example; however, you will probably want to use some sort of dynamic allocation scheme, such as linked lists, to allow the program to store long lists of varying lengths.

Currently the program has no way of sorting the mailing list. In this sense, the design of the program may not meet the needs of most users. However, this limitation may not matter to someone who does not need a sorted list. Remember who will use the program; keep your audience in mind. Even if you will be the final user, you

must satisfy your own needs. The construction of linked lists and sorting algorithms can be found in *Advanced C* by Herbert Schildt (Berkeley, Ca.: Osborne/McGraw-Hill, 1988).

FULL PROGRAM LISTING

For your convenience, the entire mailing list program is listed here:

```c
/* A simple mailing list program. */

#include "stdio.h"
#include "stdlib.h"
#include "string.h"

#define MAX 100

struct addr {
  char name[30];
  char street[40];
  char city[20];
  char state[3];
  char zip[10]; /* hold US and Canadian zips */
} list[MAX];

void load(void),save(void),search(void),display(int i);
void inputs(char *prompt, char *s, int count);
void delete(void), enter(void), show_list(void);
int find(char *name), menu_select(void);
void init_list(void);
int find_free(void);

main()
{
  int choice;

  init_list();  /* initialize the list */

  for(;;) {
    choice = menu_select(); /* get user's selection */
    switch(choice) {
```

```
        case 1: enter();   /* enter a new entry */
          break;
        case 2: delete(); /* delete existing entry */
          break;
        case 3: show_list();   /* display the list */
          break;
        case 4: search(); /* find an entry */
          break;
        case 5: save();   /* save list to disk */
          break;
        case 6: load();   /* read list from disk */
          break;
        case 7: exit(0);
      }
    }
}

/* Return user's menu selection. */
menu_select(void)
{
  char s[80];
  int c;

  printf("1. Enter a name\n");
  printf("2. Delete a name\n");
  printf("3. List the file\n");
  printf("4. Search\n");
  printf("5. Save the file\n");
  printf("6. Load the file\n");
  printf("7. Quit\n");

  do {
    printf("\nEnter your choice: ");
    gets(s);
    c = atoi(s);
  } while(c<0 || c>7);
  return c;
}

/* Enter name and address. */
void enter(void)
{
  int i;
```

```
    for(;;) {
      i = find_free();  /* find a free structure */
      if(i<0) {
        printf("list full\n");
        return;
      }

      inputs("enter name: ", list[i].name, 30);
      if(!*list[i].name) break;  /* stop entering */
      inputs("enter street: ", list[i].street, 40);
      inputs("enter city: ", list[i].city, 20);
      inputs("enter state: ", list[i].state, 3);
      inputs("enter zip: ", list[i].zip, 10);
    }
}

/* Return the index of a free structure. If none
   are free, return -1. */
find_free(void)
{
  register int i;

  for(i=0; i<MAX; i++)
    if(!*list[i].name) return i;

  return -1;
}

/* This function will input a string up to
   the length in count.  This will prevent
   the string from overrunning its space and
   display a prompting message. */
void inputs(char *prompt, char *s, int count)
{
  char str[255];

  do {
    printf(prompt);
    gets(str);
    if(strlen(str)>=count) printf("\ntoo long\n");
  } while(strlen(str)>=count);
  strcpy(s, str);
}
```

```
/* This function removes an address from the list. */
void delete(void)
{
  int i;
  char str[255];

  inputs("enter name: ", str ,30);
  i = find(str);
  if(i>=0) *list[i].name = '\0';
  else printf("not found\n");
}

/* Find a name and return its index.  Return -1
   if name not found.
*/
find(char *name)
{
  int i;

  for(i=0; i<MAX; i++)
    if(!strcmp(name, list[i].name)) break;

  if(i==MAX) return -1;  /* not found */
  else return i;
}

/* Display the list. */
void show_list(void)
{
  int i;

  for(i=0; i<MAX; i++) {
    if(*list[i].name) {
      display(i);
      printf("\n\n");
    }
  }
  printf("\n\n");
}

/* Actually output the names and addresses. */
void display(int i)
```

```
{
    printf("%s\n", list[i].name);
    printf("%s\n", list[i].street);
    printf("%s %s %s", list[i].city,
           list[i].state, list[i].zip);
}

/* Search the list. */
void search(void)
{
    int i;
    char name[30];

    inputs("enter name to find: ", name, 30);
    if((i=find(name))<0) printf("not found\n");
    else display(i);
}

/* Initialize the list by putting a null into the
   first character of the name field.
*/
void init_list(void)
{
    register int i;

    for(i=0; i<MAX; i++) *list[i].name = '\0';
}

/* Save the list. */
void save(void)
{
    FILE *fp;

    if((fp=fopen("mlist", "wb"))==NULL) {
        printf("cannot open file\n");
        return;
    }

    printf("\nsaving file\n");
    fwrite(list, sizeof list, 1, fp);
    if(ferror(fp))
        printf("An error occurred while writing file.\n");
    fclose(fp);
}
```

```
/* Load the list. */
void load(void)
{
  FILE *fp;

  if((fp=fopen("mlist", "rb"))==NULL) {
    printf("cannot open file\n");
    return;
  }

  printf("\nloading file\n");
  fread(list, sizeof list, 1, fp);
  if(ferror(fp))
    printf("An error occurred while reading file.\n");
  fclose(fp);
}
```

EXERCISES

1. Compile and run the mailing list program described in this chapter and experiment with it.

2. Rewrite the structure **addr** so that it accommodates two name fields.

3. Show how to rewrite the **save( )** and **load( )** functions so that only those elements that actually contain addresses are saved and loaded from the disk file.

4. On your own, modify the program so the second name field is used.

5. On your own, find a way to make output go to the printer.

Answers

2.
```c
struct addr {
    char name1[30];
    char name2[30];
    char street[40];
    char city[20];
    char state[3];
    char zip[10]; /* hold US and Canadian zips */
} list[MAX];
```

3.
```c
/* Save the list. */
void save(void)
{
    FILE *fp;
    register int i;
    if((fp=fopen("mlist", "wb"))==NULL) {
        printf("cannot open file\n");
        return;
    }

    printf("\nsaving file\n");

    for(i=0; i<MAX; i++) {
        if(*list[i].name)
            fwrite(&list[i], sizeof(struct addr), 1, fp);
        if(ferror(fp)) {
            printf("An error occurred while writing file.\n");
            break;
        }
    }
    fclose(fp);
}

/* Load the list. */
void load(void)
{
    FILE *fp;
    register int i;
```

```c
if((fp=fopen("mlist", "rb"))==NULL) {
  printf("cannot open file\n");
  return;
}

printf("\nloading file\n");

for(i=0; i<MAX && !feof(fp); i++) {
  fread(&list[i], sizeof(struct addr), 1, fp);
  if(ferror(fp)) {
    printf("An error occurred while reading file.\n");
    break;
  }
}
fclose(fp);
}
```

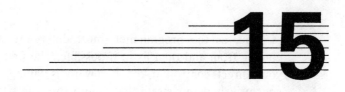

15

COMMON ERRORS

If you have made it this far you can definitely call yourself a C programmer! To conclude this book, let's look at a few common errors that plague newcomers to C. C is very robust. It has very little run time error-checking or reporting built directly into the language. Unlike BASIC, for example, which will issue a "cannot open file" message if a disk request fails, C will do nothing, unless you have expressly checked for that condition in your program. Thus, some errors are very hard to find.

There are three general categories of reasons why a program will not run correctly:

- Hardware failures

- User input data errors

- Software errors

You, as the programmer, must determine where the error is coming from and then fix it, if possible. The first category is beyond your direct control; if the hardware is failing, all you can do is conclusively demonstrate that failure so it can be fixed. However, as the programmer you can control the other two categories. Your programs should not allow user input errors to cause the program to malfunction. They should trap such input before it can cause a problem. Finally, the responsibility to produce bug-free code rests on you.

You may assume that you can easily remedy most syntax errors reported by your compiler. But having a syntactically correct program is only the first step. Your program must do what you want it to. The rest of this chapter will discuss the most common ways that errors creep into your code, plus a few unusual syntax errors.

INCREMENT AND DECREMENT OPERATOR ERRORS

The increment and decrement operators are used in most programs written in C. Remember that the order in which the operation takes place is affected by whether the operator precedes or follows the variable. Consider the following:

```
y = 10;    y = 10;

x = y++;   x = ++y;
```

These two statements are not the same. The first assigns the value of 10 to x and then increments y. The second increments y to 11 and then assigns the value 11 to x. Therefore, in the first case, x contains 10; in the second, x contains 11.

The increment and decrement operations will occur before other operations if they precede the operand; otherwise they will happen afterward.

If you are new to C programming, incorrect use of these operators can be very hard to find. Look for clues such as loops that don't run right or routines that are off by one. Another way to catch these

errors is to use a source level debugger (if one is available for your environment) to monitor your program while it executes.

POINTER PROBLEMS

A very common error in C programs is the misuse of pointers. Pointer problems fall into two general categories. The first is misuse caused by a misunderstanding of indirection and the pointer operators. The second category is the accidental use of invalid pointers. The solution to the first problem is to understand how pointers are implemented in C. The solution to the second is to always verify the validity of a pointer before it is used.

The following is a typical error that beginning C programmers make. *Do not attempt to run this program.*

```
#include "stdio.h"
#include "stdlib.h"

main()  /* this program is WRONG */
{
  char *p;

  *p = malloc(100); /* this line is wrong */

  gets(p);

  printf(p);
}
```

This program will most likely crash, probably taking the operating system with it as well. The reason is that the address returned by **malloc( )** was assigned, not to **p**, but to the memory location pointed to by **p**, which in this case is completely unknown. This is most certainly not what is wanted. To make this program correct you must substitute

```
p = malloc(100); /* this is correct */
```

for the wrong line.

However, the program also has a second, and more insidious, error. There is no run time check on the address returned by **malloc( )**. Remember, if memory is exhausted, then **malloc( )** will return 0, which is never a valid pointer in C. The malfunction caused by this type of bug is difficult to find because it will occur only rarely, when an allocation request fails. The best way to handle this is to prevent it. Here is a corrected version of the program, which includes a check for pointer validity.

```
#include "stdio.h"
#include "stdlib.h"

main()   /* this program is now correct */
{
  char *p;

  p = malloc(100); /* this is correct */

  if(!p) {
    printf("out of memory\n");
    exit(1);
  }

  gets(p);

  printf(p);
}
```

The terrible thing about "wild" pointers is that they are very difficult to track down. If you are making assignments to a pointer variable that does not contain a valid pointer address, your program may function correctly some of the time and crash other times. Also, statistically speaking, the smaller your program the more likely it will run correctly with a stray pointer. When very little of the computer's memory is in use, chances are a wild pointer will not use memory already allocated to your program. As your program grows, however, failures will become more common because the odds increase of a

wild pointer pointing to an important part of RAM. But, by the time the failures begin, you will be thinking about current additions or changes to your program, not about pointer errors. Hence, you will tend to look in the wrong spot for the bug.

The best way to recognize a pointer problem is by errors that tend to be erratic. Your program will work correctly one time, and fail the next. Sometimes other variables will contain garbage for no apparent reason. If these problems begin to occur, check your pointers. As a matter of procedure you should always check all pointers when bugs begin to occur.

Remember: Although pointers can be troublesome, they are also one of the most powerful and useful aspects of the C language and worth whatever trouble they may occasionally cause you. Make the effort early on to learn to use them correctly.

One final point to remember about pointers is that you must initialize them before they are used. This seems simple enough to remember, but many excellent C programmers will fail to do so from time to time. Consider the following code fragment:

```
int *x;

*x = 100;
```

This code would be a disaster because you don't know where **x** is pointing, and assigning a value to that unknown location would probably destroy something of value — like other code or data for your program.

BIZARRE SYNTAX ERRORS

Once in a while you will see a syntax error that you cannot understand, or that does not appear to be an error at all. Sometimes, the C compiler itself may have a bug that causes it to report false errors. The only way around that is to redesign your code. Finding other unusual errors may simply require some backtracking on your part.

One particularly unsettling error will occur when you try to compile the following code.

```
char *myfunc();   /* myfunc() returns a
                   char pointer */
main()
{


    .
     .
      .

 }


myfunc()
{
    .
     .
      .

}
```

Most compilers will issue an error message similar to "function redefined" and point to **myfunc( )**. How can this be when there is only one **myfunc( )**? The answer is that you declared **myfunc( )** to return a character pointer at the top of the program. This caused a symbol table entry to be made with that information. When the compiler encountered the **myfunc( )** function later in the program, there was no indication that it was to return anything other than an integer, the default type. Thus you were "redefining" the function. The correct program would be

```
char *myfunc();   /* myfunc() returns a
                   char pointer */

main()
{
  .
   .
    .
}

char *myfunc()
{
```

```
        .
        .
        .
}
```

   Another confusing syntax error can be generated with the following code:

```
main() /* this program has a syntax error in it */
{
   func1();
}

func1();
{
   printf("this is func1 \n");
}
```

The semicolon after the declaration of **func1( )** causes the error. The
compiler will see this as a statement outside of any function, which is
an error. However, various compilers will report this error differently. Many compilers will issue an error message such as "bad
declaration syntax" while pointing at the first open brace after
func1( ). Because you are used to seeing semicolons after statements, it might be difficult to see the source of the error.

ONE-OFF ERRORS

As you know, all C indexes start at zero. A common error involves
the use of a **for** loop to access the elements of an array. Consider the
following program, which is supposed to initialize an array of 100
integers:

```
main()  /* this program will not work */
{
   int x, num[100];

   for(x=1; x<=100; ++x) num[x]=x;
}
```

The **for** loop in this program is wrong in two ways. First, it will not initialize **num[0]**, the first element of array **num**. Second, it goes one past the end of the array, because **num[99]** is the last element in the array and the loop runs to 100. The correct way to write this program is

```
main()  /* this is right */
{
  int x, num[100];

  for(x=0; x<100; ++x) num[x] = x;
}
```

Remember, an array of 100 has elements 0 through 99.

BOUNDARY ERRORS

C and many standard library functions have very little or no run time bounds-checking. For example, it is possible to overwrite arrays, disk files, and, through pointer assignments, any variable. This type of error is unusual, but when it occurs it can be very difficult to link the symptom with the cause.

For example, consider the following program, which is supposed to read a string from the keyboard and display it on the screen.

```
#include "stdio.h"

main()
{
  int var1;
  char s[10];
  int var2;

  var1 = 10;  var2 = 10;

  get_string(s);
  printf("%s %d %s", s, var1, var2);
}
```

```
get_string(char *string)
{
  register int t;

  printf("enter twenty characters\n");

  for(t=0; t<20; ++t) *s++=getche();
}
```

Here, there are no direct coding errors. Indirectly, however, calling **get_string( )** with **s** will cause a bug. Here, **s** is declared to be 10 characters long, but **get_string( )** will read 20 characters. This will cause **s** to be overwritten. The real problem is that **s** may display all 20 characters, but either **var1** or **var2** will not contain the correct value. This happens because virtually all C compilers must allocate a region of memory for local variables, usually the stack region. The variables **var1**, **var2**, and **s** will be located in memory as shown in Figure 15-1.

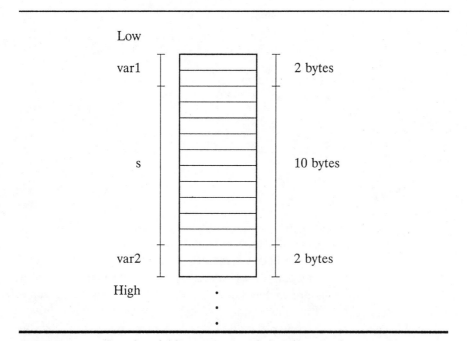

FIGURE 15-1   Local variables **var1**, **s**, and **var2** in a stack

Your C compiler may exchange the order of **var1** and **var2**, but they will still bracket **s**. When **s** is overwritten, the additional information is placed into the area that is supposed to be **var2**, destroying any previous contents. Therefore, instead of printing the number 10 for both integer variables, the one destroyed by the overrun of **s** will display something else. This will cause you to look for the problem in the wrong place.

FUNCTION PROTOTYPE OMISSIONS

Anytime a function returns a value type other than integer, the function must be declared as such by using its prototype. If you do not include a function's prototype, the compiler will assume that it returns an integer—whether it does or not. Consider the following program, which multiplies two floating-point numbers:

```
#include "stdio.h"

main() /* this is wrong */
{
  float x, y;

  scanf("%f%f", &x, &y);
  printf("%f", mul(x, y));
}

float mul(float a, float b)
{
  return a*b;
}
```

Here, **main( )** will be expecting an integer value back from **mul( )**, but **mul( )** will return a floating-point number. You will get meaningless answers because **main( )** will only copy 2 bytes out of the 4 generally needed for a **float**. Although C will catch this error if these functions are in the same file, it cannot if they are in separately compiled modules and no prototype for **mul( )** was included. In fact, the preceding program is an excellent illustration of why you should create a prototype for all functions in your program.

The way to correct this program is to include a prototype for **mul( )**. The corrected version follows:

```
#include "stdio.h"
float mul(float a, float b);

main() /* this is correct */
{
 float x, y;

  scanf("%f%f", &x, &y);
  printf("%f", mul(x, y));
}

float mul(float a, float b)
{
   return a*b;
}
```

Here, the prototype tells **main( )** to expect a floating-point value to be returned from **mul( )**.

Calling Argument Errors

You must be sure to match whatever type of argument a function expects with the type you give it. An important example is **scanf( )**. Remember that **scanf( )** expects to receive the *addresses* of its arguments, not their values. For example

```
int x;
char string[10];

scanf("%d%s", x, string);
```

is wrong, while

```
scanf("%d%s", &x, string);
```

is correct. Also remember, strings already pass their addresses to functions, so you should not use the **&** operator on them.

CONFUSING STRINGS AND CHARACTERS

Sometimes newcomers to C forget the difference between characters and strings. Remember, in C, a character occupies a single byte. A string is a null-terminated list of characters. Also, character constants are enclosed in single quotation marks, while string constants are defined by double quotes.

DEBUGGING THEORY IN GENERAL

Everyone has a different approach to programming and debugging. However, certain techniques have, over time, proven to be better than others. In debugging, incremental testing is considered to be the most cost- and time-effective method, even though it can appear to slow the development process at first.

Incremental testing is simply the process of always having working code. As soon as it is possible to run a piece of your program, you should do so, testing that section completely. As you add to the program, continue to test the new sections, as well as testing the way they connect to the known operational code. In this way you will be concentrating any possible bugs to a small area of code.

Incremental testing theory is generally based on probability and areas. As you know, area is a squared dimension. Each time you add length, you double area. Therefore, as your program grows there is an *n* squared area you must search for bugs. As a programmer, you want the smallest possible area to deal with while debugging. Through incremental testing, you are able to subtract the area already tested from the total area, thereby reducing the region where a bug may be found.

One final thought: immediate perfection is attainable only by accident. Therefore, good programmers are also good debuggers.

EXERCISES

1. What is wrong with the following code fragment?

```
/* assign numbers 0 through 9 to num */

int t, num[10];

t = 0;

 do {
   num[t] = ++t;
} while(t<10);
```

2. What is wrong with this program?

```
main()
{
  char *c;
  int t;

  c = &t;
  *c = 10;
}
```

3. Why won't this program work? Show how to fix it.

```
void swap(int a, int b);

main()  /* swap two integers */
{
  int a,b;

  a = 10;  b = 20;
  swap(a, b);
}

void swap(int x, int y)
{
  int temp;

  temp = x;
```

```
    x = y;
    y = temp;
}
```

4. Will this program ever terminate?

```
#include "stdio.h"

main()
{
  int t;

  for(t=0; t!=10; ++t) {
    printf("%d", t);
    if(t==10) t = 0;
  }
}
```

5. What is wrong in this code fragment?

```
int x;

scanf("%f", x);
```

Answers

1. Because **t** is incremented before being assigned, the numbers 1 through 10 will be placed into array **num**. The assignment line should be

   ```
   num[t] = t++;
   ```

2. It is attempting to assign, using indirection, an integer value by using a character pointer. This may be desired under certain very special circumstances, but as this program stands it is considered an error.

3. C uses call-by-value, which implies that the arguments to functions cannot be changed by those functions. To correct this program, both the call to **swap( )** and **swap( )** itself must be changed to accept pointers. Corrected, it is

```
#include "stdio.h"

void swap(int *a, int *b);

main()  /* swap two integers */
{
  int a,b;

  a = 10;  b = 20;
  swap(&a, &b);
}

void swap(int *x, int *y)
{
  int temp;

  temp = *x;
  *x = *y;
  *y = temp;
}
```

4. No.

5. Two things are wrong. First, **x** is an integer and **scanf( )** is being told to read a floating-point number. Second, and equally incorrect, **scanf( )** needs to be called with the *address* of the variable, not its value.

A

SOME COMMON
C LIBRARY
FUNCTIONS

This appendix discusses a number of the more important ANSI C library functions. If you have looked through the library section in your C compiler's manual, you are no doubt aware that there are a great many library functions. It is far beyond the scope of this book to cover each one. However, those discussed here are the ones you will most commonly need.

The library functions can be grouped into these categories:

- I/O functions
- String and character functions

- Mathematical functions

- Time and date functions

- Dynamic allocation functions

- Miscellaneous functions

The I/O functions were thoroughly covered in Chapter 10 and will not be expanded upon here.

Each function's description begins with the header file required by the function, followed by its prototype. The prototype provides you with a quick way of knowing what type of argument and how many of them the function takes and what type of value it returns.

Keep in mind that ANSI C specifies many data types, which are defined in the header files used by the functions. New type names will be discussed as they are introduced.

STRING AND CHARACTER FUNCTIONS

The C standard library has a rich and varied set of string and character handling functions. In C, a string is a null-terminated array of characters. The declarations for the string functions are found in the header file STRING.H. The character functions use CTYPE.H as their header file.

Because C has no bounds-checking on array operations, it is the programmer's responsibility to prevent an array overflow.

The character functions are declared to take an integer argument. While this is true, only the low-order byte is used by the function. Generally, you are free to use a character argument because it will automatically be elevated to **int** at the time of the call.

#include "ctype.h"
int isalnum(int ch);

DESCRIPTION   The **isalnum( )** function returns non-zero if its argument is either a letter or a digit. If the character is not alphanumeric, then 0 is returned.

EXAMPLE   This program checks each character read from **stdin** and reports all alphanumeric ones.

```
#include "ctype.h"
#include "stdio.h"
#include "conio.h"

main()
{
  char ch;

  for(;;) {
    ch = getche();
    if(ch==' ') break;
    if(isalnum(ch)) printf("%c is alphanumeric\n", ch);
  }
}
```

#include "ctype.h"
int isalpha(int ch)

DESCRIPTION   The **isalpha( )** function returns non-zero if *ch* is a letter of the alphabet; otherwise 0 is returned.

EXAMPLE   This program checks each character read from **stdin** and reports all those that are letters of the alphabet.

```
#include "ctype.h"
#include "stdio.h"
#include "conio.h"

main()
{
  char ch;

  for(;;) {
    ch = getche();
    if(ch==' ') break;
```

```
   if(isalpha(ch)) printf("%c is a letter\n", ch);
  }
}
```

#include "ctype.h"
int iscntrl(int ch)

DESCRIPTION The **iscntrl( )** function returns non-zero if *ch* is between 0 and 0x1F or is equal to 0x7F (DEL); otherwise 0 is returned.

EXAMPLE This program checks each character read from **stdin** and reports all those that are control characters.

```
#include "ctype.h"
#include "stdio.h"
#include "conio.h"

main()
{
  char ch;

  for(;;) {
    ch = getche();
    if(ch==' ') break;
    if(iscntrl(ch))
        printf("%c is a control character\n", ch);
  }
}
```

#include "ctype.h"
int isdigit(int ch)

DESCRIPTION The **isdigit( )** function returns non-zero if *ch* is a digit ('0' through '9'); otherwise 0 is returned.

EXAMPLE This program checks each character read from **stdin** and reports all those that are digits.

```
#include "ctype.h"
#include "stdio.h"
#include "conio.h"

main()
{
  char ch;

  for(;;) {
    ch = getche();
    if(ch==' ') break;
    if(isdigit(ch)) printf("%c is a digit\n", ch);
  }
}
```

#include "ctype.h"
int isgraph(int ch)

DESCRIPTION The **isgraph( )** function returns non-zero if *ch* is any printable character other than a space; otherwise 0 is returned. Printable characters are in the range 0x21 through 0x7E.

EXAMPLE This program checks each character read from **stdin** and reports all those that are printing characters.

```
#include "ctype.h"
#include "stdio.h"

main()
{
  char ch;

  for(;;) {
    ch = getche();
    if(ch==' ') break;
```

```
    if(isgraph(ch))
        printf("%c is a printing character\n",ch);
  }
}
```

#include "ctype.h"
int islower(int ch)

DESCRIPTION The **islower**( ) function returns non-zero if *ch* is a lowercase letter ("a" through "z"); otherwise 0 is returned.

EXAMPLE This program checks each character read from **stdin** and reports all those that are lowercase letters.

```
#include "ctype.h"
#include "stdio.h"
#include "conio.h"

main()
{
  char ch;

  for(;;) {
    ch = getche();
    if(ch==' ') break;
    if(islower(ch)) printf("%c is lowercase\n", ch);
  }
}
```

#include "ctype.h"
int isprint(int ch)

DESCRIPTION The **isprint**( ) function returns non-zero if *ch* is a printable character, including a space; otherwise 0 is returned. Printable characters are often in the range 0x20 through 0x7E.

EXAMPLE This program checks each character read from **stdin** and reports all those that are printable.

```
#include "ctype.h"
#include "stdio.h"
#include "conio.h"

main()
{
  char ch;

  for(;;) {
    ch = getche();
    if(ch==' ') break;
    if(isprint(ch)) printf("%c is printable\n", ch);
  }
}
```

#include "ctype.h"
int ispunct(int ch)

DESCRIPTION The **ispunct( )** function returns non-zero if *ch* is a punctuation character, excluding the space; otherwise 0 is returned. The term *punctuation,* as defined by this function, includes all printing characters that are neither alphanumeric nor a space.

EXAMPLE This program checks each character read from **stdin** and reports all those that are punctuation.

```
#include "ctype.h"
#include "stdio.h"
#include "conio.h"

main()
{
  char ch;

  for(;;) {
    ch = getche();
```

```
    if(ch==' ') break;
    if(ispunct(ch)) printf("%c is punctuation\n", ch);
  }
}
```

#include "ctype.h"
int isspace(int ch)

DESCRIPTION   The **isspace( )** function returns non-zero if *ch* is either a space, tab, vertical tab, form feed, carriage return, or new-line character; otherwise 0 is returned.

EXAMPLE   This program checks each character read from **stdin** and reports all those that are white-space characters.

```
#include "ctype.h"
#include "stdio.h"
#include "conio.h"

main()
{
  char ch;

  for(;;) {
    ch = getche();
    if(isspace(ch)) printf("%c is white-space\n", ch);
    if(ch==' ') break;
  }
}
```

#include "ctype.h"
int isupper(int ch)

DESCRIPTION   The **isupper( )** function returns non-zero if *ch* is an uppercase letter ("A" through "Z"); otherwise 0 is returned.

EXAMPLE This program checks each character read from **stdin** and reports all those that are uppercase letters.

```
#include "ctype.h"
#include "stdio.h"
#include "conio.h"

main()
{
  char ch;

  for(;;) {
    ch = getche();
    if(ch==' ') break;
    if(isupper(ch)) printf("%c is uppercase\n", ch);
  }
}
```

#include "ctype.h"
int isxdigit(int ch)

DESCRIPTION The **isxdigit( )** function returns non-zero if *ch* is a hexadecimal digit; otherwise 0 is returned. A hexadecimal digit will be in one of these ranges: 'A' through 'F', 'a' through 'f', or '0' through '9'.

EXAMPLE This program checks each character read from **stdin** and reports all those that are hexadecimal digits.

```
#include "ctype.h"
#include "stdio.h"
#include "conio.h"

main()
{
  char ch;

  for(;;) {
    ch = getche();
```

```
        if(ch==' ') break;
        if(isxdigit(ch)) printf("%c is hexadecimal\n", ch);
    }
}
```

#include "string.h"
char *strcat(char *str1, const char *str2)

DESCRIPTION   The **strcat( )** function concatenates a copy of *str2* to *str1* and terminates *str1* with a null. The null terminator originally ending *str1* is overwritten by the first character of *str2*. The string *str2* is untouched by the operation. The **strcat( )** function returns *str1*.

Remember: No bounds-checking takes place, so it is the programmer's responsibility to ensure that *str1* is large enough to hold both its original contents and those of *str2*.

EXAMPLE   This program appends the first string read from **stdin** to the second. For example, assuming the user enters "hello" and "there," the program will print "therehello."

```
#include "string.h"
#include "stdio.h"

main()
{
    char s1[80], s2[80];

    printf("enter two strings: ");
    gets(s1);
    gets(s2);

    strcat(s2, s1);
    printf(s2);
}
```

#include "string.h"
char *strchr(const char *str, int ch)

DESCRIPTION   The **strchr( )** function returns a pointer to the first occurrence of the low-order byte of *ch* in the string pointed to by *str*.

If no match is found, a null pointer is returned.

EXAMPLE   This program prints the string "This is a test."

```
#include "string.h"
#include "stdio.h"

main()
{
  char *p;

  p = strchr("this is a test", (int) ' ');
  printf(p);
}
```

#include "string.h"
int strcmp(const char *str1, const char *str2)

DESCRIPTION   The **strcmp( )** function lexicographically compares two null-terminated strings and returns an integer based on the outcome, as shown here:

Value	Meaning
less than 0	*str1* is less than *str2*
0	*str1* is equal to *str2*
greater than 0	*str1* is greater than *str2*

EXAMPLE   The following function can be used as a password verification routine. It will return 0 on failure and 1 on success.

```
#include "string.h"

password()
{
  char s[80];

  printf("enter password: ");
```

```
  gets(s);

  if(strcmp(s,"pass")) {
    printf("invalid password\n");
    return 0;
  }
  return 1;
}
```

#include "string.h"
char *strcpy(char *str1, const char *str2)

DESCRIPTION   The **strcpy( )** function is used to copy the contents of *str2* into *str1; str2* must be a pointer to a null-terminated string. The **strcpy( )** function returns a pointer to *str1*.

　　If *str1* and *str2* overlap, the behavior of **strcpy( )** is undefined.

EXAMPLE   The following code fragment will copy "hello" into string **str**.

```
char str[80];
strcpy(str, "hello");
```

#include "string.h"
size _ t strlen(const char *str)

DESCRIPTION   The **strlen( )** function returns the length of the null-terminated string pointed to by *str*. The null is not counted. The **size _ t** type is specified by ANSI and is defined in STRING.H.

EXAMPLE The following code fragment will print "5" on the screen.

```
strcpy(s, "hello");
printf("%d", strlen(s));
```

#include "stdio.h"
char *strstr(const char *str1, const char *str2)

DESCRIPTION   The **strstr( )** function returns a pointer to the first occurrence of the string pointed to by *str2* in the string pointed to by *str1* (except *str2's* null terminator). It returns a null pointer if no match is found.

EXAMPLE   This program displays the message "is is a test".

```
#include "string.h"
#include "stdio.h"

main()
{
   char *p;

   p = strstr("this is a test","is");
   printf(p);
}
```

#include "string.h"
char *strtok(char *str1, const char *str2)

DESCRIPTION   The **strtok( )** function returns a pointer to the next token in the string pointed to by *str1*. The characters making up the string pointed to by *str2* are the delimiters that determine the token. A null pointer is returned when there is no token to return.

   The first time **strtok( )** is called, *str1* is actually used in the call. Subsequent calls use a null pointer for the first argument. In this way the entire string can be reduced to its tokens.

   It is important to understand that the **strtok( )** function modifies the string pointed to by *str1*. Each time a token is found, a null is placed where the delimiter was found. In this way **strtok( )** can continue to advance through the string.

   It is possible to use a different set of delimiters for each call to **strtok( )**.

EXAMPLE This program tokenizes the string "The summer soldier, the sunshine patriot" with spaces and commas as the delimiters. The output will be "The|summer|soldier|the|sunshine|patriot".

```
#include "string.h"
#include "stdio.h"

main()
{
  char *p;

  p=strtok("The summer soldier, the sunshine patriot",
            " ,");
  printf(p);
  do {
    p = strtok('\0', " , ");
    if(p) printf("|%s", p);
  } while(p);
}
```

#include "ctype.h"
int tolower(int ch)

DESCRIPTION The **tolower( )** function returns the lowercase equivalent of *ch* if *ch* is a letter; otherwise *ch* is returned unchanged.

EXAMPLE This fragment displays "q".

```
putchar(tolower('Q'));
```

#include "ctype.h"
int toupper(int ch)

DESCRIPTION The **toupper( )** function returns the uppercase equivalent of *ch* if *ch* is a letter; otherwise *ch* is returned unchanged.

EXAMPLE   This displays "A".

```
putchar(toupper('a'));
```

THE MATHEMATICS FUNCTIONS

ANSI C defines several mathematics functions that take **double** arguments and return **double** values. These functions fall into the following categories:

- Trigonometric functions

- Hyperbolic functions

- Exponential and logarithmic functions

- Miscellaneous functions

All the math functions require that the header MATH.H be included in any program that uses them. In addition to declaring the math functions, this header defines a macro called **HUGE_VAL**. If an operation produces a result that is too large to be represented by a **double** an overflow occurs, which causes the routine to return **HUGE_VAL**. This is called a *range error*. For all the mathematics functions, if the input value is not in the domain for which the function is defined, a *domain error* occurs.

#include "math.h"
double acos(double arg)

DESCRIPTION   The **acos( )** function returns the arc cosine of *arg*. The argument to **acos( )** must be in the range −1 through 1; otherwise a domain error will occur.

EXAMPLE   This program prints the arc cosines, in one-tenth increments, of the values −1 through 1.

```
#include "math.h"
#include "stdio.h"

main()
{
  double val = -1.0;

  do {
    printf("arc cosine of %f is %f\n", val, acos(val));
    val += 0.1;
  } while(val<=1.0);
}
```

#include "math.h"
double asin(double arg)

DESCRIPTION The **asin( )** function returns the arc sine of *arg*. The argument to **asin( )** must be in the range −1 through 1; otherwise a domain error will occur.

EXAMPLE This program prints the arc sines, in one-tenth increments, of the values −1 through 1.

```
#include "math.h"
#include "stdio.h"

main()
{
  double val=-1.0;

  do {
    printf("arc sine of %f is %f\n", val, asin(val));
    val += 0.1;
  } while(val<=1.0);
}
```

#include "math.h"
double atan(double arg)

DESCRIPTION The **atan( )** function returns the arc tangent of *arg*.

EXAMPLE This program prints the arc tangents, in one-tenth increments, of the values −1 through 1.

```
#include "math.h"
#include "stdio.h"

main()
{
  double val=-1.0;

  do {
    printf("arc tangent of %f is %f\n", val, atan(val));
    val += 0.1;
  } while(val<=1.0);
}
```

#include "math.h"
double atan2(double y, double x)

DESCRIPTION The **atan2( )** function returns the arc tangent of y/x. It uses the signs of its arguments to compute the quadrant of the return value.

EXAMPLE This program prints the arc tangents, in one-tenth increments of y, from −1 through 1.

```
#include "math.h"
#include "stdio.h"

main()
{
  double y=-1.0;

  do {
    printf("atan2 of %f is %f\n", y, atan2(y, 1.0));
    y += 0.1;
  } while(y<=1.0);
}
```

#include "math.h"
double ceil(double num)

DESCRIPTION   The **ceil( )** function returns the smallest integer (represented as a **double**) that is not less than *num*. For example, given 1.02, **ceil( )** would return 2.0; given −1.02, **ceil( )** would then return −1.

EXAMPLE   This fragment prints "10" on the screen.

```
printf("%f", ceil(9.9));
```

#include "math.h"
double cos(double arg)

DESCRIPTION   The **cos( )** function returns the cosine of *arg*. The value of *arg* must be in radians.

EXAMPLE   This program prints the cosines, in one-tenth increments, of the values −1 through 1.

```
#include "math.h"
#include "stdio.h"

main()
{
  double val=-1.0;

  do {
    printf("cosine of %f is %f\n", val, cos(val));
    val += 0.1;
  } while(val<=1.0);
}
```

#include "math.h"
double cosh(double arg)

DESCRIPTION   The **cosh( )** function returns the hyperbolic cosine of *arg*. The value of *arg* must be in radians.

EXAMPLE This program prints the hyperbolic cosines, in one-tenth increments, of the values −1 through 1.

```
#include "math.h"
#include "stdio.h"

main()
{
  double val=-1.0;

  do {
    printf("cosh of %f is %f\n", val, cosh(val));
    val += 0.1;
  } while(val<=1.0);
}
```

#include "math.h"
double exp(double arg)

DESCRIPTION The **exp( )** function returns the natural logarithm *e* raised to the *arg* power.

EXAMPLE This fragment displays the value of *e* (rounded to 2.718282).

```
printf("value of e to the first: %f", exp(1.0));
```

#include "math.h"
double fabs(double num)

DESCRIPTION The **fabs( )** function returns the absolute value of *num*.

EXAMPLE This program prints "1.0 1.0" on the screen.

```
#include "math.h"
#include "stdio.h"

main()
{
  printf("%1.1f %1.1f", fabs(1.0), fabs(-1.0));
}
```

#include "math.h"
double floor(double num)

DESCRIPTION   The **floor( )** function returns the largest integer (represented as a **double**) not greater than *num*. For example, given 1.02, **floor( )** would return 1.0; given −1.02, **floor( )** would return −2.0.

EXAMPLE   This fragment prints "10" on the screen.

```
printf("%f", floor(10.9));
```

#include "math.h"
double log(double num)

DESCRIPTION   The **log( )** function returns the natural logarithm for *num*. A domain error occurs if *num* is negative and a range error occurs if the argument is 0.

EXAMPLE   This program prints the natural logarithms for the numbers 1 through 10.

```
#include "math.h"
#include "stdio.h"

main()
{
  double val=1.0;
```

```
do {
  printf("%f %f\n", val, log(val));
  val++;
} while (val<11.0);
}
```

#include "math.h"
double log10(double num)

DESCRIPTION The **log10( )** function returns the base 10 logarithm for *num*. A domain error occurs if *num* is negative and a range error occurs if the argument is 0.

EXAMPLE This program prints the base 10 logarithms for the numbers 1 through 10.

```
#include "math.h"
#include "stdio.h"

main()
{
  double val=1.0;

  do {
    printf("%f %f\n", val, log10(val));
    val++;
  } while (val<11.0);
}
```

#include "math.h"
double pow(double base, double exp)

DESCRIPTION The **pow( )** function returns *base* raised to the *exp* power (*base^exp*). A domain error occurs if *base* is 0 and *exp* is less than or equal to 0. This may also happen if *base* is negative and *exp* is not an integer. An overflow produces a range error.

EXAMPLE   This program prints the first ten powers of 10.

```
#include "math.h"
#include "stdio.h"

main()
{
  double x=10.0, y=0.0;

  do {
    printf("%f",pow(x, y));
    y++;
  } while(y<11);
}
```

#include "math.h"
double sin(double arg)

DESCRIPTION   The **sin( )** function returns the sine of *arg*. The value of *arg* must be in radians.

EXAMPLE   This program prints the sines, in one-tenth increments, of the values −1 through 1.

```
#include "math.h"
#include "stdio.h"

main()
{
  double val=-1.0;

  do {
    printf("sine of %f is %f\n", val, sin(val));
    val += 0.1;
  } while(val<=1.0);
}
```

#include "math.h"
double sinh(double arg)

DESCRIPTION   The **sinh( )** function returns the hyperbolic sine of *arg*. The value of *arg* must be in radians.

EXAMPLE   This program prints the hyperbolic sines, in one-tenth increments, of the values −1 through 1.

```
#include "math.h"
#include "stdio.h"

main()
{
  double val=-1.0;

  do {
    printf("sinh of %f is %f\n", val, sinh(val));
    val += 0.1;
  } while(val<=1.0);
}
```

#include "math.h"
double sqrt(double num)

DESCRIPTION   The **sqrt**( ) function returns the square root of *num*. If called with a negative argument, a domain error will occur.

EXAMPLE   This fragment prints "4" on the screen.

```
printf("%f", sqrt(16.0));
```

#include "math.h"
double tan(double arg)

DESCRIPTION   The **tan**( ) function returns the tangent of *arg*. The value of *arg* must be in radians.

EXAMPLE   This program prints the tangent, in one-tenth increments, of the values −1 through 1.

```
#include "math.h"
#include "stdio.h"

main()
{
  double val=-1.0;

  do {
    printf("tangent of %f is %f\n", val, tan(val));
    val += 0.1;
  } while(val<=1.0);
}
```

#include "math.h"
double tanh(double arg)

DESCRIPTION   The **tanh( )** function returns the hyperbolic tangent of *arg*. The value of *arg* must be in radians.

EXAMPLE   This program prints the hyperbolic tangent, in one-tenth increments, of the values −1 through 1.

```
#include "math.h"
#include "stdio.h"

main()
{
  double val=-1.0;

  do {
    printf("tanh of %f is %f\n", val, tanh(val));
    val += 0.1;
  } while(val<=1.0);
}
```

TIME AND DATE FUNCTIONS

The time and date functions require the header TIME.H for their prototypes. It also defines four types and two macros. The type

time _ t is able to represent the system time and date as a long integer. This is called the *calendar time.* The structure type **tm** holds date and time broken down into its elements. The **tm** structure is defined as shown here:

```
struct tm {
    int tm_sec;   /* seconds, 0-59 */
    int tm_min;   /* minutes, 0-59 */
    int tm_hour;  /* hours, 0-23 */
    int tm_mday;  /* day of the month, 1-31 */
    int tm_mon;   /* months since Jan, 0-11 */
    int tm_year;  /* years from 1900 */
    int tm_wday;  /* days since Sunday, 0-6 */
    int tm_yday;  /* days since Jan 1, 0-365 */
    int tm_isdst; /* Daylight Savings Time indicator */
}
```

The value of **tm _ isdst** will be positive if daylight saving time is in effect, 0 if it is not in effect, and negative if there is no information available. When the date and time are represented in this way, it is referred to as the *broken-down time.*

The type **clock _ t** is defined the same as **time _ t**. The header file also defines **size _ t**.

The macros defined are **NULL** and **CLK _ TCK**.

#include "time.h"
char *asctime(const struct tm *ptr);

DESCRIPTION The **asctime( )** function returns a pointer to a string that converts the information stored in the structure pointed to by *ptr* into the following form:

day month date hours:minutes:seconds year\n\0

For example:

Wed Jun 19 12:05:34 1999

The structure pointer passed to **asctime( )** is generally obtained from either **localtime( )** or **gmtime( )**.

The buffer used by **asctime( )** to hold the formatted output string is a statically allocated character array and is overwritten each time the function is called. If you want to save the contents of the string, you need to copy it elsewhere.

EXAMPLE This program displays the local time defined by the system.

```
#include "time.h"
#include "stdio.h"

main()
{
    struct tm *ptr;
    time_t lt;

    lt = time(NULL);
    ptr = localtime(&lt);
    printf(asctime(ptr));
}
```

#include "time.h"
clock_t clock(void)

DESCRIPTION The **clock( )** function returns the number of system clock cycles that have occurred since the program began execution. To compute the number of seconds, divide this value by the **CLK_TCK** macro.

EXAMPLE The following program displays the number of system clock cycles occurring since it began.

```
#include "stdio.h"
#include "time.h"
main()
{
```

```
    int i;

    for(i=0; i<100; i++) ;

    printf("%u", clock());
}
```

#include "time.h"
char *ctime(const time_t *time)

DESCRIPTION   The **ctime( )** function returns a pointer to a string
of the form

day month date hours:minutes:seconds year\n\0

given a pointer to the calendar time. The calendar time is generally
obtained through a call to **time( )**. The **ctime( )** function is equivalent to

```
asctime(localtime(time))
```

The buffer used by **ctime( )** to hold the formatted output string is
a statically allocated character array and is overwritten each time the
function is called. If you wish to save the contents of the string, you
need to copy it elsewhere.

EXAMPLE   This program displays the local time defined by the
system.

```
#include "time.h"
#include "stdio.h"

main()
{
    time_t lt;
```

```
    lt = time(NULL);
    printf(ctime(&lt));
}
```

#include "time.h"
double difftime(time _ t time2, time _ t time1)

DESCRIPTION The **difftime( )** function returns the difference, in seconds, between *time1* and *time2*. That is, *time2 − time1*.

EXAMPLE This program times the number of seconds that it takes for the empty **for** loop to go from 0 to 500000.

```
#include "time.h"
#include "stdio.h"

main()
{
    time_t start,end;
    long unsigned int t;

    start = time(NULL);
    for(t=0; t<500000L; t++);
    end = time(NULL);
    printf("required %f seconds\n", difftime(end, start));
}
```

#include "time.h"
struct tm *gmtime(const time _ t *time)

DESCRIPTION The **gmtime( )** returns a pointer to the broken-down form of *time* in the form of a **tm** structure. The time is represented in Greenwich mean time. The *time* value is generally obtained through a call to **time( )**.

The structure used by **gmtime( )** to hold the broken-down time is statically allocated and is overwritten each time the function is called. If you wish to save the contents of the structure, you need to copy it elsewhere.

EXAMPLE   This program prints both the local time and the Greenwich mean time of the system.

```
#include "time.h"
#include "stdio.h"

/* print local and GM time */
main()
{
  struct tm *local, *gm;
  time_t t;

  t = time(NULL);
  local = localtime(&t);
  printf("local time and date: %s", asctime(local));
  gm = gmtime(&t);
  printf("Greenwich time and date: %s", asctime(gm));
}
```

#include "time.h"
struct tm *localtime(const time_t *time)

DESCRIPTION   The **localtime( )** function returns a pointer to the broken-down form of *time* in the form of a **tm** structure. The time is represented in local time. The *time* value is generally obtained through a call to **time( )**.

The structure used by **localtime( )** to hold the broken-down time is statically allocated and is overwritten each time the function is called. If you wish to save the contents of the structure, you need to copy it elsewhere.

EXAMPLE   This program prints both the local time and the Greenwich mean time of the system.

```
#include "time.h"
#include "stdio.h"

/* print local and Greenwich mean time */
main()
{
  struct tm *local;
  time_t t;

  t = time(NULL);
  local = localtime(&t);
  printf("local time and date: %s", asctime(local));
  local = gmtime(&t);
  printf("Greenwich time and date: %s", asctime(local));
}
```

#include "time.h"
time_t time(time_t *time)

DESCRIPTION The **time( )** function returns the current calendar time of the system. If the system has no time keeping mechanism, then −1 is returned.

The **time( )** function can be called either with a null pointer or with a pointer to a variable of type **time_t**. If the latter is used, then the argument will also be assigned the calendar time.

EXAMPLE This program displays the local time defined by the system.

```
#include "time.h"
#include "stdio.h"

main()
{
  struct tm *ptr;
  time_t lt;

  lt = time(NULL);
```

```
    ptr = localtime(&lt);
    printf(asctime(ptr));
}
```

DYNAMIC ALLOCATION

There are two primary ways a C program can store information in the main memory of the computer. The first uses global and local variables — including arrays and structures. In the case of global and static local variables, the storage is fixed throughout the run time of your program. For dynamic local variables, storage is allocated from the stack space of the computer. Although these variables are efficiently implemented in C, they require the programmer to know in advance the amount of storage needed for every situation. The second way information can be stored is with C's dynamic allocation system. In this method, storage for information is allocated from the free memory area as it is needed.

The proposed ANSI standard specifies that the header information necessary to the dynamic allocation system will be found in STDLIB. In this file, the type **size_t** is defined. This type is used extensively by the allocation functions and is essentially the equivalent of **unsigned**.

#include "stdlib.h"
void *calloc(size_t num, size_t size);

DESCRIPTION   The **calloc( )** function returns a pointer to the allocated memory. The amount of memory allocated is equal to *num**size. That is, **calloc( )** allocates sufficient memory for an array of *num* objects of size *size*.

The **calloc( )** function returns a pointer to the first byte of the allocated region. If there is not enough memory to satisfy the request, a null pointer is returned. It is always important to verify that the return value is not a null pointer before attempting to use it.

EXAMPLE   This function returns a pointer to a dynamically allocated array of 100 **float**s.

```
#include "stdlib.h"
#include "stdio.h"

float *get_mem()
{
  float *p;

  p = (float *) calloc(100, sizeof(float));
  if(!p) {
    printf("allocation failure - aborting");
    exit(1);
  }
  return p;
}
```

#include "stdlib.h"
void free(void *ptr)

DESCRIPTION   The **free( )** function deallocates the memory pointed to by *ptr*. This makes the memory available for future allocation.

It is imperative that **free( )** only be called with a pointer that was previously allocated using one of the dynamic allocation system's functions, such as **malloc( )** or **calloc( )**. Using an invalid pointer in the call will probably destroy the memory management mechanism and cause a system crash.

EXAMPLE   This program first allocates room for the user-entered strings and then frees them.

```
#include "stdlib.h"
#include "stdio.h"

main()
{
  char *str[100];
```

```
int i;

for(i=0; i<100; i++) {
  if((str[i] = (char *)malloc(128))==NULL) {
    printf("allocation error - aborting");
    exit(0);
  }
  gets(str[i]);
}

/* now free the memory */
for(i=0; i<100; i++) free(str[i]);
}
```

#include "stdlib.h"
void *malloc(size_t size)

DESCRIPTION   The **malloc( )** function returns a pointer to the first byte of a region of memory of size *size* that has been allocated from the heap. (Remember the heap is a region of free memory managed by C's dynamic allocation subsystem.) If there is insufficient memory in the heap to satisfy the request, **malloc( )** returns a null pointer. It is always important to verify that the return value is not a null pointer before attempting to use it. Attempting to use a null pointer will usually result in a system crash.

EXAMPLE   This function allocates sufficient memory to hold structures of type **addr**.

```
#include "stdlib.h"
#include "stdio.h"

struct addr {
  char name[40];
  char street[40];
  char city[40];
  char state[3];
  char zip[10];
};
```

```
      .
      .
      .
struct addr *get_struct(void)
{
   struct addr *p;

   if((p=(struct addr *)malloc(sizeof(struct addr)))==NULL)
{
      printf("allocation error - aborting");
      exit(0);
   }
   return p;
}
```

#include "stdlib.h"
void *realloc(void *ptr, size ⎯ t size)

DESCRIPTION The **realloc( )** function changes the size of the allocated memory pointed to by *ptr* to that specified by *size*. The value of *size* may be greater or less than the original. A pointer to the memory block is returned since it may be necessary for **realloc( )** to move the block to increase its size. If this occurs, the contents of the old block are copied into the new block—no information is lost.

If there is not enough free memory in the heap to allocate *size* bytes, a null pointer is returned and the original block is freed (lost). This means it is important to verify the success of a call to **realloc( )**.

EXAMPLE This program first allocates 17 characters, copies the string "this is 16 chars" into the space, and then uses **realloc( )** to increase the size to 18 in order to place a period at the end.

```
#include "stdlib.h"
#include "stdio.h"
#include "string.h"

main()
{
   char *p;
```

```
    p = (char *) malloc(17);
    if(!p) {
      printf("allocation error - aborting");
      exit(1);
    }

    strcpy(p,"this is 16 chars");

    p = realloc(p,18);
    if(!p) {
      printf("allocation error - aborting");
      exit(1);
    }

    strcat(p, ".");

    printf(p);

    free(p);
}
```

MISCELLANEOUS FUNCTIONS

The functions discussed in this section are all standard functions that don't easily fit in any other category.

#include "stdlib.h"
void abort(void)

DESCRIPTION   The **abort( )** function causes immediate termination of a program. Whether it closes any open files is defined by the implementation, but generally it won't.

EXAMPLE   In this program, if the user enters an "A," the program will terminate.

```
#include "stdlib.h"
#include "stdio.h"
#include "conio.h"

main()
{
  for(;;)
    if(getche()=='A') abort();
}
```

#include "stdlib.h"
int abs(int num)

DESCRIPTION   The **abs( )** function returns the absolute value of the integer *num*.

EXAMPLE   This function converts a user-entered number into their absolute values.

```
#include "stdlib.h"
#include "stdio.h"

get_abs(void)
{
  char num[80];

  gets(num)

  return abs(atoi(num));
}
```

#include "stdlib.h"
double atof(const char *str)

DESCRIPTION   The **atof( )** function converts the string pointed to by **str** into a **double** value. The string must contain a valid floating point number. If this is not the case, the returned value is 0.

The number may be terminated by any character that cannot be part of a valid floating point number. This includes white-space characters, punctuation (other than periods), and characters other than "E" or "e". Thus, if **atof( )** is called with "100.00HELLO," the value 100.00 will be returned.

EXAMPLE   This program reads two floating point numbers and displays their sum.

```
#include "stdlib.h"
#include "stdio.h"

main()
{
  char num1[80], num2[80];

  printf("enter first: ");
  gets(num1);
  printf("enter second: ");
  gets(num2);
  printf("the sum is: %f",atof(num1)+atof(num2));
}
```

#include "stdlib.h"
int atoi(const char *str)

DESCRIPTION   The **atoi( )** function converts the string pointed to by **str** into an **int** value. The string must contain a valid integer. If this is not the case, the returned value is 0.

The number may be terminated by any character that cannot be part of an integer. This includes white-space characters, punctuation, and other characters. Thus, if **atoi( )** is called with "123.23," the integer value 123 will be returned and the 0.23 ignored.

EXAMPLE   This program reads two integers and displays their sum.

```
#include "stdlib.h"
#include "stdio.h"

main()
{
    char num1[80], num2[80];

    printf("enter first: ");
    gets(num1);
    printf("enter second: ");
    gets(num2);
    printf("the sum is: %d",atoi(num1)+atoi(num2));
}
```

#include "stdlib.h"
int atol(const char *str)

DESCRIPTION   The **atol( )** function converts the string pointed to by **str** into a **long int** value. The string must contain a valid long integer. If this is not the case, the returned value is 0.

The number may be terminated by any character that cannot be part of an integer. This includes white-space characters, punctuation, and other characters. Thus, if **atol( )** is called with "123.23," the integer value 123 will be returned and the 0.23 will be ignored.

EXAMPLE   This program reads two long integers and displays their sum.

```
#include "stdlib.h"
#include "stdio.h"

main()
{
    char num1[80], num2[80];

    printf("enter first: ");
    gets(num1);
    printf("enter second: ");
```

```
    gets(num2);
    printf("the sum is: %ld",
           atol(num1)+atol(num2));
}
```

#include "stdlib.h"
void *bsearch(const void *key, const void *base, size _ t num, size _ t size, int (*compare)(const void *, const void *))

DESCRIPTION The **bsearch( )** function performs a binary search on the sorted array pointed to by *base* and returns a pointer to the first member that matches the key pointed to by *key*. The number of elements in the array is specified by *num* and the size (in bytes) of each element is described by *size*. (The **size _ t** type is defined in STDLIB.H and is essentially the equivalent of **unsigned**.)

The function pointed to by *compare* is used to compare an element of the array with the key. The form of *compare* must be

> *func _ name*(const void *arg1*, const void *arg2*)

It must return the following values:

> If *arg1* is less than *arg2* then return less than 0.
> If *arg1* is equal to *arg2* then return 0.
> If *arg1* is greater than *arg2* then return greater than 0.

The array must be sorted in ascending order with the lowest address containing the lowest element.

If the array does not contain the key, then a null pointer is returned.

EXAMPLE This program reads characters entered at the keyboard (assuming buffered keyboard I/O) and determines whether they belong to the alphabet.

```
#include "stdlib.h"
#include "ctype.h"
#include "stdio.h"
int comp();

char *alpha="abcdefghijklmnopqrstuvwxyz";

comp(const char *ch, const char *s);

main()
{
  char ch;
  char *p;
  int comp();

  do {
    printf("enter a character: ");
    scanf("%c%*c",&ch);
    ch = tolower(ch);
    p = (char *) bsearch(&ch,alpha, 26, 1, comp);
    if(p) printf("is in alphabet\n");
    else printf("is not in alphabet\n");
  } while(p);
}

/* compare two characters */
comp(const char *ch, const char *s)
{
  return *ch-*s;
}
```

#include "stdlib.h"
void exit(int status)

DESCRIPTION   The **exit( )** function causes immediate normal termination of a program.

The value of *status* is passed to the calling process, usually the operating system, if the environment supports it. By convention, if the value of *status* is 0, normal program termination is assumed. A non-zero value may be used to indicate an error.

EXAMPLE   This function performs menu selection for a mailing list program. If "Q" is selected, the program is terminated.

```
menu(void)
{
  char choice;

  do {
    printf("Enter names (E)\n");
    printf("Delete name (D)\n");
    printf("Print (P)\n");
    printf("Quit (Q)\n");
  } while(!strchr("EDPQ",toupper(ch)));
  if(ch=='Q') exit(0);
  return ch;
}
```

#include "stdlib.h"
long labs(long num)

DESCRIPTION   The **labs( )** function returns the absolute value of the **long int** *num.*

EXAMPLE   This function converts the user-entered numbers into their absolute values.

```
#include "stdlib.h"
#include "stdio.h"

long int get_labs()
{
  char num[80];

  gets(num)

  return labs(atol(num));
}
```

#include "setjmp.h"
void longjmp(jmp_buf envbuf, int val);

DESCRIPTION   The **longjmp( )** instruction causes program execution to resume at the point of the last call to **setjmp( )**. These two functions are the way ANSI C provides for a jump between functions. Notice that the header SETJUMP.H is required.

The **longjmp( )** function operates by resetting the stack as described in *envbuf*, which must have been set by a prior call to **setjmp( )**. This causes program execution to resume at the statement following the **setjmp( )** invocation—the computer is "tricked" into thinking that it never left the function called **setjmp( )**. (As a somewhat graphic explanation, the **longjmp( )** function "warps" across time and space (memory) to a previous point in your program, without having to perform the normal function-return process.

The buffer *envbuf* is of type **jmp_buf**, which is defined in the header SETJMP.H. The buffer must have been set through a call to **setjmp( )** prior to calling **longjmp( )**.

The value of *val* becomes the return value of **setjump( )** and may be interrogated to determine where the long jump came from. The only value not allowed is 0.

It is important to understand that the **longjmp( )** function must be called before the function called **setjmp( )** returns. If not, the result is technically undefined; in actuality, a crash will almost certainly occur.

By far the most common use of **longjmp( )** is to return from a deeply nested set of routines when a catastrophic error occurs.

EXAMPLE   This program prints "1 2 3".

```
#include "setjmp.h"
#include "stdio.h"

void f2(void);

jmp_buf ebuf;

main()
{
```

```
    char first=1;
    int i;

    printf("1 ");
    i = setjmp(ebuf);
    if(first) {
      first = !first;
      f2();
      printf("this will not be printed");
    }
    printf("%d", i);
}

void f2(void)
{
 printf("2 ");
 longjmp(ebuf, 3);
}
```

#include "stdlib.h"
void qsort(void *base, size_t num, size_t size,
int (*compare)(const *void, const *void))

DESCRIPTION The **qsort( )** function sorts the array pointed to by
base using a QuickSort (developed by C. A. R. Hoare). The Quick-
Sort is generally considered the best general-purpose sorting algorithm. Upon termination, the array will be sorted. The number of
elements in the array is specified by *num* and the size (in bytes) of
each element is described by *size*. (The **size_t** type is defined in the
header file STDLIB.H and is essentially the equivalent of **unsigned**.)

The function pointed to by *compare* is used to compare an
element of the array with the key. The form of *compare* must be

func_name(const void *arg1*, const void *arg2*)

It must return the following values.

If *arg1* is less than *arg2* then return less than 0.
If *arg1* is equal to *arg2* then return 0.
If *arg1* is greater than *arg2* then return greater than 0.

The array is sorted in ascending order with the lowest address containing the lowest element.

EXAMPLE   This program sorts a list of integers and displays the result.

```
#include "stdlib.h"
#include "stdio.h"

int comp();

int num[10]= {
  1,3,6,5,8,7,9,6,2,0
};

main()
{
  int i;

  printf("original array: ");
  for(i=0; i<10; i++) printf("%d ", num[i]);

  qsort(num, 10, sizeof(int), comp);

  printf("sorted array: ");
  for(i=0; i<10; i++) printf("%d ", num[i]);
}

/* compare the integers */
comp(const int *i, const int *j)
{
  return *i-*j;
}
```

#include "stdlib.h"
int rand(void)

DESCRIPTION   The **rand**( ) function generates a sequence of pseudo-random numbers. Each time it is called, an integer between

0 and **RAND_MAX** is returned. The **RAND_MAX** macro is defined in STDLIB.H. The ANSI standard stipulates that **RAND_MAX** will have a value of at least 32767.

EXAMPLE   This program displays ten pseudo-random numbers.

```
#include "stdlib.h"
#include "stdio.h"

main()
{
  int i;

  for(i=0; i<10; i++)
    printf("%d ",rand());
}
```

#include "setjmp.h"
void setjmp(jmp_buf envbuf);

DESCRIPTION   The **setjmp( )** function saves the contents of the system stack in the buffer *envbuf* for later use by **longjmp( )**.

The **setjmp( )** function returns 0 upon invocation. However, **longjmp( )** passes an argument to **setjmp( )** when it executes, and it is this value (always non-zero) that will appear to be **setjmp( )**'s value after a call to **longjmp( )**.

See the **longjmp( )** section for additional information.

EXAMPLE   This program prints "1 2 3".

```
#include "setjmp.h"
#include "stdio.h"

void f2(void);

jmp_buf ebuf;

main()
{
```

```
      char first=1;
      int i;

      printf("1 ");
      i = setjmp(ebuf);
      if(first) {
        first = !first;
        f2();
        printf("this will not be printed");
      }
      printf("%d",i);
}

void f2(void)
{
 printf("2 ");
 longjmp(ebuf, 3);
}
```

#include "stdlib.h"
void srand(unsigned seed)

DESCRIPTION   The **srand( )** function is used to set a starting point
for the sequence generated by **rand( )**. (The **rand( )** function returns
pseudo-random numbers.)

   Generally **srand( )** is used to allow a program to be run several
times using different sequences of pseudo-random numbers.

EXAMPLE   This program uses the system time to randomly initialize the **rand( )** function using **srand( )**.

```
#include "stdio.h"
#include "stdlib.h"
#include "time.h"

/* Seed rand with the system time
   and display the first 100 numbers.
*/
main()
{
```

```
int i, utime;
long  ltime;

/* get the current calendar time */

ltime = time(NULL);
utime = (unsigned int) ltime/2;
srand(utime);
for(i=0; i<10; i++) printf("%d ", rand());
}
```

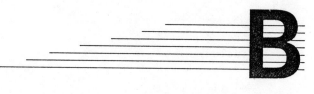

C KEYWORD
SUMMARY

As defined by the ANSI standard, these are the 32 keywords, which, combined with the formal C syntax, form the C language. These keywords are shown in Figure B-1.

All C keywords are lowercase. In C, uppercase and lowercase are different; for instance, "else" is a keyword, "ELSE" is not.

An alphabetical summary of each of the keywords follows.

auto

auto is used to create temporary variables that are created upon entry into a block and are destroyed upon exit.

```
#include "stdio.h"
#include "conio.h"

main()
{
  for(;;) {
    if(getche()=='a') {
      auto int t;
      for(t=0; t<'a'; t++)
        printf("%d ", t);
    }
  }
}
```

In this example, the variable **t** is created only if the user strikes an "a". Outside the **if** block, **t** is completely unknown and any reference to it would generate a compile time syntax error.

break

break is used to exit from a **do**, **for**, or **while** loop, bypassing the normal loop condition. In addition, it is used to exit from a **switch** statement.

auto	double	int	struct
break	else	long	switch
case	enum	register	typedef
char	extern	return	union
const	float	short	unsigned
continue	for	signed	void
default	goto	sizeof	volatile
do	if	static	while

FIGURE B-1 Keyword list

An example of **break** in a loop is shown here:

```
while(x<100) {
  x = get_new_x();
  if(kbhit()) break;   /* key hit on
                          keyboard */
  process(x);

}
```

Here, if a key is typed, the loop will terminate no matter what the value of **x** is.

A **break** always terminates the innermost **for, do, while,** or **switch** statement, regardless of the way it is nested. In a **switch** statement, **break** effectively keeps program execution from "falling through" to the next **case.** (Refer to the **switch** section for details.)

case

case is covered in conjunction with **switch.**

char

char is a data type used to declare character variables. For example, to declare **ch** to be a character type, you would write

```
char ch;
```

In C, a character is 1 byte long.

const

The **const** modifier is used to tell the compiler the variable that follows cannot be modified. It is also used to prevent a function from modifying the object pointed to by one of its arguments.

continue

continue is used to bypass portions of code in a loop and force the conditional test to be performed. For example, the following **while** loop will simply read characters from the keyboard until an "s" is typed.

```
while(ch=getche()) {
  if(ch!='s') continue;  /* read another char */
  process(ch);
}
```

The call to **process( )** won't occur until **ch** contains the character "s".

default

default is used in the **switch** statement to signal a default block of code to be executed if no matches are found in the **switch**. See the **switch** section.

do

The **do** loop is one of three loop constructs available in C. The general form of the **do** loop is

```
do {
  statements block
} while(condition);
```

If only one statement is repeated, the braces are not necessary, but they add clarity to the statement.

The **do** loop is the only loop in C that will always have at least one iteration because the condition is tested at the bottom of the loop.

A common use of the **do** loop is to read disk files. The following code will read a file until an EOF is encountered.

```
do {
  ch = getc(fp);
  printf("%c", ch);
} while(!feof(fp));
```

double

double is a data type specifier used to declare double precision floating point variables. To declare **d** to be of type **double** you would write

```
double d;
```

else

See the **if** section.

enum

The **enum** type specifier is used to create enumeration types. An enumeration is simply a list of objects. Hence, an enumeration type specifies what that list of objects consists of. Further, an enumeration type variable may only be assigned values that are part of the enumeration list. For example, the following code declares an enumeration called **color** and a variable of that type called **c** and performs an assignment and a condition test.

```
#include "stdio.h"

enum color {red, green, yellow};
enum color c;

main()
{
  c = red;
  if(c==red) printf("is red\n");
}
```

extern

The **extern** data type modifier is used to tell the compiler that a variable is declared elsewhere in the program. This is often used in conjuction with separately compiled files that share the same global data and are linked together. In essence, it notifies the compiler of a variable without redeclaring it.

As an example, if **first** was declared in another file as an integer, then in subsequent files the following declaration would be used.

```
extern int first;
```

float

float is a data type specifier used to declare floating point variables. To declare **f** to be of type **float** you would write

```
float f;
```

for

The **for** loop allows automatic initialization and incrementation of a counter variable. The general form is

> for(*initialization*; *condition*; *increment*) {
>   *statement block*
> }

If the *statement block* is only one statement, the braces are not necessary.

Although the **for** allows a number of variations, generally the *initialization* is used to set a counter variable to its starting value. The *condition* is generally a relational statement that checks the counter variable against a termination value, and the *increment* increments (or decrements) the counter value.

The following code will print the message "hello" ten times.

```
for(t=0; t<10; t++) printf("hello\n");
```

goto

The **goto** causes program execution to jump to the label specified in the **goto** statement. The general form of the **goto** is

```
    goto label;
    .

    .

    .
    label:
```

All labels must end in a colon and must not conflict with keywords or function names. Furthermore, a **goto** can only branch within the current function, and not from one function to another.

The following example will print the message "right" but not the message "wrong."

```
goto lab1;
  printf("wrong");
lab1:
  printf("right");
```

if

The general form of the **if** statement is

```
    if(condition) {
      statement block 1
    }
    else {
      statement block 2
    }
```

If single statements are used, then the braces are not needed. The **else** is optional.

The condition may be any expression. If that expression evaluates to any value other than 0, then *statement block 1* will be executed; otherwise, if it exists, *statement block 2* will be executed.

The following code fragment can be used for keyboard input and to look for a "q," which signifies "quit."

```
ch = getche();
if(ch=='q') {
  printf("program terminated");
  exit(0);
}
else  proceed();
```

int

int is the type specifier used to declare integer variables. For example, to declare **count** as an integer you would write

```
int count;
```

long

long is a data type modifier used to declare double length integer variables. For example, to declare **count** as a long integer, you would write

```
long int count;
```

register

The **register** modifier is used to request that a variable be stored in the way that allows the fastest possible access. In the case of characters or integers, this usually means a register of the CPU. The

register modifier can only be used on local variables. To declare **i** to be a **register** integer, you would write

```
register int i;
```

return

The **return** statement forces a return from a function and can be used to transfer a value back to the calling routine. For example, the following function returns the product of its two integer arguments.

```
mul(int a, int b)
{
   return(a*b);
}
```

   Keep in mind that as soon as a **return** is encountered, the function will return, skipping any other code in the function.

short

short is a data type modifier used to declare short integers. For example, to declare **sh** to be a short integer you would write

```
short int sh;
```

signed

The **signed** type modifier is used to specify a **signed char** data type.

sizeof

The **sizeof** keyword is a compile time operator that returns the length of the variable or type it precedes. If it precedes a type, then

the type must be enclosed in parentheses. For example,

```
printf("%d", sizeof(int));
```

will print "2" for many C implementations.

The **sizeof** statement's principal use is in helping to generate portable code when that code depends on the size of the C built-in data types.

static

The **static** keyword is a data type modifier used to instruct the compiler to create permanent storage for the local variable that it precedes. This enables the specified variable to maintain its value between function calls. For example, to declare **last_time** as a **static** integer, you would write

```
static int last_time;
```

struct

The **struct** statement is used to create complex or conglomerate variables, called structures, that are made up of one or more elements of the seven basic data types. The general form of a structure is shown in the following:

```
struct struct_name {
    type element1;
    type element2;

        .
        .
        .
    type elementN;
} structure_variable_name;
```

The individual elements are referenced using the dot or arrow operators.

switch

The **switch** statement is C's multi-way branch statement. It is used to route execution in one of several ways. The general form of the statement is

```
switch(variable) {
    case (constant1): statement set 1;
    break;
    case (constant2): statement set 2;
    break;
        .

        .

        .

    case (constant N): statement set N;
    break;
    default: default statements;


}
```

Each *statement set* may be one or many statements long. The **default** portion is optional.

The **switch** works by checking the **variable** against all the constants. As soon as a match is found that set of statements is executed. If the **break** statement is omitted execution will continue until the end of the **switch**. You can think of the **case**s as labels. Execution will continue until a **break** statement is found or the **switch** ends.

The following example can be used to process a menu selection:

```
ch = getche();

switch (ch) {
  case 'e': enter();
       break;
  case 'l': list();
       break;
  case 's': sort();
       break;
  case 'q': exit(0);
default: printf("unknown command\n");
```

```
        printf("try again\n");

}
```

typedef

The **typedef** statement allows you to create a new name for an existing data type. The data type may be one of the built-in types or a structure or union name. The general form of **typedef** is

typedef *type_specifier new_name*;

For example, to use the word "balance" in place of "float," you would write

```
typedef float balance;
```

union

The **union** keyword is used to assign two or more variables to the same memory location. The form of the definition and the way an element is referenced are the same as for **struct**. The general form is

union *union_name* {
  type *element1*;
  type *element2*;
    .
    .
    .
  type *elementN*;
} union *variable_name*;

unsigned

The **unsigned** type modifier tells the compiler to eliminate the sign bit of an integer and to use all bits for arithmetic. This has the effect

of doubling the size of the largest integer. However, unsigned variables may hold only positive numbers. For example, to declare **big** to be an unsigned integer you would write

```
unsigned int big;
```

void

The **void** type specifier is primarily used to explicitly declare functions that return no (meaningful) value. It is also used to create **void** pointers (pointers to **void**) that are generic pointers capable of pointing to any type of object.

volatile

The **volatile** modifier is used to tell the compiler that a variable may have its contents altered in ways not explicitly defined by the program. Variables that are changed by hardware such as real-time clocks, interrupts, or other inputs are examples.

while

The **while** loop has the general form

```
while(condition) {
    statement block
}
```

If a single statement is the object of the **while**, the braces may be omitted.

The **while** tests its *condition* at the top of the loop. Therefore, if the *condition* is false to begin with, the loop will not execute at all. The *condition* may be any expression.

An example of a **while** follows. It will read 100 characters from a disk file and store them in a character array.

```
t = 0;

while(t<100) {
  s[t] = getc(fp);
  t++;
}
```

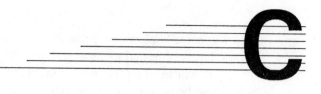

THE GOTO

The **goto** is ANSI's unconditional jump statement. This book has not made use of the **goto**, however, because in a language like C, which has a rich set of control structures and allows additional control using **break** and **continue**, there is little need for the **goto**. In fact, there is no programming situation in which the **goto** is absolutely required.

The chief concern most programmers have about the **goto** is its tendency to confuse a program and render it nearly unreadable. This is mainly why the **goto** was only mentioned in passing in the main text of this book. However, there may be times when the use of the

goto will actually clarify program flow, for example, in exiting from several layers of nested loops when some catastrophic error occurs.

If you will be using C as a replacement for assembly language, you should be introduced to the **goto** because, under certain circumstances, it enables code to be very small and fast. Remember, however, that it must always be used with caution.

The **goto** requires a label for operation. A *label* may be any valid identifier. The label name must be followed by a colon. For example, a loop from 1 to 100 could be written using **goto**s this way:

```
x = 1;

loop1:
   x++;
   if(x<100) goto loop1;
```

The **goto** can only be used to jump to a label within the same function. For non-local jumps, see the **longjmp( )** standard library function.

TRADEMARKS

FORTH®	FORTH, Inc.
IBM® PC	International Business Machines Corporation
DEC™	Digital Equipment Corporation
QuickC™	Microsoft Corporation
Turbo C®	Borland International, Inc.
UNIX®	AT&T
UNIX C®	AT&T

INDEX